The Feminization of Famine

Expressions of the Inexpressible?

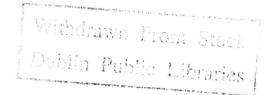

The Feminization of Famine

Expressions of the Inexpressible?

Margaret Kelleher

Duke University Press
Durham 1997

First published in 1997
in the United States by
Duke University Press,
Durham, NC 27708
and in Ireland by
Cork University Press
Crawford Business Park
Crosses Green
Cork

Library of Congress Cataloging-in-Publication Data

Kelleher, Margaret.
 The feminization of famine: expressions of the inexpressible?
/ Margaret Kelleher.
  p. cm.
 Includes bibliographical references and index.
 ISBN 0–8223–2032–0 (cloth : alk. paper). – ISBN 0–8223–2045–2
(pbk. : alk. paper)
1. English fiction—Irish authors—History and criticism.
2. Women—Ireland—History—19th century—Historiography.
3. Famines—India—Bengal—History—20th century. 4. Women—India—
Bengal—History—20th century. 5. Famines—Ireland—History—19th
century. 6. Women and literature—Ireland—History. 7. Famines in
literature. 8. Narration (Rhetoric) 9. Women in literature. I. Title.
PR8807.W6K45 1997
823.009'352042—dc21   96–53220
                                                                                      CIP

ISBN 0–8223–2032–0 hardcover
0–8223–2045–2 paperback

Typeset by Seton Music Graphics, Bantry, Co. Cork
Printed by ColourBooks, Baldoyle, Co. Dublin.

To Jo, Michael and Gemma Kelleher

Contents

Acknowledgements

This project began as part of my doctoral work in Boston College: I owe special gratitude to my supervisor Rosemarie Bodenheimer and readers Adele Dalsimer and Jenny Sharpe; to the Irish Studies programme – colleagues and friends, Adele Dalsimer, Philip O'Leary and Kevin O'Neill; and to William Neenan, S. J., Academic Vice-President. My thanks also to Eleanor Byrne, David Buckley, Kathleen Cahill, Joyce Flynn, Mary-Jo Kietzman, Katherine O'Donnell, Kathy O'Malley, Laurel Rus, Robert Savage, Dawn Skorczewski, Mary-Ann Smith, Terri Trafas, Maura Twomey and Eilís Ward, and with special memories of Ann Burke and Margaret Dever.

I would like to thank my colleagues in Mater Dei Institute of Education who saw this book through to its fruition, the Board of Mater Dei Institute for facilitating my research, and, in particular, John Devitt, Anne Kenna and Richard Hayes for their continual encouragement and concrete suggestions. My thanks also to Luke Dodd, Anne Fogarty, Colbert Kearney, Gerardine Meaney, Chris Morash, Christopher Murray, Cormac Ó Gráda, Tim P. O'Neill, Cathal Póirtéir, Peggy Preston, Kate Sweeney and the late Augustine Martin.

From friends in Dublin and Cork I received much support; special thanks to Maeve Lewis, Máire Ní Mhaonaigh, Teresa O'Hara, Íde O'Carroll and Unn Villius for their insight and counsel, and to Jenny Storey and Fergus Sullivan for their help in the final stages of production.

I acknowledge, with gratitude, the staff of the National Library of Ireland, the library of Trinity College Dublin, the India Office Library, London, and the Centre for South Asian Studies, Cambridge University, for their assistance. To John Behan, I am indebted for permission to use his sculpture 'Famine mother and children' as cover image, and Tom Kenny for bringing this work to my attention.

Finally, very special thanks to Andy Storey for his perspicacity, support and constant belief in this project.

Margaret Kelleher, November 1996
St Patrick's College, Maynooth

A version of one section of chapter 1, on the subject of Trollope's *Castle Richmond*, appeared in *Irish University Review* 25, 2 (1995); and one section of chapter 2, concerning the famine writings of Asenath Nicholson, previously appeared in *Fearful Realities: New Perspectives on the Famine*, edited by Chris Morash and Richard Hayes (Irish Academic Press, 1995); my thanks to their editors and publishers.

Note: in light of varying typographical conventions, both within Irish historiography and internationally, I have chosen to use lower-case 'f' for 'the [Irish, Bengal] famine'.

I hardly dare to voice the notion which, if it did not come to me then comes to me now, the insane notion that perhaps it was on her, on Sybil, our bright bitch, that the sorrow of the country, of those baffled people in the rotting fields, of the stricken eyes staring out of hovels, was visited against her will and even without her knowledge so that tears might be shed, and the inexpressible expressed. Does that seem a ridiculous suggestion? But I do not suggest, I only wonder.

John Banville

The issue of women's economic and social inferiority and her simultaneous elevation in the form of mother or *Grihalakshmi* or *Sakti* is basically one of ideological mystification, that is, masking the reality with imaginary relation.

Ujjal Dutta

A famine's no place for a woman.

Rudyard Kipling

Introduction

The nymph, borne through the air in her borrowed chariot, came to Scythia, and on a bleak mountain-top which men call Caucasus, unyoked her dragon steeds. Seeking out Famine, she saw her in a stony field, plucking with nails and teeth at the scanty herbage. Her hair hung in matted locks, her eyes were sunken, her face ghastly pale; her lips were wan and foul, her throat rough with scurf; her skin was hard and dry so that the entrails could be seen through it; her skinny hip-bones bulged out beneath her hollow loins, and her belly was but a belly's place; her breast seemed to be hanging free and just to be held by the framework of the spine; her thinness made her joints seem large, her knees were swollen, and her ankles were great bulging lumps.

Ovid, *Metamorphoses*, Book VIII[1]

The final tale in Book VIII of Ovid's *Metamorphoses* relates the story of Erysichthon who earns the wrath of Ceres, goddess of agriculture, when he cuts down a mighty oak sacred to her; his punishment, Ceres ordains, is to be racked by 'dreadful Famine'. Since the goddess cannot go to where Famine lives, 'for the fates do not permit Ceres and Famine to come together', she sends a messenger to Scythia, and although, as Ovid reminds his readers, the tasks of Famine and Ceres 'are ever opposite', Famine agrees to fulfil Ceres' wish. Erysichthon is filled with a hunger which is insatiable until, finally, he feeds himself 'by consuming his own body'. In the extract reproduced above, Fames[2] is first seen, personified as woman, grotesquely plucking 'with nails and teeth at the scanty herbage'. On her body may be read the traces of famine, features which will recur throughout later famine scenes: breasts 'hanging', joints horribly swollen and her belly 'but a belly's place'. Later, when she

I

encounters Erysichthon, she will fill him 'with herself', but, already, her very appearance testifies to her own deadly power, making her at once the incarnation of Famine and one of its victims.

Ovid's Fames is one of the earliest written examples of what may be termed 'the feminization of famine', i.e. the representation of famine and its effects through images of women. The prevalence of figures of mother-and-child is obvious from even the most cursory look at today's media representations of disaster and catastrophe, or relief agencies' fund-raising campaigns. Depictions of the dry-breasted mother unable to feed her child, of a woman unable to bury her child, of a mother torn between the competing claims of her children, or of a child suckling the breast of its dead mother occur not only throughout present-day accounts but also embody the worst consequences of famine in literary and historical texts. This study takes as its subject the representations of women in famine narratives, examining in detail the literature arising from two historical famines, the first being the Irish 'Great Famine' of the 1840s whose literary depictions continue to emerge, and the second, occurring a century later, in 1940s Bengal.

One of the first questions raised by a study of famine literature is that of the very possibility of representation: is it possible to depict the horror and scale of an event such as famine; are literature and language adequate to the task? As early as 1846 and 1847, many of the visitors to famine-stricken areas of Ireland expressed doubts as to the possibility of conveying what they had seen. William Carleton, author of the famine novel *The Black Prophet*, first published in instalments between May and December 1846, interrupts his portrait of a famine-stricken family, in the final instalment of his novel, with the exclamation 'But how shall we describe it?'[3] The difficulty of representation in the face of an overwhelming spectacle, what George Steiner, in reference to the Holocaust, would later call 'the failure of the word',[4] is powerfully conveyed in the narrative of William Bennett, an Englishman who travelled around Ireland for six weeks in the spring of 1847:

> STARVATION, – a word that has now become so familiar, as scarcely to awaken a painful idea, – is NOT being two or three days deficient of food. *It is something quite different*; and the effects of dwindling and

insufficient nourishment upon a whole population, – upon the mass
of men, women, and the little children; the disease, – the emaciation, – the despair, – are utterly past the powers of description, or
even of imagination, without witnessing. I am in possession of details
beyond anything that has appeared in print, or I believe, in private
circulation; in fact, for the sake of poor humanity, unfit to communicate. My mind was at times so struck down, that for days together
the pen has refused its office; the appalling spectacles have seemed to
float between, whenever I attempted it, and to paralyse every effort.[5]

Over a hundred years later, the novelist John Banville would term
the representation of famine 'the inexpressible expressed'.[6]

The existence of an unspeakable or inexpressible reality, one
which defies artistic depiction, is famously addressed by George
Steiner, in the following comment: 'The world of Auschwitz lies
outside speech as it lies outside reason. To speak of the *unspeakable*
is to risk the survivance of language as creator and bearer of humane,
rational truth.'[7] Not alone does Steiner challenge the possibility of
aesthetic representation, he also questions the ethics of such an
attempt, fearing that it may lessen and trivialize the horror. In his
words, 'The aesthetic makes endurable.'[8] The writings of an
Auschwitz survivor, Primo Levi, have further questioned the
possibility of witness, since the true witnesses, 'those who saw the
Gorgon, have not returned to tell about it, or have returned
mute'.[9] Dangers exist that analogies between the Holocaust and
the 1840s Irish famine, for example, may become trite and
simplistic and obscure the complexities of both catastrophes, but
the issues raised by Holocaust writers, in particular concerning the
ethics and potential of representation, have significant implications
for famine literature.[10] In response to the challenges delivered by
Steiner, critics such as Lawrence Langer and Paul Ricoeur have
defended the potential of the literary imagination to make real and
present the events of the past, to render them imaginatively
accessible to later generations of readers. Literature therefore
possesses the power to make the reality of the past 'possible' for the
imagination, 'giving eyes', in Ricoeur's phrase, to narrator and
reader through 'the quasi-intuitiveness of fiction'.[11] In that regard,
one may view literature, as Julia Kristeva has argued, as that which

'represents the ultimate coding of our crises, of our most intimate and most serious apocalypses'.[12]

Levi's words have a particular resonance in the Irish context since the events of the 1840s have been obscured by silence at a number of levels: in popular memory, in Irish historiography which, until recently, contained little extensive work on famine, and in literature.[13] Such a silence may denote depths of pain, of shame and of guilt on the part of those who survived, and a necessary repression of the past in order to move forward. The apparent scarcity of literary representations, whether at the time or in the succeeding generations, has led one critic to define the Great Famine as 'the threatened death of the signifier'.[14] In his essay 'Heathcliff and the Great Hunger', Terry Eagleton argues that a 'repression or evasion' has been at work in Irish literary culture: 'There is a handful of novels and a body of poems, but few truly distinguished works. Where is the Famine in the literature of the Revival? Where is it in Joyce?' and, echoing Steiner, asserts that 'the event strains at the limits of the articulable, and is truly in this sense the Irish Auschwitz'.[15]

Yet the extent of such a silence or repression in the Irish literary tradition runs the risk of being overstated. As Seán Ryder persuasively argues in his work on the Nation poets, references to the impossibility of communication were frequently a rhetorical tool.[16] Even the powerful and eloquent disclaimers given by an eyewitness such as William Bennett are always succeeded by an attempt at representation, the prefacing remarks thus serving to heighten and focus a reader's interest. The extent to which Irish literature contains references to the famine depends, very simply, on where one looks. Chris Morash's anthology, *The Hungry Voice*, has revealed the existence of a body of poetic writing contemporary with the famine, written largely by the professional classes; his recent work, *Writing the Famine*, a study of the themes of progress and providentialism, further demonstrates the extent of literary and historical writing about the events of the 1840s, continuing in the succeeding generation.[17] Though the 1840s famine is, as Eagleton states, curiously absent from the work of Yeats and Joyce – writers separated from its events by only one generation – a wider definition of what constitutes 'famine' material – for example, references to fertility in Joyce's work – has yielded some interesting discoveries.[18] The famine is certainly present in the work of many writers of the Literary Revival: in Maud Gonne's dramatic and journalistic writings, in Rosa Mulholland's fiction and poetry, in the Irish-language drama of Father Patrick Dinneen, the fiction of Somerville and Ross and the historical reflections of Emily Lawless.[19] In the years after the famine, beginning as early as 1851 and through the second half of the nineteenth century, the events of the 1840s were the subject of a significant number of fictional works, the majority of which were written by women. Although, as the second chapter will explore in more detail, many of these writers were separated geographically and/or economically from hunger and starvation, their work played an important role in keeping the memory of the Great Famine alive. In the twentieth century, fiction continues to be 'in the service of the unforgettable',[20] evidenced most famously in Liam O'Flaherty's novel, *Famine*. Throughout this period, many Irish-language famine texts emerge, their existence rarely mentioned in references to famine literature. These works range from writings contemporary with the famine to twentieth-century stories by Seosamh Mac Grianna and Máirtín Ó Cadhain, and are the subject of significant recent studies by Niall Buttimer and Máirín Nic Eoin.[21] Much also remains to be learnt from a comparative study of the famine literatures which have emerged from other countries; the example chosen in this volume is the extensive body of literature treating of the 1940s Bengal famine.[22]

Given the existence of this body of literature, the types of representation which result and the strategies employed deserve closer and more careful attention. The story of famine may be told as one of resistance or of passive victimization; more rarely, some writers explore the complex means through which people attempt to survive. At their most successful, famine narratives encourage their readers to imagine what the experience of famine may have been like, exposing the gaps left by the historical record and offering insights into the possible as well as the known. But perhaps the most significant aspect of a literary famine text is its potential to individualize the crisis, to depict, in the words of one Indian critic, 'a vast and horrible social phenomenon – the destitution of a whole people – in terms of individual human experience' without 'reducing the frightful proportions of the tragedy'.[23] The individuation of famine through the portrayal of single victims is, as this study will show, a necessary and, on occasion, very effective strategy. In Primo Levi's eloquent words, 'to all of us there remains in the best of cases, only the sporadic pity addressed to the single individual, the *Mitmensch*, the co-man: the human being of flesh and blood standing before us, within the reach of our providentially myopic senses'.[24] Yet, in envisioning the individual's relationship with the overall crisis, writers may fall far short of the ideal combination of 'historical explanation and individuation through horror' outlined by Paul Ricoeur.[25] The question is even more acute given that, in the majority of famine representations, the 'single individual', the victim of famine who is the subject of a detailed description, is female. A key strategy for those who seek to convey the event of famine is the feminization of its effects; why and to what effect will be the central concerns of this work.

Feminist critics such as Alice Jardine and Jacqueline Rose have drawn attention to the frequency with which 'the unspeakable' is characterized as female; again and again, images of women are used to figure moments of breakdown or crisis – in the social body, in political authority, or in representation itself[26] – thus expressing what in Lacanian psychoanalysis is called the '*pas tout*', or the 'point of impossibility', of any system. Rose observes: 'in so far as the system closes over that moment of difference or impossibility, what gets set up in its place is essentially an image of the woman'.[27] This association of women's experience with a crisis in representation can have various results; on the one hand, it suggests the existence of a 'wild zone' outside conventional expression, a distinctively female space, which has become the source of inspiration for some women writers;[28] yet it also may produce a much more constricting role, with women as 'bearers of meaning, not makers of meaning', through whom others' words take form.[29] The work of African–American novelist Toni Morrison is particularly significant in this regard; highlighting the sense of 'an unspeakable' in the history of slavery, most often associated with women's experience, she also reveals the ways in which this may cover over the 'unspoken', that which needs to be spoken, to be remembered and retold.[30] In the specific context of famine literature, one encounters both writers' sense of 'an unspeakable', that which is too awful to relate, and also, as emphasized above, their attempts to give it form; in this regard, female images emerge, as John Banville acknowledges, so that 'tears might be shed and the inexpressible expressed'.[31]

Banville's succinct formulation emphasizes not only the representational strategies inherent in the female image, but also its affective power. This aspect of the female image, its power to move the reader or spectator, should not be underestimated nor evaded. As Maud Ellmann has explored in her suggestive and provocative work, *The Hunger Artists*, 'there is something about hunger, or more specifically about the *spectacle* of hunger, that deranges the distinction between self and other'.[32] The spectacle of hunger created in famine texts generates related questions concerning the source of its affective power: what, in the famine scene, compels the recognition and identification of its readers? Does the spectacle of woman and child appeal, as Ellmann suggests, 'to our forgotten past, to the famished and abandoned infant in ourselves'?[33] A pyschoanalytical interpretation of the effect of the famine image, particularly when it involves the maternal body, might emphasize its evocation of what Kristeva calls the 'primal shelter' that 'ensured the survival of the newborn'.[34] Yet famine scenes are very frequently depictions of the failure or collapse of this primal shelter, of the mother's inability to nourish or protect her child. In this regard, the maternal image develops a much more unsettling and threatening quality, and becomes an expression of 'the unthinkable', extending from the mother's inability to feed her child, to cases of abandonment, desertion, even infanticide.

The depictions of maternity, to be found in famine texts, reproduce an ambivalence at the very heart of the maternal figure. The archetype of the Great Mother may also manifest itself as the bad or, in Erich Neumann's words, the 'Terrible Mother': giver of life and of death, source of nurture and protection, but also possessing the power to deprive, devour or destroy.[35] As Neumann observes, the Great Mother, as represented in the primordial world, 'is the protectress, the good mother, who feeds man with fruits and tubers and grains, but also poisons him and lets him hunger and thirst in times of drought, when she withdraws from living things'.[36] Bengali famine texts vividly illustrate this doubleness through the mythical figures of Lakshmi, goddess of prosperity, and Kali, goddess of destruction. To some extent, the famine victim herself may possess an allegorical function, embodying the fate of mother earth, the mother/land, even nation. Yet, in the context of nineteenth-century Irish famine literature, the sense of 'woman as nation' appears more frequently in poetry than narrative;[37] while, in the novels of writers such as Carleton and Trollope, the individual female victim clearly 'stands for' the plight of many others, an interpretation of her significance in national terms is problematic. To read female characterizations too readily as allegorical figures may be simplistic and reductive. In twentieth-century retellings of the story of famine, however, the female victim, both lower and upper-class, gains a more explicit collective function, figuring both the crisis of famine and society's survival. Women's sacrificial identity is similarly prevalent in Bengali literature of the famine, with interesting relations to developments in the national sphere.

An important point to emphasize is that representations of women victims are not the only images of famine. Contemporary depictions of the 1840s Irish famine, for example, include recurring motifs such as the 'walking dead', descriptions of children prematurely aged or with mouths stained green from eating grass, and horrific references to bodies eaten by rats or dogs; many writers later repeat and enlarge these images to give famine literary form. But where famine's effects are given a detailed, physical description, where the individual spectacle of a hungry body is created, this occurs, predominantly, through images of women. In this regard, famine literature is another example of a very old tradition whereby the female is what Marina Warner calls 'a vehicle of attributed meaning': 'On to the female body have been projected the fantasies and longings and terrors of generations of men and through them of women, in order to conjure them into reality or exorcize them into oblivion.'[38] The specific nature of famine images, as inscribed onto the female body, demands quite urgent attention, not only because of what these images embody but also because of what they may obscure, the universal significance which they purport to relate and the more particular messages they convey.

What might seem an obvious answer to the question of why female images are prevalent in famine literature is that they reflect the historical reality of women's experience of famine. A closer look, however, at the historical findings with regard to famine mortality, both in Ireland and in Bengal, and specifically its gender breakdown, reveals a much more complex relationship between the historical event and its literary versions. One general assumption which appears throughout famine studies is that women are more resilient than men during times of disaster. In 1849, Sidney Godolphin Osborne, an English philanthropist, reporting in *The Times* of his recent journey to Ireland and the conditions there, remarked that 'the girls and women bear it better than the males'.[39] Similarly, Sir Charles Elliot, a nineteenth-century famine commissioner based in India, observed that 'all the authorities seem agreed that women succumb to famine less easily than men'.[40] This belief continued into the twentieth century with, for example, many commentators during the 1940s Bengal famine emphasizing the occurrence of much higher mortality among men; in its report, the department of anthropology in Calcutta University called this 'a very sinister and significant feature' of the famine.[41] The accuracy of this assumption continues to be the subject of much debate: while nutritionists argue that women have a greater relative ability to cope with temporary distress situations, sociological and economic studies emphasize the special vulnerability of women caused by patterns of discrimination and exploitation within household structures.[42]

Turning specifically to the 1840s Irish famine, Boyle and Ó Gráda have shown that the heaviest mortality was experienced by the young and the very old who accounted for less than one-third of the population but three-fifths of the deaths. Their figures for famine mortality, when examined in terms of gender, reveal that, in absolute terms, there were slightly more excess deaths among males, but this differential is very small.[43] Interestingly, this trend represented a change in pre-famine and post-famine situations when women had a higher mortality rate than men. Yet, as Boyle and Ó Gráda demonstrate, the differential is so small that not much should be made of it. What is significant, however, is the disparity between the historical reality of famine, with mortality relatively more severe among males,[44] and literature's focus on individual female victims. As chapter one and two will explore, a curious ambivalence results from these depictions: women frequently appear as the sole adult survivor, having outlived their male relatives and now lacking their support, suggesting at once a greater resilience and a particular vulnerability.

The views expressed by commentators during the Bengal famine that male mortality greatly outweighed female deaths have since been challenged by the economist Amartya Sen. Sen shows that the proportion of men in excess mortality in 1943 (fifty-four per cent) was slightly higher than the pre-famine average (fifty-two per cent), but the difference is small, and over the larger period of 1943–46, mortality was the same as the pre-famine average. And, while in absolute terms, more men died during the famine, women, relative to their proportion of the population, had a marginally lower chance of survival.[45] Once again, one must be cautious about drawing large conclusions from tentative figures but what is clear is that they do not bear out the contemporary perception that the famine fell much more heavily on men. In literary depictions of the famine, female sufferers are once again predominant, with references to male relatives as dead, gone elsewhere for employment or imprisoned; thus, to some extent, the contemporary assumption of greater male mortality is reinforced. This results, in the case of Bengali famine literature, in an emphasis more on the strategies for survival employed by women to withstand famine, both their failure and their success, as well as their implications for the future of society. The nature of these depictions, and how they contrast with those prevalent in Irish famine literature, will be illustrated in detail in chapter four.

Beginning with contemporary representations of the 1840s Irish famine, chapters one and two will explore the spectacle of famine constructed by male and by female observers. Chapter three examines the types of famine representation, and the significance of female images, in twentieth-century 'retellings' of Irish famine. In chapter four, another historical event, the Bengal famine of 1943–44 and its literary depictions become the focus of discussion. A significant body of literature exists with regard to the Bengal famine, with many novels and stories written at the time or in succeeding years. Of the texts to be discussed, approximately half were written in English, the remainder in Bengali or Urdu. English translations exist of these texts, some of which appeared within a short time of the original publication. The restrictions of reading in translation must be acknowledged. In addition, the dangers of a comparative reading becoming a reductive one are also acutely relevant. The Bengali texts emerge from a very different cultural and political perspective; the historical event to which they refer is also of a radically dissimilar nature. While points of comparison may appear, the purpose of chapter four is to study, in its integrity, a body of famine representations and the specific figures which emerge.

This study cannot answer what the famine, in Ireland or Bengal, meant for women at the time, nor recover their particular and various experiences. Much of this detail would seem irretrievably lost, although recent research on the general trends affecting women, both historically and in the present, provides some suggestive insights.[46] What emerges from these recent studies is a much more complex picture of woman and famine than traditional images of passive victimization, on the one hand, or generalized comments on women's biological resilience, on the other.[47] The subject of this volume is the history of famine representations in literature, the long narrative tradition which lies behind present-day manifestations. It will explore how women's experience of famine has been imagined, the various and recurring forms in which authors have portrayed the 'possible', or what may have been. These representations, as the following chapters will reveal, have a crucial role in shaping our very notion of famine.

NOTES AND REFERENCES

1. Ovid's *Metamorphoses*, translated by Frank Justus Miller, Loeb Classical Library (London, 1916), pp. 456–67.

2. Literally 'Hunger' and, by extension, 'Famine'; I am indebted to John Devitt for this reference.

3. William Carleton, *The Black Prophet* ([1847]; Shannon, 1972, facsimile of 1899 edition), p. 344.

4. George Steiner, *Language and Silence: Essays 1958–1966* ([1967]; London, 1985), p. 71.

5. William Bennett, *Narrative of a recent journey of six weeks in Ireland in connexion with the subject of supplying small seed to some of the remoter districts . . .* (London and Dublin, 1847), pp. 132–33.

6. John Banville, *Birchwood* ([1973]; London, 1987), p. 143.

7. Steiner, *Language and Silence*, p. 146. See also Theodor Adorno's article, 'Cultural Criticism and Society', in *Prisms* (1955), trans. Samuel and Shierry Weber (Cambridge, Mass., 1981), which includes the famous comment 'To write poetry after Auschwitz is barbaric'. Among the many responses to the issues raised by Steiner, Lawrence L. Langer's *The Holocaust and the Literary Imagination* (New Haven and London, 1975) deserves particular mention; see also Joan Ringelheim, 'The Holocaust: Taking Women into Account', in *Jewish Quarterly*, 39, 3 (1992), pp. 19–24. My thanks to Ronit Lentin for this reference.

8. Steiner, *Language and Silence*, p. 191.

9. Primo Levi, *The Drowned and the Saved* (1986), trans. Raymond Rosenthal (London, 1989), p. 64.

10. The extent to which the consciousness of 'our own time, of World War II, concentration camps, and race-murder' shapes our readings of a past event like the Irish famine is the theme of Steven Marcus's provocative essay, 'Hunger and Ideology', in *Representations: Essays on Literature and Society* ([1975]; New York and Oxford, 1990), pp. 3–16.

11. Paul Ricoeur, *Time and Narrative* ([1985]; Chicago, 1988), iii, p. 188; see also Langer, *The Holocaust and the Literary Imagination*, pp. 1–30.

12. Julia Kristeva, *Powers of Horror: An Essay on Abjection* (1980); trans. Leon S. Roudiez (New York, 1982), p. 208.

13. For recent studies of the famine in folk memory, see Cormac Ó Gráda's *An Drochshaol: Béaloideas agus Amhráin* (Baile Átha Cliath, 1994) and Cathal Póirtéir, 'Folk Memory and the Famine', in *The Great Irish Famine* (Cork and Dublin, 1995). Interesting comments on the scarcity of reference to famine, in Irish historiography, are made by Ó Gráda in his *Ireland Before and After the Famine: Explorations in Economic History 1800–1930* ([1988]; Manchester, 1993), pp. 98–101; see also his engrossing '"Making History" in Ireland in the 1940s and 1950s: the Saga of *The Great Famine*', in *Irish Review*, 12 (1992), pp. 87–

107. Though famine literature has, until recently, received little attention, the existence of a 'small genre of retrospective literature' is briefly discussed in Malcolm Brown, *The Politics of Irish Literature* (London, 1972), pp. 144–47.

14. Terry Eagleton, *Heathcliff and the Great Hunger: Studies in Irish Culture* (London, 1995), p. 11.

15. Ibid., pp. 12–13.

16. Sean Ryder, 'Reading Lessons: Famine and the *Nation*, 1845–1849', in Chris Morash and Richard Hayes (eds.), *'Fearful Realities': New Perspectives on the Famine* (Dublin, 1996), pp. 151–63. A strong challenge to the 'fashionable' theory of 'incommunicability' is also delivered by Primo Levi in *The Drowned and the Saved* (pp. 68–69): 'Except for cases of pathological incapacity, one can and must communicate . . . To say that it is impossible to communicate is false; one always can.'

17. Chris Morash (ed.), *The Hungry Voice: The Poetry of the Irish Famine* (Dublin, 1989), and Morash, *Writing the Irish Famine* (Oxford, 1995).

18. See, for example, Mary Lowe-Evans, *Crimes Against Fecundity: Joyce and Population Control* (New York, 1989), pp. 5–29.

19. As chapter three will explore in more detail, the literature of the Irish Revival is more extensive than Eagleton's comments (*Heathcliff and the Great Hunger*, p. 11) suggest.

20. Ricoeur, *Time and Narrative*, iii, p. 189.

21. Neil Buttimer, 'A Stone on the Cairn: the Great Famine in Later Gaelic Manuscripts', in Morash and Hayes (eds.), *'Fearful Realities'*, pp. 93–109; Antain Mac Lochlainn, 'The Famine in Gaelic Tradition', in *Irish Review*, 17/18 (1995), pp. 90–108, and Máirín Nic Eoin, 'Ar an Trá Fholamh – an Gorta Mór in Litríocht Ghaeilge na hAoise seo', in Cathal Póirtéir (ed.), *Gnéithe den Ghorta* (Dublin, 1995), pp. 107–30.

22. A number of nineteenth-century Anglo-Indian stories also provide interesting treatments of the subject of famine, including Rudyard Kipling, 'William the Conqueror', in *The Day's Work* ([1898]; London, 1988), and the title-story in C. H. Crosthwaite's *Thakur Pertah Singh and Other Tales* (Edinburgh, 1913), first published in *Blackwood's Magazine*, 1895.

23. Kwaja Ahmad Abbas, preface to Krishan Chandar, *Ann Dātā*, (Poona, 1944/5).

24. Levi, *The Drowned and the Saved*, p. 40.

25. Ricoeur's warning against a 'ruinous dichotomy between a history that would dissolve the event in explanation and a purely emotional retort that would dispense us from thinking the unthinkable' is acutely relevant to Irish famine historiography, as is the ideal alternative which he posits: 'The more we explain in historical terms, the more indignant we become; the more we are struck by the horror of events, the more we seek to understand them', from *Time and Narrative*, iii, p. 188.

26. See Alice Jardine, *Gynesis: Configurations of Woman and Modernity* (Ithaca and London, 1985), chapter 2, and Jacqueline Rose, *Sexuality in the Field of Vision* (London, 1986), chapter 9.

27. Rose, *Sexuality in the Field of Vision*, p. 219.

28. See Elaine Showalter's discussion of the function of the 'wild zone' or 'female space' in women's writing, in 'Feminist Criticism in the Wilderness', *Critical Inquiry*, 8, 1 (1981), pp. 179–205, reprinted in Showalter (ed.), *The New Feminist Criticism* (New York, 1985); and Elizabeth Abel (ed.), *Writing and Sexual Difference* (Brighton, 1982).

29. See Margaret Homans, *'Bearing the Word': Language and Female Experience in Nineteenth-Century Women's Writing* (Chicago and London, 1986). Similar concerns are expressed in the poetry and prose writings of Eavan Boland, including *Object Lessons: The Life of the Woman and the Poet in Our Time* (Manchester, 1995) and 'A Kind of Scar: The Woman Poet in a National Tradition', LIP pamphlet (Dublin, 1989). The phrase 'bearers of meaning' comes from Laura Mulvey's 'Visual Pleasure and Narrative Cinema', *Screen*, 16, 3 (1975), pp. 6–18.

30. See Toni Morrison, *Playing in the Dark: Whiteness and the Literary Imagination* ([1992]; London, 1993) and Morrison, 'Site of Memory', in William Zinsser (ed.), *Inventing the Truth: The Art and Craft of Memoir* (Boston, 1987).

31. Banville, *Birchwood*, p. 143.

32. Maud Ellmann, *The Hunger-Artists: Starving, Writing and Imprisonment* (London, 1993), p. 54. Ellmann examines in detail the 'codings' of the hungry body which occur in two contexts, that of anorexia and hunger-strike.

33. Ellmann, *The Hunger-Artists*, p. 54.

34. Julia Kristeva, 'Stabat Mater' (1977), reprinted and translated in Toril Moi (ed.), *The Julia Kristeva Reader* (Oxford, 1986), p. 176.

35. As Neumann writes, in *The Great Mother: An Analysis of the Archetype* (London, 1955), 'The Feminine appears as great because that which is contained, sheltered, nourished, is dependent on it and utterly at its mercy' (p. 43).

36. Neumann, *The Great Mother*, p. 52.

37. Two interesting examples of an allegorization of Ireland's 'griefs' may be seen in *Howitt's Journal*, the short-lived London radical journal: George Cooper's 'The Irish Mother's Lament over Her Child', in *Howitt's Journal*, 23 October 1847, and Ferdinand Freiligrath, 'Ireland' (translated by Mary Howitt), in *Howitt's Journal*, 3 April 1847.

38. Marina Warner, *Monuments and Maidens: The Allegory of the Female Form* ([1985]; London, 1987), pp. 37, 225.

39. Sidney Godolphin Osborne, letter to *The Times*, 9 July 1849, pp. 4–5.

40. Quoted in Amartya Sen, *Poverty and Famines: An Essay on Entitlement and Deprivation* ([1981]; Oxford, 1982), pp. 210–11.

41. Cited by Sen, *Poverty and Famines*, p. 211, n. 29.

42. See E. Margaret Crawford, 'Subsistence Crises and Famines in Ireland: A Nutritionist's Views', in Crawford (ed.), *Famine: The Irish Experience 900–1900* (Edinburgh, 1989), p. 201. The existence of 'two – possibly opposite – tendencies' determining women's mortality has been identified by Jean Drèze

and Amartya Sen in *Hunger and Public Action* (Oxford, 1989): 'On the one hand, there is considerable evidence that the proportionate increase of mortality is typically *lower* for women than for men in famine situations . . . On the other hand, a number of studies also bring out the fact that, in many societies, the priorities of the family are often pro-male in distress situations' (p. 55).

43. See Phelim P. Boyle and Cormac Ó Gráda, 'Fertility Trends, Excess Mortality and the Great Irish Famine', *Demography*, 23, 4 (1986), pp. 543–59. Boyle and Ó Gráda suggest a differential of between 16,000 and 37,000 deaths, based on an estimated excess mortality, i.e. deaths directly attributable to famine, of about one million people. See also Mary Daly, *The Great Famine in Ireland* (Dublin, 1986), pp. 100–01; Daly speculates that the greater vulnerability of men 'may be due to the pressure of relief works, particularly for bodies deprived of food, or may simply reflect the fact that men have higher calorie requirements than women and thus faced greater difficulties in coping with scarcity' (p. 100).

44. Boyle and Ó Gráda, 'Fertility Trends', pp. 4, 26–27. This general picture, that 'women were less likely to succumb than men; is confirmed by historian David Fitzpatrick: 'Females accounted for 48.1 per cent of estimated excess mortality, being outnumbered by males in every reported age-band. The discrepancy was negligible for young children, but substantial among the elderly.' See Fitzpatrick, 'Women and the Great Famine', in Margaret Kelleher and James H. Murphy (eds.), *Separate Spheres?: Gender and Nineteenth-Century Ireland* (Dublin, forthcoming 1997). More generally Fitzpatrick contests arguments regarding women's greater vulnerability during famine, and suggests an extension of Sen's theory of entitlements to include less material or non-monetary resources, including 'household and family *services*'.

45. See Amartya Sen, *Poverty and Famines*, appendix D, pp. 210–13. As Sen notes, the male population exceeded the female population in Bengal (p. 211, n. 30).

46. See, for example, Megan Vaughan, *The Story of an African Famine: Gender and Famine in Twentieth-Century Malawi* (Cambridge, 1987). Recent works in the Irish context include Dympna McLoughlin's work on pauper women – see her 'Workhouses and Irish Female Paupers, 1840–70', in Maria Luddy and Clíona Murphy (eds.), *Women Surviving* (Dublin, 1989), pp. 117–47; Robert Scally's observations on 'The Missing' in *The End of Hidden Ireland* (New York and Oxford, 1995), pp. 121–27; and Maria Luddy's work on philanthropy, *Women and Philanthropy in Nineteenth-Century Ireland* (Cambridge, 1995), a topic discussed in more detail in chapter two of this book.

47. For a succinct discussion of this topic see David Arnold, *Famine: Social Crisis and Historical Change* (Oxford and New York, 1988), pp. 86–91.

— 1 —

'Appalling Spectacles'[1]:
Nineteenth-Century Irish Famine Narratives

This chapter will examine the representations of famine victims constructed by what have become the two most famous nineteenth-century famine novels: William Carleton's *The Black Prophet* and Anthony Trollope's *Castle Richmond*. Yet Carleton's and Trollope's narratives reflect only a very small part of the many writings of the time which were concerned with the subject of famine: literary, historiographical and journalistic. A sense of the general discourse from which these novelists drew, and, more specifically, the relationship between their texts and other contemporary depictions of famine victims, may be obtained from a survey of some of the published testimonies of the period. These eye-witness reports constitute a rich but frequently neglected source with regard to the 1840s Irish famine. In late 1846 and 1847, as readers first encountered William Carleton's novel, detailed and vivid descriptions of famine conditions were appearing in newspapers, in government correspondence and in the published accounts of observers. By 1860, when Trollope's novel, *Castle Richmond*, was published, controversies regarding the accuracy and status of such reports were long underway, debates in which Trollope actively intervened.

CONTEMPORARY TESTIMONIES

The majority of published eye-witness accounts were written by visitors to Ireland, usually from Britain and occasionally from

America. Some of the most significant and detailed testimonies come from members of the Society of Friends, men such as William Forster and his son William Edward Forster, and James Tuke and William Bennett who were sent by Quaker colleagues in England to 'obtain trustworthy information as to the real state of the more remote districts, and through what agency to open suitable channels for relief'.[2] Other visits were of a more individual nature. In February 1847, for example, Frederick Blackwood, later Marquess of Dufferin and Ava, then a twenty-year old student in Oxford, visited Ireland, together with his friend, G.F. Boyle, 'in order to ascertain with our own eyes the truth of the reports daily publishing of the misery existing there'. On their return, the young men recounted what they had seen in a short pamphlet entitled *Narrative of a Journey from Oxford to Skibbereen during the Year of* the *Irish Famine*.[3] Later in the famine period, in 1849 and in 1850, Sidney Godolphin Osborne, a clergyman and philanthropist, visited Ireland and published accounts of his travels in the columns of the *Times* and in a book entitled *Gleanings in the West of Ireland*.[4] Other significant newspaper reports were written by Irish observers, often clergymen or doctors, such as Reverend Webb's description of conditions in Caheragh, West Cork, first published in the *Southern Reporter* in February 1847, while the letter of a Cork magistrate, Nicholas Cummins, written to the Irish-born Duke of Wellington, appeared in the *Times* on Christmas Eve, 1846.

Again and again, famine observers emphasize the difficulty, even impossibility, of recording the horrors which they have witnessed. 'I can find no language or illustration sufficiently impressive to portray the spectacle', wrote Elihu Burritt, the American philanthropist, with regard to his visit to Ireland in February 1847; 'I have lain awake for hours, struggling mentally for some graphic and truthful similes, or new elements of description, by which I might convey to the distant reader's mind some tangible image of this object.'[5] Many other writers utter similar comments, apologizing for their inability to capture in words the overwhelming sights seen, defending themselves against charges of exaggeration, and emphasizing the 'factual' nature of their accounts. Thus, William Bennett, narrating his six-week journey to Ireland in

March and April 1847, breaks his description of 'Erris cabins' with
the following exclamations:

> And now language utterly fails me in attempting to depict the state
> of the wretched inmates. I would not willingly add another to the
> harrowing details that have been told; but still they are the FACTS of
> actual experience, for the knowledge of which we stand account-
> able. I have certainly sought out one of the most remote and
> destitute corners; but still it is within the bounds of our Christian
> land, under our Christian government, and entailing upon us –
> both as individuals and as members of a human community – a
> Christian responsibility from which no one of us can escape. My
> hand trembles while I write. The scenes of human misery and
> degradation we witnessed still haunt my imagination, with the
> vividness and power of some horrid and tyrannous delusion, rather
> than the features of a sober reality.[6]

Later, in another impassioned discourse, he declares the effects of
starvation to be 'past the powers of description, or even of imagination, without witnessing', and 'in fact, for the sake of poor
humanity, unfit to communicate'.[7]

Bennett's address to the reader, while apologetic as to the paucity of his language, also acknowledges and defends his narrative's
disturbing quality, its continuing affective power. Immediately succeeding these comments is a detailed account of what he has seen:

> We entered a cabin. Stretched in one dark corner, scarcely visible,
> from the smoke and rags that covered them, were three children
> huddled together, lying there *because they were too weak to rise*, pale
> and ghastly, their little limbs – on removing a portion of the filthy
> covering – perfectly emaciated, eyes sunk, voice gone, and evi-
> dently in the last stage of actual starvation. Crouched over the turf
> embers was another form, wild and all but naked, scarcely human
> in appearance. It stirred not, nor noticed us. On some straw,
> soddened upon the ground, moaning piteously, was a shrivelled old
> woman, imploring us to give her something, – baring her limbs
> partly, to show how the skin hung loose from the bones, as soon as
> she attracted our attention. Above her, on something like a ledge,
> was a young woman, with sunken cheeks, – a mother I have no

doubt, – who scarcely raised her eyes in answer to our enquiries, but pressed her hand upon her forehead, with a look of unutterable anguish and despair. Many cases were widows, whose husbands had recently been taken off by the fever, and thus their only pittance, obtained from the public works, entirely cut off. In many the husbands or sons were prostrate, under that horrid disease, – the results of long-continued famine and low living, – in which first the limbs, and then the body, swell most frightfully, and finally burst. We entered fifty of these tenements. The scene was one and invariable, differing in little but the number of the sufferers, or of the groups, occupying the several corners within . . .⁸

As this extract graphically illustrates, writers, however unsure as to the adequacy of language, *do* attempt famine representations, their prefacing remarks serving to sharpen the reader's attention. More interestingly, these comments attest to a double fear: both of language's inadequacy *and* its dangerous power.

The images provided by Bennett's sketch are prevalent throughout contemporary depictions: his emphasis on children's suffering, the delineation of 'scarcely human' forms, the disturbing nakedness of women, and the predominant characterization of adult famine victims as mothers and widows. The narrative's focus on the young and old, as well as widows and young mothers, clearly relates to the particular vulnerability and destitution experienced by these groups. In November 1846, a Waterford correspondent and member of the Society of Friends noted that 'the distressed and destitute may be classed under several heads':

The first comprises the aged, infirm, and widows. This class have been accustomed to subsist partly on the produce of a little knitting, but principally on 'the charity of the neighbours'; and this latter source being now from the pressure of the times wholly dried up, they may be looked upon as really the most destitute, and consequently to them the attention of the Friends here has been in the first instance directed. Another class comprises the poorest of the peasantry, compelled by dire necessity to seek refuge in the towns. They mostly consist of women with children, the husband being perhaps employed at a distance on some of the public works, and whose weekly stipend is insufficient to support them . . . The

remaining class consists of families of the men employed in public
works, whose earnings are inadequate to provide sufficient food,
at its present high prices, for their large families.[9]

Other contemporary commentators pay particular attention to
the destitution experienced by widows, by women who have been
deserted by their husbands or by those whose husbands are
employed at a distance.[10] In 1850, Sidney Godolphin Osborne
emphasized the presence in workhouses of many able-bodied
women who had been deserted by their husbands. Describing
scenes of eviction, he noted:

> It is a rare thing to find any males at these scenes of desolation; in
> the majority of cases, I fear, they desert their families, go to seek
> work at a distance, perhaps in England; very often they start for
> America as soon as they find they are to be ejected. A very large
> proportion of the families in the workhouse are deserted families.[11]

Women's vulnerability is thus seen as arising directly from the
absence of male support. For Osborne, however, the presence of so
many women in the workhouse was also evidence of females'
greater ability to survive famine situations:

> No one has yet I believe been able to explain, why it is, that men
> and boys, sink sooner under famine, than the other sex; still, so it is;
> go where you will, every officer will tell you, it is so. In the same
> workhouse, in which you will find the girls and women looking
> well, you will find the men and boys, in a state of the lowest physical
> depression; equal care in every way being bestowed on both sexes.[12]

In a letter to the *Times,* published a year earlier, Osborne similarly
observed, 'the girls and women bear it better than the males'.[13]
Studies of famine mortality support, to some extent, Osborne's
remarks; as the introduction discussed, male deaths from famine
appear slightly higher than those of females, but only marginally
so.[14] In the context of individualized depictions of famine victims,
however, women are clearly predominant, reflecting a view of the
female subject's particular vulnerability, on the one hand, and a
belief in women's greater ability to survive hunger, on the other.

Depictions of famine victims, however, very rarely explore the strategies employed by the poor to withstand or defer privation. Even where observers like Osborne credit women with a greater ability to survive, representations of passive and apathetic victims recur, with women somehow, and only briefly, outliving their husbands. The majority of sketches situate poor women within their cabins; the male, upper-class visitor, guided to the scene by a local clergyman or doctor, stands, observing, on the threshold. The following extract from Dufferin and Boyle's tour of cabins in Skibbereen, in the company of Mr Townsend, a local clergyman, provides one example:

> So universal and virulent was the fever, that we were forced to choose among several houses to discover one or more which it would be safe to enter. At length, Mr Townsend singled out one. We stood on the threshhold [*sic*] and looked in; the darkness of the interior was such, that we were scarcely able to distinguish objects . . . We entered another at no great distance: over a few peat embers a woman was crouching, drawing her only solace from their scanty warmth; she was suffering from diarrhoea: there seemed scarcely a single article of furniture or crockery in any part of the hut. The woman answered the enquiries of Mr Townsend in a weak and desponding voice; and from what we could gather, there seemed to be several other human beings in different corners of the hovel, but in the darkness we were totally unable to distinguish them.[15]

On other occasions, the famine scene is viewed from a carriage, the onlooker's vision framed by the window. The following report was given by James Mahony, artist for the *Illustrated London News*, and published 13 February 1847. Observing a crowd of 'famished poor' surrounding his coach, Mahony notes that

> amongst them was a woman carrying in her arms the corpse of a fine child, and making the most distressing appeal to the passengers for aid to enable her to purchase a coffin and bury her dear little baby. This horrible spectacle induced me to make some inquiry about her, when I learned from the people of the hotel that each day brings dozens of such applicants into the town.[16]

Over and over again in these narratives, the 'spectacle' of famine reproduces what Laura Mulvey, in the context of film criticism, has termed 'woman as image, man as bearer of the look'.[17] These scenes thus emerge as 'appalling spectacles' not alone because of the wretched and distressing nature of what is seen but also in the spectacle which observers themselves construct in their attempts at representation. The following extract from Osborne's narrative, *Gleanings in the West of Ireland*, published in 1850, provides a graphic example. Travelling through Clare, Osborne encounters a number of recently-evicted families:

> One of these lately 'tumbled out' colonies, though a very wretched spectacle, is sometimes a very picturesque one; the women in the red petticoat of the country, the said garment ever in tatters, with the dark bodice only just sufficiently patched to make a bare covering to the bosom; their long dark parted hair; bare legs and feet; the attitudes of the old, crouching under the bank or wall; of the less aged, in active work, drawing the smoke-blackened wood from beneath the thatch; the baby, half out of the queer-looking, half-box, half-boat, called a cradle; the younger children, half naked, romping around the ruins, or climbing about the furniture on the road-side . . . a painter could find no little beauty in a scene, which to one, who looks not at the picture, but at its cost, is only a very ugly page in the history of the exercise of man's power, over those who are themselves powerless.[18]

While Osborne's concluding comment is quite forceful politically, castigating 'the exercise of man's power', his representation of the famine scene gives it a type of exotic life of its own. Details of children 'romping', of the 'smoke-blackened wood' and 'red petticoat' create 'a picturesque' and romanticized version of wretchedness.

One of the most frequent figures in famine texts is that of a hunger-stricken mother, holding a child at her breast. Mahony's illustration of a woman carrying the corpse of her child, entitled 'Woman Begging at Clonakilty', to which the above-cited text served as explanatory note, is one of the best known. The translation from verbal text, with its realistic detail, to visual image is an interesting one. The spectacle of mother and child becomes iconic, with strong evocations of the Madonna and Child; traces of famine are inscribed on the face of this Irish Madonna through her wrinkled skin, drooping lip and 'staring' eye. Many of Mahony's contemporaries employed similar images, in verbal form, emphasizing the woman's inability to feed her child, the absence of nourishment from the mother's breast. Thus James Tuke refers, in December 1846, to an 'unfortunate mother' who is 'so far reduced as to be unable to afford the natural supply of nourishment'.[19] In some depictions, the mother has died with the child still attempting to suckle at her breast.[20] Other observers report, with horror, mothers nursing sons of fifteen or eighteen so that the son may have the strength to work. Writing one generation after these events, in his history of the Great Famine, first published in 1875, Canon John O'Rourke acknowledges his own hesitation in reproducing the following 'illustration of the unprecedented misery to which the people had sunk' given by Rev. B. O'Connor to his fellow-members of the Killarney Relief Committee:

> He [O'Connor] said: 'A man employed on the public works became sick. His wife had an infant at her breast. His son, who was fifteen years of age, was put in his place upon the works. The infant at the mother's breast', said the reverend gentleman, amid the sensation of the meeting, *'had to be removed,* in order that this boy might receive sustenance from his mother, to enable him to remain at work.'[21]

The great power which this image possesses to unsettle observer and reader is intriguing; it suggests a discomfort, even disgust, in the idea of an almost adult son feeding at his mother's breast, usurping the infant's place, but also portrays a particular and rare form of male vulnerability.

When the maternal body, scene of 'the primal shelter that ensured the survival of the newborn',[22] becomes the place of death, a primordial breakdown has occurred. This tragic inversion of life and death-giving forces is eloquently conveyed in William Carleton's sketch of a famine mother, published in December 1846, in the last instalment of *The Black Prophet,* as the 'dying struggles' of an infant 'fast perishing at the now exhausted fountain of its life'.[23] Throughout contemporary accounts, changes and challenges to the mother–child relationship function as a sign of the wider crisis. While many observers detail women's desperate efforts to save their own children or those of other women through heroic acts of self-sacrifice,[24] others allude to more 'fearful realities'. Dr Daniel Donovan, a Skibbereen doctor, memorably writes of a general collapse in family structures: 'I have seen mothers snatch food from the hands of their starving children; known a son to engage in a fatal struggle with his father for a potato; and have seen parents look on the putrid bodies of their offspring without evincing a symptom of sorrow.'[25] In May 1847, R. D. Webb, a correspondent of the Society of Friends, writing from Belmullet, records 'instances of women wilfully neglecting their young children, so that they died' and delivers the following comment: 'Poor things! I can wonder at nothing I hear, after what I have seen of their fearful wretchedness and destitution. None of us can imagine what change would be wrought in ourselves if we had the same shocking experience'.[26] The act of infanticide remains, as recent writings by Toni Morrison and Adrienne Rich show, one of the most 'unthinkable' of human experiences;[27] Webb's report bears gentle witness to its existence during the Irish famine.[28]

The female figure, as scene of hunger and 'bearer of meaning', receives a detailed physical inspection, never matched in characterizations of male famine victims. Observers highlight the woman's nakedness or quasi-nakedness, often with references to their own, resulting, discomfort. In the above extract from Osborne, the narrator's gaze lingers on the 'dark bodice only just sufficiently patched to make a bare covering to the bosom'. The 'exercise of power', denounced by Osborne, is disturbingly apparent in his own account, particularly in his description of visits to Irish workhouses. On a number of occasions he approvingly notes the efforts taken by women and young girls to hide their bodies from his scrutiny; one woman 'positively naked to the waist, but with the instinctive modest quickness of her race, as she talked to us, by crossing her arms and hitching up some of the rags which hung about her; she extemporised a bodice'.[29] Viewing children who were 'walked out into the yard for me to see them better', Osborne notices 'one child actually, whether of herself, or by order, put her hand across to hold the rags together in front of the poor thing who walked with her, that we might not be more shocked than she could by such ingenuity prevent'.[30] Maud Ellmann, in her work *The Hunger-Artists*, suggests that 'the spectacle of nakedness titillates the clothed with the delusion of their own superiority'.[31] Certainly, in Osborne's account, the extent of intrusion represented by the visitors is made unintentionally clear as is their power to require a closer inspection. Recalling his visit to a women's workhouse, Osborne exclaims: 'No power of pen can describe the state of the clothing of this seething mass of female pauperage; there were some, that the others, for shame's sake, would not let stand up before us; some I felt ashamed to ask to do so, though with more rags on.'[32] While these passages attest to the narrator's own discomfiture, their most memorable details are the efforts by women and children to evade inspection.

References to women's nakedness pervade famine accounts. For William Bennett, the 'miserably clad female forms we met along the public road were disgraceful, – disgusting'.[33] In the case of Nicholas Cummins, it is reluctantly conveyed:

> . . . decency would forbid what follows, but it must be told. My clothes were nearly torn off in my endeavour to escape from the throng of pestilence around, when my neckcloth was seized from behind by a gripe [*sic*] which compelled me to turn, I found myself grasped by a woman with an infant just born in her arms and the remains of a filthy sack across her loins – the sole covering of herself and baby.[34]

Occasionally, famine reports give some indication of what has led to this extremity, for example the pawning or sale of clothing in order to obtain food; one member of the Society of Friends notes that the women were 'unable to get out' having 'pawned almost every article'.[35] Yet, as one reads these accounts, the focus on women's nakedness itself becomes troubling. In the case of a writer like Osborne, the concern with women's unclothed bodies emerges as a marked obsession, moving his narrative into the realm of pornography. Writing with regard to the state of Irish workhouses, he cites over and over again the nakedness of female inmates. His fear of the consequences of the 'promiscuous, almost naked contact' of women crammed together in the workhouse wards comes to dominate his account:

> I can conceive nothing more indecently offensive, than such a space of ground, so closely covered with women, nearly nude – for I am told night dress, in these houses, too often may be taken to be just the covering of the bed clothes . . . Were it necessary or fitting, I could prove, from good evidence, taken in three different houses, that the cramming of these large dormitories with women, of every adult age, has proved itself to be, in itself, a monster evil.[36]

In *Monuments and Maidens*, Marina Warner cautions that the 'slipped chiton' is 'a most frequent sign that we are being pressed to accept an ulterior significance, not being introduced to the body as person';[37] in the case of famine narratives, this is strikingly, and disturbingly, so.

Many of the famine observers acknowledge the unsettling effects of what they have witnessed. For some visitors, such as Eli Burritt, Dufferin and Boyle, the overwhelming nature of the 'spectacle' of famine, as well as the fear of contagion, led them to cut short their journeys and return hurriedly to England. In his letter to the Duke of Wellington, Nicholas Cummins recalls being 'surrounded' by at least two hundred 'phantoms', 'such frightful spectres as no words can describe';[38] he proceeds with the account, cited above, of how his own clothes were 'nearly torn off' in his endeavour to escape, his neckcloth 'seized' by the woman's forceful 'gripe'. The physical distance which Cummins attempts to maintain is clearly threatened, both by the woman's compelling 'grasp' and the threat of nakedness posed to the observer himself. In this regard, famine accounts support Ellmann's observation that 'there is something about hunger, or more specifically about the spectacle of hunger, that deranges the distinction between self and other'.[39] A famous account, written on 24 December 1846, the very day Cummins' letter appeared in the *Times*, demonstrates this 'derangement' in a graphic way. Writing from West Clare to his superior in the Board of Works, Captain Wynne delivered the following report:

> I ventured through that parish [Clare Abbey] this day, to ascertain the condition of the inhabitants, and, although a man not easily moved, I confess myself unmanned by the extent and intensity of suffering I witnessed, more especially amongst the women and little children, crowds of whom were to be seen scattered over the turnip fields, like a flock of famishing crows, devouring the raw turnips, mothers half naked, shivering in the snow and sleet, uttering exclamations of despair, whilst their children were screaming with hunger; I am a match for any thing else I may meet with here, but this I cannot stand.[40]

The emotional force of Wynne's letter is still palpable and it is hardly surprising that this passage has become one of the most frequently-cited contemporary comments. The narrator's use of the word 'unmanned' is obviously striking; the intensity of his response to the scene of suffering women and children is such that it threatens his own identity as secure, male observer.

Wynne's description of the 'flock of famishing crows', grubbing for turnips in the field, is reminiscent of a much older passage: the figure of Famine 'plucking with nails and teeth at the scanty herbage' in Ovid's tale.[41] A more troubling aspect is its continuance of the dehumanizing language to be found throughout famine depictions. Female characters veer between a fatal passivity or, as in Cummins' account, a terrifying activity. Even the rare occasions when women are shown at work possess their own disturbing quality. Thus, in March 1847, William Bennett describes the employment of women and girls on the public works in Ballina as an offence against decency, the very witnessing of the scene 'melancholy and degrading':

> Independently of the moral effects of useless labour, – which it is impossible should be otherwise than listlessly pursued, – it was melancholy and degrading in the extreme to see the women and girls withdrawn from all that was decent and proper, and labouring in mixed gangs on the public roads. Not only in digging with the

spade, and with the pick, but in carrying loads of earth and turves on their backs, and wheeling barrows like men, and breaking stones, are they employed. My heart often sunk within me at the obviously deteriorating effects of such occupation, while the poor neglected children were crouched in groups around the bits of lighted turves in the various sheltered corners along the line.'[42]

Perhaps one of the most disturbing of all famine scenes is that recorded by Osborne in his *Gleanings from the West of Ireland*. Journeying with a companion from Leenane to Westport, he encounters an 'instance' of what he terms the 'wonderful way in which the Irish can, in hopes of ever so small a gift, sustain exertion in the practice of "running"':

> A girl of about twelve years of age, of course barefooted; dressed in a man's old coat, closely buttoned; ran beside our car, going at times very fast; for a distance, quite surprising: she did not ask for anything, but with hands crossed, kept an even pace, only adapting it, to our accidental change of speed; we, as a rule, refused all professional mendicants; we told her again and again, we would give her nothing; she never asked for anything: I saw my friend melting, I from time to time tried to congeal him, by using arguments against encouraging such bad habits, &c. He was firm, astonished at her powers, not so irritated, as I was, by her silent, wearying importunity; on she went, as we went; he shook his head at her; every quarter of a mile I thought the said shake softened in its negative character; I read fresh lectures on the evil of being led from right principles, by appeals to our pity, through the exhibition of what excited our wonder; the naked spokes of those naked legs, still seemed to turn in some mysterious harmony, with our wheels; on, on she went ever by our side, using her eyes only to pick her way, never speaking, not even looking at us; she won the day – she got very hot, coughed – but still ran with undiminished speed; my companion gave way – that cough did it, he gave her a fourpenny; I confess I forgave him – it was hard earned, though by a bad sort of industry.[43]

The dramatic energy of this piece is unforgettable: the girl's 'silent' running outside the carriage and the growing tension within; the various reactions of the spectators – one astonished, the other irritated; inside, the conflict between 'pity' and 'right principles' as, outside, she continues to run, 'never speaking, not even looking at us'; and the eventual 'giving way'. Osborne's own depiction of the scene has a seductive, rhythmic quality, yet, as one rereads the passage, its 'exhibition' becomes increasingly troubling: 'the naked spokes of those naked legs', turning in 'some mysterious harmony, with our wheels', the cough of the young girl, and the final judgement – 'a bad sort of industry'.

The spectacle of famine, as early as the 1840s, is thus frequently constructed through female figures, its traces inscribed on hunger-ravaged, unclothed bodies. Women's function as 'bearer of mean-ing', in these famine texts, possesses a number of aspects. Most obviously, the maternal body displays the absence of nourishment, the failure of 'primal shelter' and sustenance. The mother's milk is a central metaphor of the gift of life; her dry breast is thus one of famine's deepest horrors, expressive of a primal fear, where the 'fountain of life' is now death-giving. Milk is also, as Marina Warner and Julia Kristeva suggest, a metaphor 'of non-speech, of a "semiotics" that linguistic communication does not account for'.[44] The maternal body, with its particular associations with the 'unspoken' or 'non-speech', can thus function as the 'strange fold that changes culture into nature, the speaking into biology'.[45] The individual figure stands for a general breakdown or crisis, not only in society, but also in representation itself.

Many of these motifs continue in Carleton and Trollope's novels. Yet these narratives also offer a significant opportunity to study the effect of these scenes within a wider representation of famine. The question of how depictions of famine victims relate to the vexed question of famine's causation, how they determine interpretations of famine, will form the subject of the remainder of this chapter.

WILLIAM CARLETON'S *THE BLACK PROPHET*

Although published in 1846, Carleton's *The Black Prophet* is set during an earlier period, employing details from the famines of 1817 and 1822. Its analysis of famine's causation is of particular relevance to the times within which the novel first appeared, with forceful criticisms of the British legislature for its 'long course of illiberal legislation and unjustifiable neglect'[46] together with a strong condemnation of those, within Ireland, guilty of exploitation. The novel's characterization of the effects of famine, however, is significantly at odds with its treatment of its origins; the depiction of famine victims is coloured by Carleton's growing alarm at the implications of his own analysis. In this context, the narrative's representation of female victims has a key role.

The Black Prophet first appeared, in eight instalments, in the *Dublin University Magazine* from May to December 1846, and was published in book form, the following year, by Simms and M'Intyre of Belfast and London.[47] Although set some twenty years in the past, the novel was itself to have a prophetic quality. The first chapters were published in the summer of 1846, thus anticipating what would prove to be the fatal recurrence of blight – in Carleton's words, 'the fearful visitation' – only a few months later. By December, when the final instalment was published, the contemporary relevance of this 'Tale of Irish Famine' was acutely clear: 'The sufferings of that year of famine we have endeavoured to bring before those who may have the power in their hands of assuaging the similar horrors which have revisited our country in this.'[48]

Carleton's novel has a strong interventionist role, made explicit in the 1847 single-volume edition. Dedicating the volume to Lord John Russell, 'Prime Minister of Great Britain and Ireland', the author explains that his narrative is 'calculated to awaken those who legislate for us into something like a humane perception of a calamity that has been almost perennial in this country'. In an address to the prime minister, heavy with irony, he notes that action by Russell and his government would ensure that this famine novel, 'the first Tale of Irish Famine that ever was dedicated to an English Prime Minister', would also be the last, since such an 'enlarged and enlightened policy' would 'put it out of the power of any succeeding author ever to write another'.[49]

Carleton's preface to the 1847 edition, written in February of that year, defines the purpose of his novel both as memorial to the past and as a means of stimulating action in the present. In providing an 'authentic history' of previous periods of famine, it seeks to maintain these 'national inflictions' in the public memory. The record of past sufferings serves, in turn, to generate relief for those in present need, 'exciting', through its scenes of famine, 'a strong interest in the breasts of all those who can sympathize' and 'stirring' that 'sympathy into active and efficient benevolence'. The reader is thus cast in the role of potential donor, possessing the ability to sympathize with and to actively intervene in this calamity. The novel is, Carleton explains, his own contribution to 'that Great Fund of Benevolence', in the hope that its circulation 'among the higher and wealthier classes may, in the amplest sense, fulfil the objects for which it was written'.⁵⁰ The very purchase of the novel by readers, inevitably members of 'the higher and wealthier classes', becomes equivalent to a charitable act, this some 150 years before the 'pioneering' Band-aid appeal!

The subject of famine in *The Black Prophet*, as in other nineteenth-century novels treating of this theme, constitutes only one of the novel's plots; in Carleton's narrative it is accompanied by a conventional love story and murder mystery. Mave Sullivan and Sarah M'Gowan are rivals in their love for Con Dalton; while Jerry Sullivan and Condy Dalton, the fathers of Mave and Con, are enemies due to the belief that Dalton is guilty of the murder of Sullivan's brother, some twenty years earlier. Readers quickly infer that the key to the mystery's solution involves the 'Black Prophet', Donnel Dhu, father of Sarah. The unsolved murder cannot remain buried but rises to the surface in the next generation, with obvious parallels to the theme of famine, also returning to the present after some twenty years. As the novel develops, and in particular as it draws to a close, the differing, even competing requirements of its various plots become apparent; the conventions of love-story and murder-mystery demand complete resolution, the famine material defies such closure. Thus, while the good fortune of the Sullivan and Dalton families will be assured in the novel's conclusion, the fate of the thousands of starving people invoked by the novel remains unclear.

The difficulties faced by Carleton in reconciling the various plots are evident when, on a number of occasions in the novel, long discourses on the causes and effects of famine interrupt the novel's other story-lines. These interventions by the narrator, often directly addressed to the reader, include a bitter castigation of those responsible, either through negligence or exploitation, for the country's 'present' state, as in the following extract from chapter twenty:

> Indeed, one would imagine that after the many terrible visitations which we have had from destitution and pestilence, a legislature sincerely anxious for the health and comfort of the people, would have devoted itself, in some reasonable measure, to the humane consideration of such proper sumptuary and sanitary enactments, as would have provided not only against the recurrence of those evils, but for a more enlightened system of public health and cleanliness, and a better and more comfortable provision of food for the indigent and the poor. As it is at present, provision-dealers of all kinds, mealmongers, forestallers, butchers, bakers and huxters, combine together, and sustain such a general monopoly in food, as is at variance with the spirit of all law and humanity, and constitutes a kind of artificial famine in the country; and surely these circumstances ought not to be permitted, so long as we have a deliberative legislature, whose duty it is to watch and guard the health and morals of the people.[51]

With such comments, the narrative bursts out of its setting, 'some twenty years in the past', to address directly the causes of the famine now raging in 1846. Carleton's emphasis on the role of a legislature to provide 'food for the indigent and the poor' and to 'watch and guard the health and morals of the people' contrasts sharply with definitions of government responsibility held by many of his contemporaries. Early in 1847, Lord Brougham warned, in the House of Lords, that 'nothing could be worse for Ireland herself than that . . . the whole empire should contribute to the removal of a temporary misfortune which no human agency had brought upon Ireland'.[52] Carleton's insistence, in contrast, on the responsibilities of the legislature and the consequences of its neglect is also a significant reminder that non-interventionist views did not constitute the only ideas current in the political discourse of the time.

The people responsible for the 'general monopoly of food' are identified more fully in chapter seventeen; here Carleton carefully distinguishes between those observing the laws of the market and those guilty of wilful exploitation. While the activities of 'strong farmers, with bursting granaries and immense haggards' are implicitly criticized for their habit of storing large quantities of provisions 'until a year of scarcity arrives, when they draw upon their stock precisely when famine and prices are both at their highest', they are surpassed by a 'still viler class', those 'hard-hearted and well-known misers' who 'at every time, and in every season, prey upon the distress and destitution of the poor'.[53] Carleton's identification of 'a kind of artificial famine',[54] resulting from monopoly rather than food shortage, is particularly striking when read in the context of recent work on the significance of food distribution and entitlements. His famine discourses provide a detailed answer to the following question posed some one hundred and fifty years later: 'to say that starvation depends "not merely" on food supply but also on its "distribution" would be correct enough, though not remarkably helpful. The important question then would be: what determines distribution of food between different sections of the community?'[55]

The progressive nature of *The Black Prophet*'s analysis of famine's causation initially carries over into a sympathetic depiction of its victims, people 'impelled by hunger and general misery'.[56] At first, in a direct address to his readers, Carleton declares it 'not surprising' that people should, 'in the ravening madness of famine', 'forget those legal restraints, or moral principles, that protect property under ordinary or different circumstances'. He acknowledges that the sight of vessels 'laden with Irish provisions' leaving the ports presented, to 'destitute and starving multitudes', such a temptation 'as it was scarcely within the strength of men, furious with famine, to resist'.[57] Yet the actions of these 'starving multitudes', however understandable, and the specific threat they pose to property and its owners, become a growing source of alarm. The pressure on language to record the author's ambivalence is apparent in the profusion of oxymoron and other dualisms: the famine crowds are characterized by 'excited stupefaction', 'dull but frantic tumult', and, notably, 'an expression which seemed partly the wild excitement of temporary frenzy, and partly the dull, hopeless apathy of fatuity'.[58]

These representations of famine victims display features familiar in colonial descriptions, such as the conjunction of passive and threateningly active qualities, of human and animal terms: 'There is no beast, however, in the deepest jungle of Africa itself, so wild, savage and ferocious, as a human mob, when left to its own blind and headlong impulses.'[59] As the work of Homi Bhabha highlights, the ambivalences that so frequently inscribe the colonized subject reveal the contradictions of an authority which seeks to construct an 'other' which is at once different and sufficiently identical to justify control.[60] One of the most frequent conjunctions in colonial stereotypes is that of apathy and undisciplined action, where the colonized is both idle and frighteningly active; while idleness and ingratitude threaten an indifference to authority, the alternative poses an ever more fearful challenge.

Similarly, in *The Black Prophet*, fears as to the potentially violent 'impulses' of the starving 'mob' yield descriptions which are less and less sympathetic. Scenes of pillage produce disgusting and self-inflicted results: 'sickness of various descriptions, giddiness, retchings, fainting-fits, convulsions, and, in some cases, death itself, were induced by this wolfish and frightful *gluttony* on the part of the *starving* people' (emphases added).[61] The hungry poor now appear less as victims of a neglectful legislature and more as creatures dangerously misguided: 'victims of a quick and powerful contagion which spread the insane spirit of violence' as well as victims of disease and starvation. 'Respect for order' and the 'moral safety of society' are endangered by 'the great tyrannical instinct of self preservation' – one of Carleton's most curious constructions.[62]

In the context of the threat posed by famine protests and hence the text's decreasingly sympathetic presentation of famine crowds, the characterization of female victims has a central role. *The Black Prophet* contains two individualized and detailed portraits of famine victims, both of whom are women. The first, Margaret Murtagh, is a mother who is unmarried; her death occurs in chapter six of the novel after she is denied credit by the money-lender and miser,

Darby Skinadre, whose 'lank and sallow appearance', together with his exploitation of misery, render him 'like the very Genius of Famine'.[63] At first, Margaret attempts to comfort her lover as he lies in her arms, in a pietà-like scene:

> Margaret, on seeing him fall, instantly placed her baby in the hands of another woman, and, flying to him, raised his head and laid it upon her bosom . . . the young woman bent her mouth down to his ear, and said, in tones that were wild and hollow, and that had more of despair than even of sorrow in them –
> 'Tom, oh Tom, are you gone? – hear me –'
> But he replied not to her.
> 'Ah! there was a day,' she added, looking with a mournful smile around, 'when he loved to listen to my voice; but that day has passed for ever.'
> He opened his eyes as she spoke; hers were fixed upon him. He felt a few warm tears on his face, and she exclaimed in a low voice, not designed for other ears –
> 'I forgive you all, Tom dear – I forgive you all.'
> He looked at her, and, starting to his feet, exclaimed –
> 'Margaret, my own dear Margaret, hear me! She is dyin'!' he shouted, in a hoarse and excited voice – 'she is dyin' with want. I see it all. She's dead!'[64]

In an awkward and bewildering shift, the comforting mother herself becomes the martyr. The narrator's succeeding comment on her death occurs with a striking equivocation: 'It was too true: the unhappy girl had passed into another life; but whether from a broken heart, caused by sin, shame and desertion, or from famine and the pressure of general destitution and distress, could never be properly ascertained.' Thus two possibilities exist for Margaret's death: a broken heart or starvation; Carleton refuses to choose. The first explanation contains her death within a conventional female representation and removes the woman from the sphere of political victimization suggested by the second alternative, 'general destitution and distress'. Because of the 'sin' of her unmarried status, Margaret's vulnerability and victimization are of a moral rather than socio-economic nature, further obscuring details of her starvation.

Carleton's other detailed presentation of a famine victim also involves a mother figure. In the episode in which this description occurs, Nelly, one of the novel's chief characters, and a priest are on a journey whose purpose relates to another of the novel's plots, the murder mystery. The encounter with a famine victim thus adds to the gathering suspense, delaying both the end of their journey and the solution of the murder. This chapter also opens the final instalment of the novel; entitled 'A Picture for the Present' and offering 'a scene of appalling misery', it serves to remind readers of the famine which is happening in the novel's outer frame, late 1846. The narrator's opening exclamation, 'But how shall we describe it?',[65] heightens the reader's expectations of an horrific famine scene.

Many of the features present in this account echo the accounts of the 1840s famine, discussed earlier. Common motifs include a woman unable to bury her dead child, a woman divided between her children, often forced to choose between them, and, most typically, references to a woman unable to feed her child. In this cameo scene, the 'group of misery' consists of a mother and her three children, two of whom are dying, one is dead. Carleton's depiction of the family is harrowing; perhaps most memorable is the account of the woman, 'unhappy and perishing creature', 'divided or rather torn asunder, as it were, by the rival claims of affection' of her two surviving children:

> Lying close to her cold and shivering breast was an infant of about six months old, striving feebly, from time to time, to draw from that natural source of affection the sustenance which had been dried up by chilling misery and want. Beside her, on the left, lay a boy – a pale, emaciated boy – about eight years old, silent and motionless, with the exception that, ever and anon, he turned round his heavy blue eyes, as if to ask some comfort or aid, or even some notice from his unfortunate mother, who, as if conscious of these affectionate supplications, pressed his wan cheek tenderly with her fingers, to intimate to him that, as far as she could, she responded to, and acknowledged these last entreaties of the heart; whilst again, she felt her affections called upon by the apparently dying struggles of the infant that was, in reality, fast perishing at the now exhausted fountain of its life.[66]

The description of the dying infant at its mother's breast, as already mentioned, underlines the horror that the child's source of life has become the location of its death. The final part of this 'awful scene' is the body of the young girl, laid out by her mother; at this point, the narrator's voice exclaims, 'and oh, great God! what a task for a mother, and under what circumstances must it have been performed!'

As Carleton's attempt to represent this 'group of misery' develops, his language becomes increasingly strained, evidenced by curious and complex oscillations between 'high' and 'low', subhuman and human terms:

> Between these two claimants was the breaking heart of the woful mother divided, but the alternations of her love seemed now almost wrought up to the last terrible agonies of *mere animal instinct*, when the sufferings are strong in proportion to that debility of reason which supervenes in such deaths as arise from famine, or under these feelings of indescribable torture which tore her affection, as it were, to pieces, and *paralysed her higher powers of moral suffering.* (emphases added)[67]

The mother is the subject of a detailed physical description; from her body – 'her knit and painful eyebrows, over her shrunken upper forehead, upon her sharp cheek-bones, and along the ridge of her thin, wasted nose . . . her skeleton arms, pointed elbows and long-jointed fingers' – may be read the expression of 'gaunt and yellow famine in all its most hideous horrors'.[68] She is characterized as both rational and irrational, 'half-conscious and half-instinctive':

> Her eyeballs protruded even to sharpness, and as she glared around her with a half-conscious and half-instinctive look, there seemed a fierce demand in her eye that would have been painful were it not that it was occasionally tamed down into something mournful and imploring by a recollection of the helpless beings that were about her. Stripped, as she then was, of all that civilized society presents to a human being on the bed of death – without friends, aid of any kind, comfort, sympathy, or the consolations of religion – she

might be truly said to have sunk to the mere condition of animal life – whose uncontrollable impulses had thus left their startling and savage impress upon her countenance, unless, as we have said, when the faint dawn of consciousness threw a softer and more humane light into her features.[69]

The effects of famine are written on and by means of the maternal body; in case we have missed the point, the woman utters one word: 'very feebly and indistinctly, the word – *hunger*'.[70] By the end of the episode, the infant lies 'still at her breast', its death is quickly followed by that of its mother who dies in 'solemn joy' and 'sorrowful serenity'.[71] Of the four family members, only one child, the boy, survives. The novel quickly returns to the murder plot; no other reference is made to this scene nor, save for one paragraph in the concluding chapter, to the subject of famine.

This 'picture for the present' provides an undeniably graphic and moving description of famine suffering. Yet the terms in which the famine mother is presented are curiously ambivalent; she has 'sunk to the mere condition of animal life' and its 'uncontrollable impulses' but occasionally reveals 'a softer and more humane light'. The 'fierce demand' in her eye is potentially 'painful' to the observer; thus narrator and reader also become vulnerable to her gaze. In a significant qualification, this fierceness is 'tamed down' into 'something mournful and imploring'. The taming occurs as a result of the same trait which has prevented her sinking to the 'mere condition of animal life': what Carleton calls 'the faint dawn of consciousness', the recollection that she is a mother.[72] Underlying the passage is the suggestion that the woman's 'look' is too powerful and must be restrained, returned to a safe register of 'sorrowful' and maternal 'serenity'. Thus, as the text makes explicit, the identity of motherhood has a domesticating or taming role, modifying the woman's fierceness *and* the pain in observing her.

Motherhood constitutes the chief identifying characteristic of both female victims of famine; in both descriptions, economic or political factors receive little or no emphasis. The demonstrably powerful enactment of deaths from hunger remains curiously unrelated to the narrative's wider discussion of famine and its causes.

Instead Carleton's use of a woman's maternal body to portray famine's impact contains the representation within local and domestic terms, separating the women's starvation from issues of legislative responsibility and political causation. Perversions of the maternal ideal, a woman unable to feed her child, who outlives her child, who cannot bury her child, are the dominant features of scenes which are physically immediate but politically isolated.

With Carleton's novel a further aspect to the feminization of famine is revealed. The characterization of famine mothers, through the associations of domesticity and natural instinct, together with connotations of sin, even of madness, allows the author to move the discourse on famine away from the political and economic spheres and into a moral register. The suggestion of 'nature' being the special provenance of motherhood, both less and more than human, is particularly significant. As Warner and many other feminist critics have emphasized, the 'conflation of nature and woman only continues the false perception that neither is inside culture, that women do not participate in it, let alone create it'.[73] The figure of woman can thus serve to restrain the challenges delivered earlier in the famine novel, through the 'strange fold that changes culture into nature',[74] politics into morality.

ANTHONY TROLLOPE'S *CASTLE RICHMOND*

Castle Richmond, one of Trollope's four Irish novels, was first published in 1860.[75] Its author had lived in Ireland from 1841 to 1850, and intermittently in the 1850s, as surveyor for the British postal service.[76] On the eve of his departure from Ireland in 1859, he wrote his famine novel, *Castle Richmond*, set on the borders of Cork and Kerry, near the towns of Kanturk and Mallow, and covering the period 1846 to 1847 – what Trollope calls 'the famine year'.

Like *The Black Prophet*, famine in *Castle Richmond* provides the backdrop to a conventional love-story. Many critics of Trollope's novel thus view its references to famine as peripheral, possessing only a casual link with the main plot.[77] One of the novel's first reviews, published in the *Saturday Review* on 19 May 1860, wittily condemned Trollope's mixture of subjects: 'It is of course impossible to persuade him to give up a practice which he appears to have adopted in principle, but the milk and the water really should be in separate pails.'[78] Yet, in a rare interpretation of the novel, the reviewer went on to argue that the famine material constituted Trollope's primary interest:

> Perhaps the most curious part of the book is that which relates to the Irish famine. It is impossible not to feel that that was the part of it about which Mr Trollope really cared, but that, as he had to get a novel out of it, he was in duty bound to mix up a hash of Desmonds and Fitzgeralds with the Indian meal on which his mind was fixed as he wrote.

To date, most accounts of the novel have overlooked the significance of its famine material; yet, both the context within which Trollope's famine representations emerged and the particular, often troubling, characterizations which he offers deserve much closer attention.

Castle Richmond was not Trollope's first contribution to the historiography of the Irish famine. Between August 1849 and June 1850, the *Examiner*, a liberal Sunday paper, published seven letters written by the young author on 'the subject of Ireland, her undoubted grievances, her modern history, her recent sufferings, and her present actual state'.[79] Trollope's articles focused, in particular, on the causes of the recent famine and the measures taken to alleviate distress, partially in response to a series of letters on Ireland published by Sidney Godolphin Osborne in the *Times*, in June and July of 1849.[80] In his autobiography, Trollope recalled the purpose and unhappy fate of his letters:

> S.G.O. was at that time denouncing the Irish scheme of the Administration in the Times, using very strong language, – as those who remember his style will know. I fancied then – as I still think – that I understood the country much better than he did; and I was anxious to show that the steps taken for mitigating the terrible evil of the times were the best which the Minister of the day could have adopted . . . They [the letters] were favourably entertained, – if the printing and publication be favourable entertainment. But I heard no more of them. The world in Ireland did not declare that

the Government had at last been adequately defended, nor did the treasurer of the *Examiner* send me a cheque in return.[81]

Trollope's continuing determination to communicate his view of 'the terrible evil of the times', and to as wide an audience as possible, provided a crucial motivation for the writing of *Castle Richmond*. Much of the novel's material, such as its portrayal of the relief-schemes, its treatment of famine's causes and consequences, echoes the *Examiner* letters and develops their refutation of Osborne's analysis. The letters also, however, provide another context to the novel, one which has received little or no comment, demonstrating Trollope's critical views of previous representations of famine.

In his first letter to the *Examiner*, published 25 August 1849 and titled 'Irish Distress', Trollope mentions the 'fearfully graphic' and 'awfully familiar' pictures of famine and plague given by Osborne and 'by almost every class of people able to narrate what they have seen'.[82] The first section of this chapter has given some idea of the type of 'pictures' to which he is alluding: sketches of famine conditions which appeared in newspapers at the time or in the published memoirs of visitors to Ireland. While conceding that 'much good has arisen from these vivid narrations', Trollope strictly limits their potential significance: 'What do such tales, true as they are, prove to us, but that there has been a famine and a plague in the land?' Furthermore, he fears, they have conveyed an overly pessimistic view of Ireland, where there is 'no hope left for the people who had been afflicted'.[83] By 6 April 1850, when the third letter appeared, Trollope's attitude to the 'vivid narrations' and 'recital of horrors' by contemporary newspapers is much more critical. No longer 'true' tales, they are condemned for their exaggeration and inaccuracy:

> During the whole period of the famine I never saw a dead body lying exposed in the open air, either in a town or in the country . . . I feel that apology is due for such a subject; but you will remember that the Irish newspapers of the time teemed with the recital of such horrors, – that the air was said to be polluted by

unburied corpses; that descriptions were given of streets and lanes in which bodies lay for days on the spots where the starved wretches had last sunk; and that districts were named in which the cabins were fabled to contain more dead than living tenants.[84]

In a deliberate challenge to newspapers' claims to provide factual accounts, Trollope characterizes their representations of famine as 'horrid novels':

> The Irish press is not proverbial for a strict adherence to unadorned truth; and, under the circumstances, it was perhaps not surprising that writers habituated to disdain facts should exaggerate and compose novels; but those horrid novels were copied into the English papers, and were then believed by English readers.

By 1849, the first generation of historiographical debate on the famine was clearly underway, with debates not merely involving the causes of famine, but also concerning the accuracy of earlier representations. Throughout the *Examiner* letters, Trollope emphasizes his own credentials as 'eye-witness' to the misery of the period. At some moments, his writing betrays a defensive tone:

> Now it may be said that if I did not enter cabins, I could not see the horrid sights which were to be met within; but such a remark cannot apply to that which is said to have been of such frequent occurrence out under the open sky. The whole period was spent by me in passing from one place to another in the south and west of Ireland.[85]

Curiously, he emphasizes his ability, as 'eye-witness of the misery of the period', to 'point out what did not happen, and tell of scenes which were not of frequent occurrence';[86] in other words, his function is primarily one of exposing others' fictions. Ten years later, Trollope was to engage once more, this time in fictional form, with the 'vivid narrations' of his contemporaries. And, as the following reading will demonstrate, his narrative, *Castle Richmond*, came to provide its own version of the 'horrid novel'.

The love-plot of *Castle Richmond* does involve, in the words of its early reviewer, 'a hash of Desmonds and Fitzgeralds', with three central characters, Clara Desmond, Owen Fitzgerald and Herbert Fitzgerald. Clara, sister of the young Earl of Desmond whose family, previously 'great', is now bankrupt, is initially attracted to Owen, member of a younger branch of the Fitzgerald family. Herbert, Owen's cousin, is heir to the Fitzgerald name and property, a position threatened for much of the novel because of the possible illegitimacy of his parents' marriage. The novel details Clara and Owen's ill-fated attraction, the supplanting of Owen by Herbert, and Herbert's eventual securing of both his inheritance and love-object.

The event of famine first connects with the love plot in providing an occupation for Clara following her family's refusal to allow her marriage to Owen. She becomes involved in philanthropic work, specifically relief-schemes initiated by Herbert; thus famine is also the means through which the future lovers, Clara and Herbert, are brought together: 'She had devoted herself from the first to do her little quota of work towards lessening the suffering around her, and the effort had been salutary to her.'[87] As the narrative progresses, Herbert's work in famine relief emerges as a crucial factor in his becoming the novel's champion. Trollope clearly faces difficulty in transferring Clara's preference from the more rugged Owen to the character of Herbert – acknowledged by Trollope himself in his autobiography as a prig.[88] Consequently, Herbert's efforts to relieve the sufferings of those affected by famine have a crucial narrative function, supporting his claims to the status of hero.

The narrative's sub-plot, the threat to Herbert's family fortune and status, also develops simultaneously with the spread of famine; when the Fitzgerald patrimony is most in danger, the famine is at its worst. On one occasion, the text comes close to suggesting that the ill-fortune of the tenants derives from their landlord: 'To them, the Miss Fitzgeralds, looking at the poverty-stricken assemblage, it almost seemed as though the misfortune of their house had brought down its immediate consequences on all who had lived within their circle; but this was the work of the famine.'[89] The narrator is clearly anxious to dismiss this connection and determinedly blames the misfortune of the poor on 'the famine', a force totally separate from the Fitzgerald family. The relationship between lower-class famine victim and upper-class characters, however, continues to trouble the narrative.

Trollope's analysis of the origins of famine is elaborated in chapter seven of his novel, entitled 'The Famine Year'. Directly engaging with contemporary debates, he strongly rejects popular views of the famine as caused by 'the idolatry of popery, or of the sedition of demagogues, or even mainly by the idleness of the people'.[90] The destruction of the potato he attributes to 'the work of God', echoing providentialist views of the blight which were current in the 1840s. Unlike many of his contemporaries, Trollope dismisses any suggestion that this is an 'exhibition of God's anger', arguing instead that it exemplifies only 'his mercy'.[91] The underlying responsibility for famine is firmly assigned to the practice of sub-division, in particular the sub-letting of land by large tenants.[92] The author strongly condemns this class who, not consenting to be 'farmers', 'looked to be gentlemen living on their property, but who should have earned their bread by the work of their brain, or failing that, by the sweat of their brow':

> And thus a state of things was engendered in Ireland which discouraged labour, which discouraged improvements in farming, which discouraged any produce from the land except the potato crop; which maintained one class of men in what they considered to be the gentility of idleness, and another class, the people of the country, in the abjectness of poverty.[93]

'With thorough rejoicing, almost with triumph', he reports that this 'idle, genteel class' has been 'cut up root and branch' by the famine.

Yet Trollope's discourse on famine's causation contains some curious contradictions, particularly in relation to the characters within his own story. Ironically, the closest example within *Castle Richmond* to the 'genteel idler', castigated as the cause of famine, could be considered to be Herbert, the novel's hero. Herbert is not a tenant; yet he comes to resemble those Irish who see themselves wrongly as 'gentlemen' since, as an illegitimate son, Herbert too 'owned no properties and had no places when the matter came to be properly sifted'.[94] The story does not cause Herbert to be 'cut up root and branch' as befalls the 'idle, genteel class'; yet, for the time that he is nameless and without a career, he is perilously close to 'the gentility of idleness'. Although the later restoration of Herbert's name and position clearly limits such an interpretation of his character, a curious tension remains in the text between the 'gentility' which marks the story's hero and that which identifies those responsible for famine's origin.

In this context, Herbert's work to relieve the sufferings of famine victims defends the 'gentleman' hero against the charge of 'idleness'. With the emphasis on Herbert's activity comes a corresponding insistence on the 'idleness' or apathy of the poor, part of the narrative's increasing focus on famine victims:

> And now the great fault of those who were the most affected was becoming one which would not have been at first expected. One would think that starving men would become violent, taking food by open theft – feeling, and perhaps not without some truth, that the agony of their want robbed such robberies of its sin. But such was by no means the case . . . The fault of the people was apathy.[95]

On two occasions in the novel, Herbert as famine benefactor directly encounters the apathetic, male recipients of his aid. Both of these scenes take place at public relief-works, in the winter of 1846–47. A close reading of Trollope's depiction of these encounters reveals interesting tensions regarding power and its operation.

In chapter eighteen, Herbert meets a gang of labourers waiting to begin work on cutting away a hill, one of the deliberately 'unproductive' projects of the time. The men's presence is vaguely threatening: 'wretched-looking creatures, half-clad, discontented, with hungry eyes, each having at his heart's core a deep sense of injustice done personally upon him'; yet their characterization also includes more passive qualities: they are 'melancholy, given to complaint, apathetic, and utterly without interest in what they were doing'.[96] Their reported speech, transcribed in dialect form, such as the explanation of their inability to start work because 'we did not exactly know whether yer honer'd be after beginning at the top or the bothom',⁹⁷ emphasizes their comic stupidity and situates them as objects of ridicule. Underlying the narrator's indulgent humour, however, is the implication that the men, through ignorance and apathy, have contributed to their own wretchedness: one man, 'cold, however, as he was', would 'do nothing towards warming himself, unless that occasional shake can be considered as a doing of something'.⁹⁸ Yet later we are told that 'an Irishman would despise himself' for the 'low economy'⁹⁹ of putting down a wheelbarrow while speaking.

The stereotypes employed in characterizing these men, listlessness combined with extravagance of energy, clearly contradict each other in what Homi Bhabha has called the 'productive ambivalence of the object of colonial discourse'.¹⁰⁰ Undisciplined energy and idle apathy, the presentation remains ambivalent. Yet both characterizations imply that a controlling force is necessary, to motivate and govern the men's activity. The confusion within colonial stereotypes carries over to those holding authority; the representative of imperial power, the engineer of the relief works, is 'bewildered'.¹⁰¹ Interestingly, the engineer also initially fails to distinguish Herbert, holder of power and privilege, from the labourers: 'He had not observed, or probably, had not known Herbert Fitzgerald.'¹⁰²

The suggested link between Herbert, as upper-class spectator, and the men he observes becomes clearer in a later encounter also set on the relief-works. This meeting's position in the narrative is significant: Herbert, now believing himself to be illegitimate, is on his way to acquaint the Desmonds with his loss of fortune and his loss of the 'things which money buys': 'outward respect, permission to speak with authority among his fellow-men, for power and place, and the feeling that he was prominent in his walk of life'.¹⁰³ When he meets the gang of 'road-destroyers', Herbert receives the chance to recover his status, 'to be in advance of other men', by entering into dialogue with the men and by allowing them the chance to voice their complaints. Significantly, he is now on foot, and thus is physically closer to the men. Unlike previous meetings, he refuses to 'discourse' with them, 'running the gauntlet through them as best he might, and shaking them off from him, as they attempted to cling round his steps', and loses or refuses the opportunity to demonstrate his prominence.[104] In seeking to distance himself from the famine victims, ironically he comes closer to their position.

These two episodes trace, in suggestive ways, both the operations of privilege and its limitations. Herbert's feeling of being 'prominent' does not exist in and of itself; instead he depends on others recognizing and assigning to him this position.[105] Power-relations are produced by 'discoursing' with others; as the narrative continues to demonstrate, they are acts of enunciation which require an assenting audience.

In *Castle Richmond*, Trollope provides a number of detailed characterizations of individual famine victims through encounters with the upper-class characters, Herbert and/or Clara. A series of pairings results: the first is between female benefactor and female victim; then Herbert and Clara together encounter a woman seeking charity. As Clara fades into insignificance, Herbert meets other men, in the episodes discussed above; finally, the upper-class man, alone, encounters a starving woman late in the novel. Women's hungry bodies emerge as the central object, famine's effects most graphically imaged through the construction of female spectacle.

The narrative's pairing of upper and lower-class woman occurs, not in the roadworks, an exclusively male location, but in a little store where the three women, Clara and the two Fitzgerald sisters, sell food to non-labourers, women and old men. Here, as Trollope approvingly explains, food is sold rather than given away, to prevent 'hundreds' getting it 'who were not absolutely in want, and would then sell it'.[106] These upper-class women thus dispense the political decisions of governing men, while they receive from poor women the coins earned by their male relations. Within this female exchange of the currency of men, Clara, an upper-class woman, meets a woman suffering from the effects of famine.

The description of the lower-class woman, as in the contemporary representations discussed earlier, outlines her maternal and partially-naked form: 'a woman came into the place with two children in her arms and followed by four others of different ages. She was a gaunt, tall creature, with sunken cheeks and hollow eyes, and her clothes hung about her in unintelligible rags'.[107] The structure of the passage pairs Clara and the poorer woman; the woman

rubs her 'forefinger' in the food and invites Clara to do likewise.
Clara obeys, 'looking into the woman's face, half with fear and half
with pity, and putting, as she spoke, her pretty delicate finger down
into the nasty daubed mess of parboiled yellow flour';[108] her feelings
are ambivalent, fearful and pitying, sympathetic yet removed. The
narrator's view initially follows a similar pattern, allowing the
woman 'reason for her complaints', but seeing her as 'one of many
thousands' with similar grievances.[109]

As the episode progresses, however, the dominant aspect in the
characterization of the poor woman emerges as her ingratitude.
This 'thanklessness', we are told, is the 'hardest burden which had
to be borne by those who exerted themselves at this period'. In a
lengthy intervention, the narrator acknowledges some basis for this
ingratitude yet quickly restrains the force of his comments by
detailing the 'hard task' of other more 'delicate' women:

> To call them ungrateful would imply too deep a reproach, for their
> convictions are that they were being ill used by the upper classes.
> When they received bad meal which they could not cook, and
> even in their extreme hunger could hardly eat half-cooked; when
> they were desired to leave their cabins and gardens, and flock into
> the wretched barracks which were prepared for them; when they
> saw their children wasting away under a suddenly altered system of
> diet, it would have been unreasonable to expect that they should
> have been grateful. Grateful for what? Had they not at any rate a
> right to claim life, to demand food that should keep them and their
> young ones alive? But not the less was it a hard task for delicate
> women to work hard, and to feel that all the work was unappreci-
> ated by those whom they so thoroughly commiserated, whose
> sufferings they were so anxious to relieve.[110]

The above extract begins as a forceful articulation of the 'rights' of
the starving, then veers sharply away from the implications of this
argument with an extraordinary attempt to render equally sympathetic the efforts of upper-class, 'delicate' women. The more lethal
'delicacy' of those who are starving is obscured. On the one hand,
the comparison insists on the relationship of the two groups, since
one's sufferings directly results from the other's ingratitude. Yet the

other side of this equation, the origin of the poor woman's hunger, is not explored; instead the narrator is at pains to illustrate the upper-class women as 'anxious to relieve' sufferings. Thus Clara, as philanthropic woman, exists as an example of her class's dedication and power – to dispense charity. A disturbing implication lingers: that those with the power to 'relieve' suffering possess other, deeper responsibilities.

In the novel's second presentation of a famine woman, Herbert and Clara encounter 'a sight' which, as Trollope explains, 'for years past had not been uncommon in the south of Ireland, but which had become frightfully common during the last two or three months'.[111] The 'sight' is a woman's body and receives, from the gaze of the narrator, an unprecedented physical inspection. Firstly, the description emphasizes both her rags and the nakedness which such rags have failed to conceal from the examining eye: 'A woman was standing there, of whom you could hardly say that she was clothed, though she was involved in a mass of rags which covered her nakedness. Her head was all uncovered, and her wild black hair was streaming round her face.' Like the earlier 'unintelligible rags', a complex phrase such as 'involved in a mass of rags' only partially covers the nakedness exposed. The passage continues with an evaluation of the woman's lack of 'comeliness' and a close scrutiny of her body: 'She was short and broad in the shoulders, though wretchedly thin; her bare legs seemed to be of nearly the same thickness up to the knee, and the naked limbs of the children were like yellow sticks.' The description of the individual woman then gives way to a general meditation on 'the kinds of physical develop-ment among the Celtic peasantry in Ireland'; the controlling factor remains 'what is attractive to the eye':

It is strange how various are the kinds of physical development among the Celtic peasantry in Ireland. In many places they are singularly beautiful, especially as children; and even after labour and sickness shall have told on them as labour and sickness will tell, they still retain a certain softness and grace which is very nearly akin to beauty. But then again in a neighbouring district they will be found to be squat, uncouth, and in no way attractive to the eye.[112]

Significantly, the group of which the woman is part is a biological species named 'Celtic'; her male counterparts, in their relation to the world of waged labour, are part of a political grouping named 'Irish'.[113]

Throughout the scene, the male narrator as observer carries the power to inspect and judge, to define what is attractive and repulsive. The spectacle thus created once again presents 'woman as image, man as bearer of the look'; as Laura Mulvey argues: 'In a world ordered by sexual imbalance, pleasure in looking has been split between active/male and passive/ female.'[114]

The episode continues with Herbert and Clara's conversation with the woman; this dialogue, although dominated by Herbert's interrogation, also conveys the differing reactions of male and female spectators. Both Herbert and Clara initially fail to recognize her, although she insists, identifying herself as Bridget Sheehy, that 'shure an' it's yer honour knows me well enough; and her ladyship too'.[115] Clara, to whom Bridget initially directs her appeal, reacts with sympathy: 'Clara looked at them piteously and put her hand towards her pocket. Her purse was never well furnished, and now in these bad days was usually empty. At the present moment it was wholly so.' Like Bridget, Clara lacks money and joins her in beseeching Herbert to intervene. Both women's appeals go temporarily unanswered by Herbert, possessor of money and the caretaker of political argument. Instead Herbert's response is mediated by larger arguments of political economy, particularly the view that charity in the form of money must not be given.[116] 'Herbert had learned deep lessons of political economy and was by no means disposed to give promiscuous charity on the road-side.'[117] The conclusion of the chapter, when Herbert finally succumbs to Bridget's request, will expose these political arguments to be untenable, a revelation whose full implications for the prevailing system of famine relief remain unacknowledged: 'But the system was impracticable, for it required frames of iron and hearts of adamant. It was impossible not to waste money in almsgiving.'[118]

Gender and economics thus separate this meeting with a begging woman from Herbert's encounters with men at work on the roads. To give work and wages to a male labourer involves a relationship near to the type of waged economy desired by the narrator, however useless or deliberately unproductive the work. To give money to a mother is charity and, intriguingly, 'promiscuous'. The reference to promiscuity, with its connotations of casual and indiscriminate activity, attributes to the woman a lack of chastity in begging, a suggestion reinforced by reference to her nakedness. Yet the phrase contains an interesting ambiguity as to whether donor or recipient of charity risks promiscuity.

Trollope's narrative thus configures issues of sexuality and charity, the sexuality of the object viewed and the charity of the spectator, in such a way as to suggest that the act of giving reinforces deviant or uncontrolled sexuality. Anxiety increasingly characterizes Herbert's reaction to the woman; her threat is twofold: economically problematic *and* sexually different. Laura Mulvey argues that 'woman as icon, displayed for the gaze and enjoyment of men, the active controllers of the look, always threatens to evoke the anxiety it originally signified'.[119] In Mulvey's analysis, the original anxiety concerns sexual difference; in Trollope's narrative, the woman represents both economic and sexual difference, threatening the fragile discipline of the male observer and a male-dominated political system.

Later in the novel, in a chapter called 'The Last Stage', a similar episode occurs which reinforces the power of the male character and in which a woman's body even more clearly functions as icon and spectacle. In this scene, Herbert is the sole observer. The picture of a female victim is filtered through his perspective much more than in the earlier scene; as male protagonist he both 'articulates the look and creates the action'.[120]

Nameless and fortuneless, Herbert is on his way to see Clara on the day before his departure to England; he takes a circuitous route, prolonging the gratification of his meeting with her. Seeking shelter from 'a squall of rain', Herbert enters a cabin. His 'glance' and body frame the description of what is inside: 'Beneath his feet was the damp earthen floor, and around him were damp, cracked walls, and over his head was the old lumpy thatch.'[121] After some time he perceives that:

the place was inhabited. Squatting in the middle of the cabin, seated on her legs crossed under her, with nothing between her and the wet earth, there crouched a woman with a child in her arms. At first, so dark was the place, Herbert hardly thought that the object before him was a human being.

From the first details, the woman is scarcely human: squatting animal-like, her eyes 'gleaming' with a 'dull, unwholesome brightness'. Closer scrutiny by the male observer reveals her nakedness:

> And then he looked at her more closely. She had on her some rag of clothing which barely sufficed to cover her nakedness, and the baby which she held in her arms was covered in some sort; but he could see, as he came to stand close over her, that these garments were but loose rags which were hardly fastened round her body. Her rough short hair hung down upon her back, clotted with dirt, and the head and face of the child which she held was covered with dirt and sores. On no more wretched object, in its desolate solitude, did the eye of man ever fall.

Herbert's gaze thus governs the view of the woman's body; the perspective from which we are told that rags 'barely sufficed to cover her nakedness' is clearly his – 'the eye of man'.

Trollope's narration of this encounter between upper-class male and the unnamed woman graphically illustrates Michel Foucault's definition of the power inherent in the deployment, and inspection, of sexuality:

> this form of power demanded constant, attentive and curious presences for its exercise; it presupposed proximities; it proceeded through examination and insistent observation; it required an exchange of discourses, through questions that exhorted admissions, and confidences that went beyond the questions that were asked. It implied a physical proximity and an interplay of intense sensations . . . It wrapped the sexual body in its embrace.[122]

As Herbert comes to 'stand over' the woman, his gaze wraps her body 'in its embrace'; only his turning his face away can 'relieve her from her embarrassment'.[123]

From 'insistent observation', Herbert proceeds to an interrogation, a series of 'questions that exhorted admissions', to which the woman responds with silence or in monosyllables. This exchange, or more accurately, its absence, provides interesting insights into Herbert's own position. The narrator stresses, repeatedly and sympathetically, the discomfort and dilemma caused for Herbert by the woman's lack of communication:

> For a while Herbert stood still, looking round him, for the woman was so motionless and uncommunicative that he hardly knew how to talk to her. That she was in the lowest depth of distress was evident enough, and it behoved him to administer to her immediate wants before he left her; but what could he do for one who seemed to be so indifferent to herself?[124]

A note of censure appears in accounts of the woman's indifference and her failure to 'show any of those symptoms of reverence which are habitual to the Irish when those of a higher rank enter their cabins'.[125] Ironically the narrator fails to acknowledge that, at this position in the narrative, Herbert has lost his 'higher rank' and fortune. More significantly, the repeated emphasis on Herbert's inability to act reveals that Herbert does not possess the all-encompassing power one might expect from one in his position; instead he depends on the object of his gaze to speak and act. Because of her silence and lack of response, he does not know how to behave.

> For a minute or two he said nothing – hardly, indeed, knowing how to speak, and looking from the corpse-like woman back to the life-like corpse back to the woman, as though he expected that she would say something unasked . . . He felt that he was stricken with horror as he remained there in the cabin with the dying woman and the naked corpse of the poor dead child. But what was he to do? He could not go and leave them without succour. The woman had made no plaint of her suffering and had asked for nothing.[126]

The operation of Herbert's power in giving charity thus depends on the woman articulating a request; as in the earlier road-work scenes, the relationship of famine victim and potential donor emerges, not as a simple form of superiority, but as a complex form of interdependence.

Other moments in the episode serve to re-establish Herbert's power: in order to see the woman's child, he moves the straw with 'the handle of his whip'. The woman's characterization, meanwhile, sinks further into animal terms, with farcical results: 'and sinking lower down upon her haunches . . . pushing back with it the loose hairs from her face, tried to make an effort at thinking'.[127] In the following passage, the most horrific event occurs:

> And he stood close over her and put out his hand and touched the baby's body. As he did so, she made some motion as though to arrange the clothing closer round the child's limbs but Herbert could see that she was making an effort to hide her own nakedness. It was the only effort that she made while he stood there beside her.[128]

In touching the child, Herbert not only approaches even closer to the woman's body but, through the child's position at her breast, touches her body. Significantly, the 'only effort' she makes is to seek to hide her nakedness from his enquiring eye. It is not difficult to recognize the intrusion, even violence, which his touch and gaze constitute; Herbert's power to cause embarrassment in a woman previously described as almost dead is horrifically clear.

Herbert's actions in the closing of the scene are quite extraordinarily ineffectual. He places a silk handkerchief over the dead child's body, barely overcoming his disgust, and gives 'a silver coin or two' to the mother. Trollope ignores the absurdity of giving coins, themselves only symbols of help, to a woman who lacks the opportunity, even life-energy, to exchange them.[129] The closing lines of the chapter, 'her doom had been spoken before Herbert had entered the cabin',[130] seek to protect any individual, specifically Herbert, from blame. The woman's death is thus deemed inevitable, though not explicitly presented and only obliquely mentioned in the chapter's closing lines.

Within this episode, the reader encounters a representation disturbingly close to being what Laura Mulvey calls a 'moment of erotic contemplation',[131] the construction of a female spectacle through the operation of a powerful yet anxious male gaze. None of the famine women reappears, thus reinforcing their status as icons. However, these encounters do crucially relate to the narrative's main concern, the relationship between Clara and Herbert. Immediately preceding the scene in which Herbert and Clara meet Bridget Sheehy, Herbert's 'sweet honeyed compliments' are unfavourably compared to the 'vigour' of Owen's affection. The succeeding famine scene thus not only solidifies the relationship of Herbert and Clara because of her recognition of his generosity, but, more problematically, enacts Clara's 'spirit's wish' to 'feel itself subdued', her dream of 'woman's subjugation'. As a consequence, Herbert's position in the narrative becomes central.[132] Similarly, the end of 'The Last Stage' provides a clear contrast between the passive spectacle of the famine woman and Herbert's active narrative role. On his way to Desmond Court, Herbert draws the following moral from the scene:

> Whatever might be the extent of his own calamity, how could he think himself unhappy after what he had seen? how could he repine at aught that the world had done for him, having now witnessed to how low a state of misery a fellow human being might be brought? Could he, after that, dare to consider himself unfortunate?[133]

This meditation ensures that the immediate consequence of the episode is a restoration of Herbert's happiness and belief in his own superiority; in Foucault's words, 'the pleasure discovered fed back to the power that encircled it'.[134]

Herbert's encounter with Clara, in the succeeding chapter, reveals a further consequence, releasing the 'erotic' suggestions implicit in the preceding famine scene.

> He came towards her respectfully, holding out his hand that he might take hers; but before he had thought of how she would act she was in his arms. Hitherto, of all betrothed maidens, she had been the most retiring. Sometimes he had thought her cold when she had left the seat by his side to go and nestle closely by his sister. She had avoided the touch of his hand and the pressure of his arm,

and had gone with him speechless, if not with anger then with dismay, when he had carried the warmth of his love beyond the touch of his hand or the pressure of his arm. But now she rushed into his embrace and hid her face upon his shoulder . . .[135]

The change in their relationship is ostensibly because of Herbert's loss of fortune. However, the main focus of the passage concerns the sexual tension, not previously acknowledged, between an aggressive Herbert and retiring Clara, a tension which can now be resolved. In both encounters, Herbert moves forward to touch a woman; the repressed eroticism of a woman, visually 'embraced' in the earlier scene, is now apparent in his meeting with Clara. From her initial identity as famine donor, Clara has come to adopt the position of famine women in *Castle Richmond*, asserting Herbert's power and attraction against suggestions to the contrary.

In *Castle Richmond*, famine is depicted through the construction of a female spectacle which is significantly more detailed and developed than any of its contemporary narratives. This provides one means of evading what may be termed the 'disjunctions and contradictions'[136] released by the narrative, the unresolved and troubling questions concerning power and responsibility. Through his characterization of female victims, Trollope seeks to present the unstoppable force of famine and the benevolent, if unsuccessful, efforts of individuals and government. A 'resisting reader', however, can identify the encounter between benefactor and victim in a very different way. Underlying these famine scenes is an anxiety which the female figure threatens to expose – the failure of a political system.

Images of women, the signs of economic and sexual difference, thus *contain*, in a double sense, a threatening potential – both possessing and restraining this power. A similar doubleness emerges with regard to the recurring question of the very possibility of representation: the figure of woman 'stands for' this crisis, providing a means of expressing *and* evading breakdown. Studies of images of women in various types of narrative have demonstrated how the female image is constructed as a guarantee against the difficulties of representation itself. Jacqueline Rose, in a discussion of cinema, cites films which 'set up the image of woman as cinema' in 'such a way as to simultaneously refer to and disavow the problem of cinema'.[137] Trollope's imaging of famine as female spectacle similarly functions to ensure that the problem of famine is at once communicated and obscured.

NOTES AND REFERENCES

1. William Bennett, *Narrative of a recent journey of six weeks in Ireland in connexion with the subject of supplying small seed to some of the remoter districts* . . . (London and Dublin, 1847), p. 133.

2. *Transactions of the Central Relief Committee of the Society of Friends during the famine in Ireland, in 1846 and 1847* (Dublin, 1852), p. 38. Reports of the visits to Ireland in 1846 and 1847 by William Forster, his son William Edward Forster, R. Barclay Fox and others, were published separately during late 1846 and early 1847; extracts from famine-observers, 'illustrative of the condition of Ireland', are also included in *Transactions*. A useful selection of contemporary documents, 1841–51, is provided by John Killen's *The Famine Decade* (Belfast, 1995).

3. Lord Dufferin and Hon. G. F. Boyle, *Narrative of a Journey from Oxford to Skibbereen during the Year of the Irish Famine* (Oxford, 1847); as the title-page notes, all proceeds of the work were to be sent to Skibbereen. Dufferin (1826–1902) was the son of Helen Selina Sheridan and great-grandson of the Irish dramatist, Richard Brinsley Sheridan; later he became governor-general of Canada (1872–78) and Viceroy of India (1884–88).

4. Sidney Godolphin Osborne (1808–89) was a well-known English philanthropist and author of 'lay sermons' in the *Times*. His letters concerning his Irish visit appeared in the *Times* on 14 and 21 June, and on 5 and 9 July 1849; the following year a single-volume account, *Gleanings in the West of Ireland* (London, 1850), appeared.

5. Elihu Burritt, an American pacifist, published his famine account, *A Visit of Three Days to Skibbereen and Its Neighbourhood*, in London in 1847; extracts from Burritt's diary, referring to his visit to Ireland in February 1847, and including the passage quoted above (p. 46), are given in Charles Northend (ed.), *Elihu Burritt: a memorial volume containing a sketch of his life and labors* . . . (New York, 1879).

6. Bennett, *Six Weeks in Ireland*, p. 26.

7. Ibid., p. 132.

8. Ibid., pp. 26–28.

9. Report from a Waterford correspondent, 25 November 1846, included in Central Relief Committee, *Distress in Ireland: Address of the Committee to the Members of the Society of Friends in Ireland, 13 November 1846*.

10. Dympna McLoughlin's article on 'Workhouses and Irish Female Paupers, 1840–70', in Maria Luddy and Clíona Murphy (eds.), *Women Surviving* (Dublin, 1989), provides some interesting information on the numbers of able-bodied women in workhouses during this period. As McLoughlin persuasively argues, the category of 'desertion' should be interpreted carefully, and could have been used as a temporary expedient to gain entry to the workhouse – a significant reminder of the various and resourceful strategies employed by famine victims (pp. 117–47).

11. Osborne, *Gleanings*, pp. 31–32.

12. Ibid., p. 19.

13. Osborne, letter to the *Times*, 9 July 1849, pp. 4–5.

14. See Phelim P. Boyle and Cormac Ó Gráda, 'Fertility Trends, Excess Mortality and the Great Irish Famine', Demography, 23, 4 (1986), pp. 543–59; see also the discussion of this topic in 'Introduction', this volume.

15. Dufferin and Boyle, *Narrative of a Journey*, pp. 12–13.

16. *Illustrated London News*, 13 February 1847; a substantial number of Mahony's sketches of famine conditions in West Cork were published in the issues of 13 and 20 February 1847.

17. Laura Mulvey, 'Visual Pleasure and Narrative Cinema', *Screen*, 16, 3 (1975), pp. 6–18.

18. Osborne, *Gleanings*, p. 30.

19. James Hack Tuke's *Narrative of the Second, Third and Fourth weeks of William Forster's visit to some of the Distressed Districts in Ireland* (London, 1847), p. 8.

20. William Edward Forster, *Narrative of William Edward Forster's Visit to Ireland* (London, 1847), p. 3.

21. Canon John O'Rourke, *The History of the Great Irish Famine of 1847, with notices of earlier Irish famines* (Dublin, 1875), p. 274.

22. Julia Kristeva, 'Stabat Mater' (1977), reprinted and translated in Toril Moi (ed.), *The Julia Kristeva Reader* (Oxford, 1986), p. 176.

23. William Carleton, *The Black Prophet: A Tale of Irish Famine* ([1847]; Shannon, 1972, facsimile of 1899 edition), p. 345.

24. See Catherine M. O'Connell, *Excursions in Ireland during 1844 and 1850* (London, 1852), where O'Connell recounts seeing a poor woman take the 'starving baby' of another woman 'to her bosom', and suckle it 'as tenderly as she did her own' (pp. 274–77).

25. D. Donovan, 'Observations on the peculiar diseases to which the famine of the last year gave origin . . .', *Dublin Medical Press*, XIX (1848), p. 67; cited in E. Margaret Crawford (ed.), *Famine: The Irish Experience, 900–1900* (Edinburgh, 1989), p. 202.

26. Letter from Richard D. Webb to the Central Relief Committee, 8 May 1847, included in *Transactions of the Central Relief Committee*, Appendix III, p. 199.

27. The story of infanticide, 'unspeakable things, unspoken', is the centre of Toni Morrison's novel, *Beloved* (New York, 1987); also see Adrienne Rich's

discussion in *Of Woman Born: Motherhood as Experience and Institution* ([1976]; London, 1992).

28. Little information is available as to how prevalent infanticide was during the famine years. The Census of 1851, using data from coroners' inquests, notes a decrease, 'so far at least as these returns show', in cases of infanticide for the period 1841–51: 340 cases in comparison with the previous decade's 620. The figures for 'desertion/exposure of infants', however, show a significant increase (314 to 508), with 1842, 1843, 1844 and 1847 being the years with highest rates, and, proportionate to population, the greatest number of exposed/deserted infants in Dublin city and counties Cork, Dublin and Kilkenny. The writers conclude that 'while it seems that immorality has increased', some differences exist between the two periods, arising 'either out of the feelings of mothers or the opinions of juries' (*Census of 1851*, V, part 1, p. 407). See also David Fitzpatrick, 'Women and the Great Famine', in Margaret Kelleher and James H. Murphy (eds.), *Separate Spheres?: Gender and Nineteenth-Century Ireland* (Dublin, forthcoming 1997), n. 54.

29. Osborne, *Gleanings*, p. 34.

30. Ibid., p. 74.

31. Maud Ellmann, *The Hunger-Artists: Starving, Writing and Imprisonment* (London, 1993), p. 102.

32. Osborne, *Gleanings*, p. 76.

33. Bennett, *Six Weeks in Ireland*, p. 20.

34. Nicholas Cummins, letter to the *Times*, 24 December 1846, p. 6; partially reproduced in Cecil Woodham-Smith, *The Great Hunger* ([1962]; London, 1987), pp. 162–63.

35. *William Dillwyn Sims's narrative, describing the Fifth and Sixth weeks of William Forster's journey to some of the Distressed Districts in Ireland* (London, 1847), p. 2.

36. Osborne, *Gleanings*, p. 98; also 'I can hardly conceive anything more thoroughly brutalizing, than the herding of this mass together at night . . . one of the most disgusting scenes of personal degradation the mind can well conceive' (pp. 76, 97).

37. Marina Warner, *Monuments and Maidens: The Allegory of the Female Form* ([1985]; London, 1987), p. 277.

38. Cummins, letter to the *Times*, 24 December 1846, p. 6.

39. Ellmann, *The Hunger-Artists*, p. 54.

40. Letter from Captain Wynne, District Inspector for Clare, to Lieut. Colonel Jones, Chairman of the Board of Works, 24 December 1846, in *Correspondence from July 1846 to January 1847, relative to the Measures adopted for the Relief of Distress in Ireland* (Board of Works series), First Part (London, 1847), pp. 434–35; reprinted in Irish University Press *Famine* Series, VI (Shannon, 1970), pp. 466–67.

41. Ovid, *Metamorphoses*, Book VIII, translated by Frank Justus Miller, Loeb Classical Library (London, 1916), p. 461; see the discussion of this piece in 'Introduction', this volume.

42. Bennett, *Six Weeks in Ireland*, pp. 9–10. By late 1846, some destitute women, often widows with families, were employed on the public works; see Woodham-Smith, *The Great Hunger*, p. 145. Christine Kinealy, in *This Great Calamity: The Irish Famine 1845–52* (Dublin, 1994), observes that in one district in Co. Louth the number of women and girls employed on the works increased from 81, in late December 1846, to over 7,000 a month later (p. 96).

43. Osborne, *Gleanings*, pp. 91–92.

44. Kristeva, 'Stabat Mater', p. 174; Marina Warner, *Alone of All Her Sex: The Myth and Cult of the Virgin Mary* ([1976]; London, 1985), pp. 192–205; as Kristeva and Warner discuss, the nursing of a child is traditionally the only natural biological function depicted in representations of the Virgin Mary.

45. Kristeva, 'Stabat Mater', p. 182.

46. William Carleton, *The Black Prophet*, dedication to Lord John Russell.

47. Representations of famine also occur in Carleton's *The Squanders of Castle Squander* (2 vols.; London, 1852) and his short story 'Fair Gurtha; or, The Hungry Grass: A Legend of the Dumb Hill', published in *Dublin University Magazine*, XLVII (1856), pp. 414–35 (see note 63 below); for a discussion of these texts, see Chris Morash, 'William Carleton and the End of Writing', in his *Writing the Irish Famine* (Oxford, 1995), pp. 155–79.

48. Carleton, *The Black Prophet*, p. 406.

49. Ibid., dedication.

50. Ibid., author's preface.

51. Ibid., pp. 220–21.

52. Cited in Cormac Ó Gráda, *Ireland Before and After the Famine: Explorations in Economic History, 1800–1930* ([1988]; Manchester, 1993), p. 127.

53. Carleton, *The Black Prophet*, p. 188.

54. Ibid., p. 220.

55. Amartya Sen, *Poverty and Famines: An Essay on Entitlement and Deprivation* ([1981]; Oxford, 1982), p. 7.

56. Carleton, *The Black Prophet*, p. 189.

57. Ibid., pp. 189–90.

58. Ibid., pp. 189, 221, 222.

59. Ibid., p. 222.

60. See Homi Bhabha, 'The Other Question', *Screen*, 24, 6 (1983), pp. 18–36, and 'Of Mimicry and Men: The Ambivalence of Colonial Discourse', *October*, 28 (1984), pp. 125–33.

61. Carleton, *The Black Prophet*, p. 223.

62. Ibid., p. 222.

63. Ibid., pp. 57, 59. In Carleton's story 'Fair Gurtha', this motif is repeated in the person of an aged man, who appears to another character as 'the very genius of famine', 'almost impossible for human language to describe'. The superstition on which the story is based receives, from Carleton, a double translation: '*fair gurtha*' or 'hungry grass' and '*far gurtha*' or 'man of hunger'. This 'man of hunger' is presented in Ovidian tones: 'something not far

removed from the very shadow of a skeleton', 'the fearful anatomical structure of his limbs and ribs' almost transparent. While in the later story, the
man 'goes about in the very shape of Hunger', personifying at once famine
and its consequence, *The Black Prophet* uses gender to separate the cause
(Darby) and consequence (Margaret) of famine.

64. Ibid., p. 80.

65. Ibid., p. 344.

66. Ibid., pp. 344–45.

67. Ibid., p. 345.

68. Ibid., p. 346.

69. Ibid.

70. Ibid., p. 347.

71. Ibid.

72. In *Uneven Developments: The Ideological Work of Gender in Mid-Victorian England*
(Chicago, 1988), Mary Poovey reproduces the following example of the
contemporary emphasis on maternal instinct: 'A woman, if removed from all
intercourse, all knowledge of all sex and its attributes, from the very hour of
her birth, would, should she herself become a mother in the wilderness,
lavish as much tenderness upon her babe, cherish it as fondly . . . sacrifice
her personal comfort, with as much ardour, as much devotedness, as the
most refined, fastidious, and intellectual mother, placed in the very centre of
civilized society' (Peter Gaskell, *The Manufacturing Population of England*
([1833]; New York, 1972; cited in Poovey, p. 7).

73. Warner, *Monuments and Maidens*, p. 324.

74. Kristeva, 'Stabat Mater', p. 182.

75. Trollope's other novels with an Irish location are *The Macdermots of
Ballycloran* (3 vols; London, 1847), *The Kellys and the O'Kellys* (3 vols;
London, 1848), *An Eye for an Eye* (2 vols; London, 1879) and his unfinished
The Landleaguers (3 vols; London, 1883).

76. During his time in Ireland, Trollope was based in a number of towns,
including Banagher, Clonmel, Mallow, Belfast and Dublin.

77. Studies of the novel include E. W. Wittig's 'Trollope's Irish Fiction', *Éire-
Ireland*, 9, 3 (1974), pp. 97–118, and Hugh Hennedy's 'Love and Famine,
Family and Country in Trollope's *Castle Richmond*', *Éire-Ireland*, 7, 4 (1972),
pp. 48–66.

78. Unsigned notice, *Saturday Review*, 19 May 1860, pp. 643–44; quoted in
Donald Smalley (ed.), *Trollope: The Critical Heritage* (London, New York,
1969), pp. 113–14.

79. 'The Real State of Ireland, No. II', *Examiner*, 6 April 1850, p. 217;
Trollope's letters to the *Examiner* are reproduced in Lance Tignay, *The Irish
Famine: Six Letters to the Examiner, 1849–1850* (London, 1987).

80. The relationship between Trollope's famine writings and Osborne's letters is
the subject of Judith Knelman's article, 'Anthony Trollope, English Journalist
and Novelist, Writing about the Famine in Ireland', *Éire-Ireland*, 23, 3 (1988),
pp. 57–67.

81. Anthony Trollope, *An Autobiography* (London, 1883), p. 84.

82. 'Irish Distress', *Examiner*, 25 August 1849, pp. 532–33.

83. Ibid.

84. 'The Real State of Ireland, No. II', *Examiner*, 6 April 1850, p. 217. Accounts of famine conditions, such as Cummins' letter to the *Times* and Dufferin and Boyle's narrative of their visit to Skibbereen, include descriptions of the type sharply criticized by Trollope in his April 1850 letter. Thus Cummins writes of the police opening the door of a house 'which was observed shut for many days, and two frozen corpses were found, lying upon the mud floor, half devoured by rats' ; also 'A mother, herself in a fever, was seen the same day to drag out the corpse of her child, a girl about twelve, perfectly naked, and leave it half covered with stones' (*The Times*, 24 December 1846, p. 6). Dufferin and Boyle's description of bodies 'lying putrifying in the midst of the sick remnant of their families' *(Narrative,* pp. 10–11) is a graphic example of the type of horror with which, according to Trollope, Irish newspapers erroneously 'teemed'.

85. 'The Real State of Ireland, No. II', *Examiner*, 6 April 1850, p. 217. Interestingly, in *Castle Richmond*, the most detailed famine-scene involves the hero's entrance into an Irish cabin.

86. Ibid., p. 217.

87. Anthony Trollope, *Castle Richmond* ([1860]; Oxford, 1989), p. 75.

88. Trollope, *An Autobiography*, p. 157.

89. Trollope, *Castle Richmond*, p. 361.

90. Ibid., p. 67.

91. Ibid., p. 65.

92. 'The wealth of Ireland was almost entirely territorial, and the income arising from that wealth had been overdrawn', in 'The Real State of Ireland, No. II', *Examiner*, 6 April 1850, p. 217.

93. Trollope, *Castle Richmond*, pp. 67–68.

94. Ibid., p. 67.

95. Ibid., p. 345.

96. Ibid., pp. 201–02.

97. Ibid., p. 205.

98. Ibid., p. 202.

99. Ibid., p. 286.

100. Bhabha, 'The Other Question', p. 19.

101. Trollope, *Castle Richmond*, p. 205.

102. Ibid., p. 204.

103. Ibid., p. 284.

104. Ibid., p. 287.

105. See Homi Bhabha's observation that colonial 'subjects are always disproportionately placed in opposition or domination through the symbolic decentering of multiple power-relations which play the role of support as well as target or adversary', in 'The Other Question', p. 24.

106. Trollope, *Castle Richmond*, p. 84.

107. Ibid.

108. Ibid., p. 85.

109. Ibid., p. 86.

110. Ibid.

111. Ibid., p. 189.

112. Ibid.

113. Ibid., p. 203.

114. Mulvey, 'Visual Pleasure and Narrative Cinema', p. 11.

115. Trollope, *Castle Richmond*, p. 190.

116. Trollope's own views, as expressed in the *Examiner* letters, were firmly against the giving of gratuitous relief: 'The supply provided should not be gratuitous, for dependence on charity for daily bread destroys the feeling of independence' ('The Real State of Ireland, No. II', *Examiner*, 6 April 1850, p. 217).

117. Trollope, *Castle Richmond*, p. 190.

118. Ibid., p. 192.

119. Mulvey, 'Visual Pleasure and Narrative Cinema', p. 13.

120. Ibid.

121. Trollope, *Castle Richmond*, p. 369.

122. Michel Foucault, *The History of Sexuality: An Introduction* ([1976]; trans. Robert Hurley (London, 1979)), p. 44.

123. Trollope, *Castle Richmond*, pp. 369, 373.

124. Ibid., pp. 370–71.

125. Ibid., p. 370.

126. Ibid., pp. 371–73.

127. Ibid., p. 371.

128. Ibid., p. 373.

129. In *Realities of Irish Life* (New York, 1868), W. Steuart Trench comments on the benevolent but ill-fated efforts of philanthropists who 'forgot that starving people could not eat sixpences or shillings': 'The people had no strength or energy to seek, purchase, or cook meal and flour, and with the silver in their hands, they died' (p. 89).

130. Trollope, *Castle Richmond*, p. 374.

131. Mulvey, 'Visual Pleasure and Narrative Cinema', p. 11.

132. As Mulvey notes, 'the split between spectacle and narrative supports the man's role as the active one of forwarding the story, making things happen' (ibid., p. 12).

133. Trollope, *Castle Richmond*, p. 374.

134. Foucault, *The History of Sexuality: An Introduction*, pp. 44–45.

135. Trollope, *Castle Richmond*, p. 380.

136. See Foucault, *The History of Sexuality: An Introduction*, p. 92.

137. Jacqueline Rose, *Sexuality and the Field of Vision* (London and New York, 1986), pp. 220–22.

— 2 —

The Female Gaze:
Nineteenth-Century Women's Famine Narratives

Chapter one looked at some of the most significant contemporary representations of the 1840s famine, both fictional and non-fictional, by male observers. This chapter will explore how famine is treated in narratives written by women during the years of the Great Famine and in the decades following. Interesting discourses on famine appear in women's private writings, for example the correspondence of novelist Maria Edgeworth and the diaries of Elizabeth Smith, wife of a Wicklow landowner. A number of women published travel narratives during this period, the most detailed account coming from an American woman named Asenath Nicholson whose writings provide significant insights into the condition of Ireland at the time.[1] The most neglected body of writing, however, is women's fictional writings, with famine stories and novels appearing throughout the second half of the nineteenth century. A number of these texts gained large audiences and a degree of critical attention scarcely reflected in later studies of nineteenth-century literature. Similarly, the existence and significance of women's nineteenth-century narratives have gone largely unnoticed in the historiography of Irish famine.

The representations of famine, discussed in chapter one, frequently demonstrated in textual form what Laura Mulvey has termed 'woman as image, man as bearer of the look'.[2] Developing Mulvey's work, other film critics have investigated the nature of a female gaze, the positioning and experience of a female spectator.[3] Women's relationship to the cinema has been summarized by one critic, Judith Mayne, in the expressive phrase, 'the woman at the keyhole':

> On one side of the corridor is a woman who peeks, on the other, the woman who is, as it were, on display . . . The history of women's relationship to the cinema, from this side of the keyhole, has been a series of tentative peeks; that threshold . . . crossed with difficulty.[4]

The keyhole or threshold marks the boundary between public and private spheres, between outside and inside, boundaries not easily transgressed by the woman 'peeking'. In famine writings, such as those discussed in chapter one, the threshold has a very concrete function, marking the physical boundary between observer and victim. More symbolically, the threshold is also the line of class difference and, frequently in fictional depictions, also of gender difference as the hungry woman is scrutinized by the male observer. Yet in a significant number of famine narratives, the authorial gaze is female; drawing from the work of film theorists such as Mayne and others, the following discussion of women's famine texts will thus examine what happens 'when a woman looks'.

WOMEN'S FAMINE FICTION

In the second half of the nineteenth century, a significant number of fictional representations of the 1840s famine were written by women.[5] As early as 1851, Mary Anne Hoare of Monkstown, Co. Cork, published *Shamrock Leaves*, a collection of tales and sketches gathered, in Hoare's words, 'from the famine-stricken fields of my native country'.[6] Her most comprehensive account occurs in 'A Sketch of Famine', first published in *Howitt's Journal,* the London radical weekly, on 24 April 1847. This quasi-fictional sketch resembles contemporary eye-witness accounts in its emphasis on the difficulties of relating what has been seen: the horrors of Dante's Ugolino's dungeon, Hoare writes, 'fade into nothingness before the every-day tragedies of our Irish cabins'.

> The peasantry, once so gay, so full of native fun and humour, that
> the phrase 'a light-hearted Irishman', has become proverbial, now
> bowed down by famine and nakedness, gaunt and haggard, faint
> and spirit-worn, are but the shadows of their former selves. *The
> food of the land is destroyed*.[7]

Shamrock Leaves was published in Dublin and London and clearly
addresses itself to 'our English brethren', emphasizing the extent of
suffering in Ireland as well as the importance of private relief.
Factual references and details, as witnessed by Hoare, are combined with more fictive stories which illustrate the sufferings of the
poor. Most troubling to the author is the realization that 'even the
proverbial kindness of the peasantry begins to fail':

> When some of the inhabitants of a crowded district were asked
> lately, why they had suffered several fellow-creatures to perish
> among them without making any effort for their relief, 'sure', they
> replied, turning their despairing eyes towards the speaker, 'it will be
> our own turn next'.[8]

Controversial issues make an early appearance in women's
famine fiction; in 1853 Mary Anne Sadlier's *New Lights* uses famine
as a backdrop to a story on the evils of proselytism.[9] Sadlier, who
emigrated to Canada in 1844, was the author of many historical and
Catholic novels and had a large Irish-American readership. *Golden
Hills*, written by Elizabeth Hely Walshe and first published in 1865,
presents, in contrast, the philanthropic work by a Protestant land-
owning family.[10] Walshe's novel offers a detailed account of, what its
author terms, this 'national scourging'; the relief-system is outlined,
and defended, as are the benevolent actions of landowners who,
subject to numerous agrarian outrages, riots and assassinations, 'went
in daily peril of their lives'. The sufferings endured by the land-
owning class during the famine and the financial ruin experienced
by many form a central subject throughout these novels. One
example is Margaret Brew's 1884 novel, *The Chronicles of Castle
Cloyne*, which emphasizes 'the universal action' of the famine:

> But it was not the very poor alone who suffered from the ruin
> caused by the blight in the potatoes, though, as a matter of course,

they were the first to suffer. The farmers, and the shopkeepers, and
the tradesmen, whose business was ruined for want of customers,
and the great accumulation of bad debts that could never be
recovered; and, lastly, the landed proprietors, whose tenants had
become hopelessly insolvent, and whose lands, impoverished and
untilled, were like a howling wilderness. To this last class, with
very few exceptions, the ruin, if it had come more slowly, did not
come the less surely or pitilessly.[11]

Despite its universalizing intention, however, Brew's novel is
largely a lament for an old order, embodied by the gentry who
were 'swamped' and 'rooted out' by the famine. Brew's perspective is shared by many of her fellow-authors, themselves members
of the landed classes; thus, Louise Field, in 1896, dedicated her
famine novel, *Denis*, to her 'kinsfolk and friends, among the
landowners of Ireland'.[12]

One of the best-known famine novels written during this
period is Annie Keary's *Castle Daly* (1875).[13] Set in the 1840s and
treating both of the famine and the 1848 rising, Keary's narrative
was extremely popular in the late nineteenth century. The *Irish
Monthly* of April 1886 recorded that it 'was singled out by so
unEnglish an Irishman as Mr John O'Leary, in a lecture at Cork, as
singularly and almost solely worthy of high praise out of the hosts
of so-called Irish novels written of late' – an interesting comment
in light of the fact that the Yorkshire-born author of *Castle Daly*
had spent a total of two weeks in Ireland![14] Keary's narrative, based
on the recollections of her Irish-born father together with her own
study of Irish history, portrays late 1840s Ireland as a time of
conflict between new systems of reform and an older, more feudal
order. Various engaging confrontations occur throughout the
novel, with national and political tensions paralleled at the domestic level. Reviews of the novel praised 'its high excellence as a
story' and, 'beyond' the story, 'its explanation of the abiding Irish
difficulty'.[15] To the journalist writing in *Graphic*, in August 1875,
Keary's famine narrative clarified political problems still current
some thirty years later, even managing to explain 'why the justice
and even generosity with which England, nowadays at least, is
fully prepared to treat Ireland meet with no better return than

continued discontent and disaffection'. The explanation which *Castle Daly* suggested to this reviewer, in an interesting combination of psychological study and enduring stereotype, is that English 'justice and generosity miss their effect by being, half unconsciously, accompanied by a certain contempt and want of sympathy, which a sensitive race like the Irish are quick to detect and resent'.[16]

Many authors, including Walshe and Brew, underline their access to the personal testimonies of those nearer to the experience of famine. Elizabeth Hely Walshe, defending herself against the potential charge of exaggeration and also, perhaps, the accusation of distance from the events, explains in her preface that she has largely used the 'personal experiences of men who lived in the midst of the troubles of those years' and bids a sceptical reader examine the historical record of the times: 'Let the files of contemporary journals, or the reports made to Parliament be examined, and it will be found that the reality was far more terrible than anything which has been told in the "Golden Hills".' The publication of the majority of these famine novels, either in London, or jointly in Dublin and London, however, suggests that they were directed primarily to a British audience. Margaret Brew's *Chronicles of Castle Cloyne*, believed by many of its first readers to be the work of 'Mr Brew', received positive notices in the *Times*, *Athenaeum*, the *Morning Post* and other journals.[17] Famine stories, as in Keary's case, were welcomed, by some reviewers, for the light they could shed on contemporary politics to readers 'perplexed by the contradictory versions of the present state of Ireland'.[18] Similarly, Louise Field, born after the famine, emphasizes, in the preface to *Denis*, the role of her narrative in throwing 'some light on circumstances and characteristics too often unknown and ignored, which yet are vital factors in that vast and ever-recurring problem, the Irish Question'. The comments by reviewers and authors indicate that the novels written by Walshe, Keary, Brew and Field, like Trollope's *Castle Richmond*, had an important role in shaping interpretations of the famine in the decades succeeding the 1840s. As is true of famine fiction in general, their precise significance, in terms of audience and the shaping of opinion, remains to be fully explored.

Women's famine fiction demonstrates many of the same challenges and choices which faced novelists such as Carleton and Trollope; famine may constitute only one of many plots, the degree of significance it receives varying from novel to novel. In their attempt to capture the 'terrible realities' of famine, many of the narratives written by women contain graphic, often harrowing, depictions of its effects. On some occasions, these representations occur as cameo scenes, with echoes of the type of sketch to be found in Carleton and Trollope's writings. In other narratives, such as Keary's *Castle Daly* and Margaret Brew's *Chronicles of Castle Cloyne*, the famine characters are more integrated through their relation to the other storylines. Ellen and Thornley, the central characters in *Castle Daly*, discover a famine-stricken dying man who is also the assassin of Mr Daly, Ellen's landlord father.[19] This famine scene, however, functions primarily within the love plot, serving, as in Trollope's novel, to bring the lovers together. Brew's novel indicates, more fully, how the famine sketch may be of significance to the rest of the text, rather than appearing as a cameo from which the novel moves quickly away. Oonagh McDermott, daughter of a farmer who has been ruined by the famine and herself a central character, discovers two of her childhood friends, one, a man, dead, the other, his wife, on the point of death:

> The unfortunate man must have been dead for many hours, for his body was as cold and rigid as marble. He had died alone! There was no kind hand near him at the last to close his eyes, for they were wide open, and their fixed and glassy stare was perfectly horrible to look on. The worn face was half covered by a stubbly black beard of a fortnight's growth, and was like nothing earthly but a yellow parchment mask, wrinkled, haggard, and careworn. The throat and chest, laid bare by having the quilt drawn down, were so thin that the bones were in a manner held together only by the skin, and could literally be counted. It was a shocking sight, the body of this poor wretch that had died of famine![20]

While Brew provides a detailed description of this 'scene of misery', together with a rare portrait of an individual male victim, the scene functions much less as spectacle than similar moments in a novel like Trollope's *Castle Richmond*. The famine victims are named characters who have appeared previously in the story and are presented, at least partly, through the perspective of a woman from the same class; structured in this way, the degree of spectacle or icon is reduced significantly.

In much of women's famine fiction, however, the by now familiar spectacle of a woman's famine body returns. Where detailed portrayals of individual victims occur, they are mostly of women – mothers and, frequently, widows. Mary Anne Hoare's tales, for example, emphasize over and over again the particular vulnerability experienced by widows and their children. 'A Sketch of Famine' begins with the moving story of a mother who brings her two infants, 'one dead, the other scarcely alive', to the church-yard.[21] Burying one in a shallow grave, she 'calmly seated herself beside the open hollow', awaiting the death of her other child; in the mother's words, '"better to stop and put him alongside his brother in the holy ground, than lay him down in the field for the rats to devour"'. Hoare's stories also refer to the strategies of survival which women and their children employ; one quasi-fictive episode tells of a widow named Sullivan who travels thirty miles with her children to the sea-shore in order to collect seaweed. Their eventual fate echoes the horrific stories of many of their con-temporaries; entering a cabin, a 'benevolent clergyman' discovers the bodies of the mother and daughter eaten 'by a colony of rats', while on her son, who is only barely alive, 'the horrid animals were preparing to prey'.[22]

Like many of her contemporaries, Mary Anne Hoare comments on the breakdown caused by famine in traditional systems of char-ity, extending to even the closest of relationships. The challenges posed to 'maternal love' are of particular horror: 'that season of famine, whose iron gripe loosed the bonds of even maternal love, and caused the mother to snatch the scanty morsel from the thin white lip of her dying child'.[23] A further illustration of the extremi-ties to which people must resort, one which clearly disturbs its narrator, is the story of a woman nursing her son of eighteen who was labouring on the roads:

A benevolent visitor entered the cabin one morning, and there discovered how the youth's strength, on which depended the wretched existence of his family, was kept up. His mother 'forgot her sucking child' in order that she might have compassion on the son of her womb. The miserable pallid infant was cast by to cry unheeded, while its elder brother drew milk from the mother's bosom.[24]

The tone and perspective offered in the passage are difficult to judge. That the woman 'forgets' her child is, as the author's use of quotation marks signals, an inadequate interpretation. The narrator's sympathy appears to oscillate between a recognition of the needs of the 'wretched' family and a horror that the infant is 'cast by'. Hoare's sketch is, for this reader, one of the most disturbingly evocative of famine accounts, suggesting the appalling 'choices' to be made by those suffering from hunger, the need to privilege one family member over another. The author's own dismay is unmistakable: 'This is a matter of fact: does it not rival the inventions of fiction?'[25]

Many of the motifs which Hoare and other eye-witnesses recount as 'fact' reappear in women's famine fiction. Recurring characters include the self-sacrificing famine mother and her 'monstrous' opposite. As in the narratives discussed in chapter one, depictions of maternal love receive a central position. One example is provided by Elizabeth Walshe's *Golden Hills*; in the course of the novel, a central character, Frank, encounters the dead bodies of a woman and her child in a cabin by the sea-shore:

On a table, which some neighbour had lent, lay two bodies: one, that of an attenuated woman, wrapped in an old cloak; beside her, inclosed by her arm, was a dead baby. The coroner had arrived, and they were forming a jury in the presence of the poor dead ones, whose emaciated faces and lean limbs told enough of the cause of death. Frank felt cold as he looked on the hollow eyes and claw-like fingers of the wretched mother, and the pinched, oldened features of the hapless child, whose life had yielded to the slow torments of hunger.[26]

What is to be read, primarily, from this scene is the extent of maternal love, even in death:

> 'The crathur! her arm was about him to the last,' said a by-stander. 'I'll be bound it's more of him than of hersel' she was thinkin' even in the agony – poor weenoch, his little hand is round her finger.' The women were weeping; men could scarcely repress emotion. O love, stronger than even death! O mother's instinct, more imperative than even nature's clinging to life! How does the heart warm to it, and recognize the universal brotherhood![27]

The maternal instinct, as exclaimed in the narrator's apostrophe to the reader, transcends all, even the instinct for life itself. At such a moment, the scene seems to break out of the confines of the story, compelling the reader's sympathy and recognition of a 'universal brotherhood'.

Walshe's narrative uncovers a key aspect of the maternal figure and its function in famine texts. The force of this particular female image, for author *and* reader, includes the possibility of transcending famine: to see, inscribed on the mother's body, traces beyond those of suffering and emaciation, signs instead of a death-conquering love. This passage can thus help to explain one of the recurring questions raised by this work, and by other studies of female representations, namely the source of female images' affective power.[28] How do such images, specifically maternal ones, gain recognition, or compel identification, from their viewers/readers, creating a space in which actual women, and men, experience themselves?[29] Kristeva provides one answer in her reading of the Stabat Mater, the representation of Mary, mother of Christ, at the foot of the cross: 'Man overcomes the unthinkable of death by postulating maternal love in its place'.[30] Similarly, Walshe's narrative identifies the power of maternal love, 'more imperative than even nature's clinging to life', to establish a 'universal' and death-defying 'brotherhood'; in Kristeva's words, to 'reduce social anguish' and establish a 'commonality' of readers.[31]

Rather than illustrating a 'pure' or radically different narrative gaze, women's novels, as these examples show, also employ female spectacle. One effect is the more positive and comforting representation offered by Walshe. Yet in other works, most memorably Louise Field's famine novel, the anxiety which so frequently underlies the maternal image is apparent. Field, in her novel, *Denis*, subverts idealized images of maternity with her depictions of 'ghastly' and 'horrific' scenes. One example occurs in chapter twenty-two of her novel when, similar to Walshe's scene, a jury has gathered to examine a dead woman:

> The jury, tradesmen of Moyne, said little but probably thought all the more as they viewed the body, if it were indeed a body and not some ghastly preliminary sketch or model of a woman, a word which one associates with graciously rounded outlines, knees soft to nurse little ones, arm and breast softly padded for the repose of tired curly heads. This was a bony outline, over which was painfully dragged and stretched a casing of yellow leather, ghastly to behold. But they gave this Thing the name of a respectable widow who lived in a lonely hovel, and had children in heaven – and in America.[32]

The body which is viewed and scrutinized is somehow less than real: a 'preliminary sketch' or 'outline', horribly reduced to 'a casing of yellow leather'. For jury and reader, this 'Thing' is difficult to reconcile with the person's identity as 'a respectable widow' and mother; one has to struggle to retain a sense of the woman in face of the 'ghastly' sight. Most strikingly, the ideal of motherhood, of 'graciously rounded outlines, knees soft . . . and breast softly padded', is rendered totally and painfully inadequate.

Later in the novel, Field once again confronts deeply-cherished ideals of motherhood, what Walshe has termed 'maternal instinct'. On a visit to the relief works, Mr O'Hara, a landowner, is beginning his 'luncheon' when he is surrounded by 'a family of emaciated children . . . wailing in chorus for bread, while the mother, with an infant at her shrunken breast, gazed tigerishly at the packet of food'. When O'Hara gives a sandwich to the youngest child, a scene of 'horror' ensues:

> But never did any of those who saw that scene forget the horror of the next moment, and the agonized shriek that came from the

child's blue lips. For with a bound that was like the spring of some famished wild beast upon its prey the mother had leaped upon the little one, had snatched the food from its bony fingers, and crammed it into her own mouth. The men who looked upon her face, as her eyes turned again to the child she had robbed, shuddered with a chill horror, as if they had gazed upon the face of a Medusa.[33]

In this episode, the famine mother is 'Medusa' rather than Madonna; her actions, unmotherly and inhuman, are presented as those of a 'famished wild beast', with the power to turn the horrified observer to stone. In stark contrast with Walshe's scene which depicts a death-conquering love, the maternal scene is itself the 'unthinkable'.

As Carleton's novel first hinted, in the context of famine writings, the concept of 'instinct' in relation to the 'maternal' possesses a troubling ambivalence, with the power to suggest a deep-rooted love and to uncover equally deep fears. The discourse on maternity in famine novels can thus waver between heroic, self-sacrificing attributes and dehumanized, animalistic terms. As writers attempt to represent the crisis which is famine, images of mothers are thrown into particular relief; the maternal figure displays the potential both to image disaster and deliver comfort. The breakdown in the maternal relationship, however, releases a threat which exceeds anything the political or economic register may contain.

ASENATH NICHOLSON'S FAMINE ANNALS

In December 1846, Asenath Nicholson, an American woman, aged around fifty and widowed, arrived in Dublin to begin her second extended stay in Ireland. She was to spend the next two years travelling around famine-stricken areas in the north, south and west of the country, distributing relief made available to her, on the most part, by friends and contacts in America. Nicholson's account of her travels, entitled 'The Famine of 1847, '48 and '49', was first published in 1850 and remains one of the most detailed and engaging of contemporary testimonies.[34] Read in the context of other famine narratives, her analysis of famine's causes and vivid illustration of its consequences are of special interest. In particular, using the terms coined by Judith Mayne and other theorists, her narrative provides a fascinating and detailed example of the operation of a 'female gaze', at a time when thresholds of nationality, class and gender were indeed 'crossed with difficulty'.[35]

Asenath Hatch Nicholson was born in the late eighteenth century in Vermont, where she worked as a teacher, before moving to New York in the 1830s.[36] A strict teetotaller and vegetarian, and follower of Sylvester Graham, a Presbyterian minister, she opened the Graham Temperance Boarding-house in New York, later described as 'the resort of hundreds of choice spirits from all parts of the country, including most of the names of those who were engaged in measures of social reform'.[37] In New York, she also visited the homes of Irish emigrants and later explained that 'It was in the garrets and cellars of New York that I first became acquainted with the Irish peasantry, and it was there I *saw* they were a suffering people.'[38] Nicholson first arrived in Ireland in June 1844; her book, *Ireland's Welcome to the Stranger; or, Excursions through Ireland in 1844, and 1845, for the purpose of personally investigating the condition of the poor*, first published in 1847, records her travels around Ireland, staying in lodging-houses and in cabins, including the homes of the families of servant-girls whom she had employed in New York. As well as 'personally investigating the condition of the poor', Nicholson sought to distribute and read the Bible among the Irish, having obtained a stock of Bibles, some in English and some in Irish, from the Hibernian Bible Society.[39] Beyond a general label of 'puritan' or 'protestant', however, Nicholson's own denominational affiliation remains unclear; Alfred Sheppard, author of the preface to the 1926 reprint of *Ireland's Welcome*, notes that nowhere does Nicholson give a clue to her own denomination, 'if indeed it had any other member than herself'![40]

Nicholson's independence of spirit and her ability to disturb and perplex her contemporaries are clear from the memorable editorial by Edward Nangle, published in the *Achill Herald* of June 1845:

> She lodges with the peasantry, and alleges that her object is to become acquainted with Irish character . . . This stranger is evidently a person of some talent and education; and although the singular course which she pursues is utterly at variance with the modesty and retired-

ness to which the Bible gives a prominent place in its delineation of a
virtuous female, she professes to have no ordinary regard for that holy
book. It appears to us that the principal object of this woman's
mission is to create a spirit of discontent among the lower orders and
to dispose them to regard their superiors as so many unfeeling oppres-
sors. There is nothing either in her conduct or conversation to justify
the supposition of insanity, and we strongly suspect that she is the
emissary of some democratic and revolutionary society.[41]

Nangle's editorial offers a memorable illustration of prevalent
attitudes towards women of independent spirit: such women were
judged either insane or revolutionaries. Other contemporary comments include that of William Bennett, the English Quaker, who
judged Nicholson to be 'of singular and strong character', and of
the editors of *Howitt's Journal*, who described *Ireland's Welcome* as
'one of the most extraordinary books which has appeared for
years', giving 'such a picture of cabin life as never before was given
to the world'.[42] Of its author, the radical Howitts approvingly
remarked in August 1847:

With very slender resources, she has bravely wandered far and
wide, visiting the abodes of both simple and gentle, and recording
her reception, and what she has seen, with a pen of the most
singular independence. She seems, indeed, to delight to strip away
all the self-complacency of human nature, and hold up a mirror to
the rich, which, if true, ought to startle them from their present
quiet, and rouse them while it is still day, to do something for those
whose blood will be required at their hands.[43]

Having completed the text of *Ireland's Welcome*, Nicholson
returned to the country in late 1846.[44] For the next six months she
was based in Dublin and provided relief for the destitute poor in
areas such as Cork Street, frequently cooking food in people's
homes and instructing them in the preparation of rice and Indian
meal.[45] William Bennett describes meeting this 'American lady' in
Dublin in April 1847:

I found her with limited and precarious means, still persevering from
morning to night in visiting the most desolate abodes of the poor,
and making food – especially of Indian meal – for those who did not

know how to do it properly, with her own hands. She was under much painful discouragement, but a better hope still held her up. Having a considerable quantity of arrow-root with me, at my own disposal, I left some of it with her, and £5 for general purposes.[46]

In July 1847, Nicholson began a tour of the north of Ireland, visiting Belfast, Donegal, Derry, Arranmore; the autumn of 1847 and winter 1847–48 she spent in the west, including Tuam, Ballina, Achill Island; in summer and autumn 1848 she visited Munster, before leaving Ireland in late 1848 or early 1849. Her account of what she had seen, 'The Famine of 1847, '48 and '49', was first published in London in 1850 as the third part of her historical work, *Lights and Shades of Ireland*. The following year, in April 1851, the famine section was published in New York as a separate volume, entitled 'Annals of the Famine in Ireland in 1847, 1848 and 1849'. The text's importance for an American audience was heavily underlined by its editor 'J. L.' who wrote, in his preface, that this 'tale of woe should be read by the whole American people; it will have a salutary effect upon their minds, to appreciate more fully the depth of oppression and wretchedness from which the Irish poor escape in coming to this land of plenty'.[47]

Nicholson's own preface to the full volume, *Lights and Shades*, shows a keen awareness of a reader's potential incredulity and horror and warns of the 'fearful realities' which she has witnessed. Throughout, she emphasizes the uniqueness of her perspective:

> The reader of these pages should be told that, if strange things are recorded, it was because strange things were seen; and if strange things were seen which no other writer has written, it was because no other writer has visited the same places, under the same circumstances. No other writer ever explored mountain and glen for four years, with the same object in view; . . . And now, while looking at them calmly at a distance, they appear, even to myself, more like a dream than reality, because they appear out of *common course*, and out of the order of even nature itself. But they *are* realities, and many of them fearful ones – *realities* which none but eye-witnesses can understand, and none but those who passed through them can *feel*.[48]

The distinctiveness of Nicholson's viewpoint is partly attributable to her 'foreign' or American identity; in addition, as she herself comments, her perspective is influenced by her gender: 'My task was a different one – operating individually. I took my own time and way – as woman is wont to do, when at her own option.' Although claiming that her position as outsider renders her less open to the 'danger of blind partiality', she acknowledges a bias to which she, as female observer, is particularly vulnerable: 'the danger of that excessive pity or blind fondness, which a kind mother feels for a deformed or half-idiot child, which all the world, if not the *father* himself, sets aside as a thing of nought'.[49] Nicholson's relationship to Ireland, thus outlined, first appears as a curious mixture of maternal 'fondness' and moral superiority towards this 'deformed or half-idiot child'.

As the narrative progresses, however, the author's sympathy with the victims of famine is unambiguous and usually accompanied by a vigorous denunciation of the causes of the distress of the poor. Her sketches of individuals, initially, are offered reluctantly, almost apologetically, as 'specimens, not wishing to be tedious with such narrations, only to show the character of the famine, and its effects in general on the sufferers, with whom I was conversant'.[50] Yet, as the following reading of two of these 'narrations' will show, they provide memorable and moving depictions both of the effects of famine and of Nicholson's own 'negotiations' of these encounters.

The author's first sight of 'a starving person' occurs in Kingstown/Dun Laoghaire:

> A servant in the house where I was stopping, at Kingstown, said that the milk woman wished me to see a man near by, that was in a state of actual starvation; and he was going out to attempt to work on the Queen's highway; a little labour was beginning outside the house, and fifteen-pence-a-day stimulated this poor man, who had seven to support, his rent to pay, and fuel to buy.[51]

Her description of her encounter with the starving man begins with an apostrophe to the reader, common in such accounts:

and reader, if you never have seen a starving being, *may you never!*
In my childhood I had been frighted with the stories of ghosts, and
had seen actual skeletons; but imagination had come short of the
sight of this man . . . [he] was emaciated to the last degree; he
was tall, his eyes prominent, his skin shrivelled, his manner cringing
and childlike; and the impression *then* and *there* made never *has* nor
ever *can* be effaced.[52]

The sense of a reality exceeding the possibilities of imagination and
the description of the man as 'skeleton' are, by now, familiar
motifs from other eye-witnesses. Much less frequent, however, is
Nicholson's explicit and immediate political analysis of the causes
of such suffering, evident in her ringing condemnation of official
methods of payment: 'Workmen are not paid at night on the public works, they must wait a week; and if they commence labour in
a state of hunger, they often die before the week expires.'

In further contrast to her contemporaries where encounters
with famine victims and the distribution of relief require male
authorization and mediation, usually from local ministers, priests or
doctors, Nicholson's distribution of food occurs during the family's
absence, with help provided by the servant. References to entrances
and gates, and their crucial material consequences, permeate her
narrative: the labourers are 'called in' to the kitchen for food while
others are fed at the door; the eventual locking of the gate, the
barring of access, painfully signifies the exhaustion of supplies;
while an unexpected donation from New York allows the unlock-
ing of the gate – once the 'man of the house' has left for his
business in Dublin.

Soon after this episode, and still in Dublin, Nicholson details
another encounter, on this occasion with a widow she meets
'creeping upon the street, one cold night', carrying 'a few boxes of
matches, to see if she could sell them, for she told me she could
not yet bring herself to beg; she could work, and was willing to,
could she get knitting or sewing'.[53] The woman is reluctant to give
the number of her home; having given an indirect promise to call
some future day and meaning to take the woman 'by surprise',
Nicholson recounts that 'at ten the next morning my way was

made into that fearful street, and still more fearful alley, which led
to the cheerless abode I entered'. Her journey through the city's
'retired streets and dark alleys' involves 'finding my way through
darkness and filth' until 'a sight opened upon me, which, speaking
moderately was startling'. Once again, the description of this sight,
as Nicholson's gaze travels around the room, from the dark corner
at her right to the other side of the empty grate, includes features
common in contemporary depictions: the empty fire, the woman
without a dress, pawned to pay rent, the man without a coat 'likewise pawned', and Nicholson's initial muteness at the sight. Less
frequent is the breaking of the pause by the widow encountered
earlier; very rarely in such narratives do the suffering victims speak.
In this case, a conversation takes place, one of the women is named,
and, even rarer, the encounter emerges as the first of many visits by
Nicholson: 'daily did I go and cook their food, or see it cooked'.[54]

Nicholson's repeated crossing of the threshold of this 'forbidding', 'uncomfortable' and 'wretched' abode occurs in marked
contrast to many other eye-witness accounts, examples of which
were cited in chapter one, in which the commentator remains
standing at the threshold or outside, or observes the scene from his
carriage window. The observer's reluctance to enter, and eagerness
to leave, is obvious and understandable. In this context, Nicholson's
crossing of thresholds and her return to the scene are particularly
striking; even more rarely, her visits are reciprocated: 'Often late in
the evening would I hear a soft footstep on the stairs, followed by
a gentle tap, and the unassuming Mary would enter with her
bountiful supply of fire kindling.' As part of the narrative's continued emphasis on women's desire and duty to work, Mary and
her friend are presented as 'good expert knitters and good semp-
stresses' who also repair Nicholson's clothing.

In addition to its individual sketches of famine victims, *Lights
and Shades of Ireland* contains a detailed and forceful analysis of
famine's causation. Nicholson directly engages with contemporary
views such as the attribution of famine to God's providence: 'God
is slandered, where it is called an unavoidable dispensation of His
wise providence, to which we should all humbly bow, as a chastise-
ment which could not be avoided'.[55] On a number of occasions,

she draws analogies between the position of American slaves and the Irish lower classes: 'never had I seen slaves so degraded';[56] in a keen insight into the operations of oppressive systems, she declares that existing laws

> possess the unvarying principle of fixing deeply and firmly in the heart of the oppressor a hatred towards the very being that he has unjustly coerced, and the very degradation to which he has reduced him becomes the very cause of his aversion towards him.[57]

In a letter to a friend, written from Belmullet in October 1847 and reproduced in *Lights and Shades*, she challenges England's treatment of Ireland in impassioned, if somewhat parental, rhetoric:

> Do you say she is treacherous, she is indolent, she is intriguing? Try her once more; put implements of working warfare into her hands; hold up the soulstirring stimulus of remuneration to her; give her no time for meditating plunder and bloodshed; give her no inducement to be reckless of a life that exists only to suffer. Feed her not in idleness, nor taunt her with her nakedness and poverty, till her wasted, palsied limbs have been washed and clothed – till her empty stomach has been filled; and filled too with food of her own earning, when she has strength to do it.[58]

The letter concludes with a rare, though typically sardonic, expression of despair: 'What is woman's legislating amid the din of so many wise magicians, soothsayers, and astrologers as have set up for Ireland the last two years.'

Throughout her narrative, Nicholson insists that 'sufficient' food is available, if not in Ireland then elsewhere in 'the Christian world':

> and never was a famine on earth, in *any* part, when there was not an abundance in *some* part, to make up all the deficiency; . . . Yes, unhesitatingly may it be said, that there was not a week during that famine, but there was sufficient food for the wants of that week, and *more* than sufficient.[59]

Thus, even if the 'immediate breaking forth' of famine 'could not have been foreseen or prevented, its sad effects might have been met without the loss of life'. Nicholson concludes this lengthy discussion with a bitter satire of the workings of political economy: 'the principle of throwing away life to-day, lest means to protect it tomorrow might be lessened, was fully and practically carried on and carried out'.[60] While her views as to the amount of food available may appear simplistic, greatly underestimating the force of existing economic systems, the challenge which they deliver, both to her first audience and to later readers, regarding the just distribution of resources, remains of acute relevance.

Nicholson also castigates the government systems charged with transportation and distribution of grain, her strong individual grievance being the wasting of grain on the making of alcohol, while she deems many government officials or 'hirelings' guilty of crimes ranging from unnecessary delay in distribution of relief to direct embezzlement of government funds. Towards the end of her narrative, she moves from an evaluation of relief to recount one of her most memorable encounters:

> Going out one cold day in a bleak waste on the coast, I met a pitiful old man in hunger and tatters, with a child on his back, almost entirely naked, and to appearance in the last stages of starvation; whether his naked legs had been scratched, or whether the cold affected them I knew not, but the blood was in small streams in different places, and the sight was a horrid one.[61]

'Interrogated' as to why he 'took such an object into sight', the man explains that he has travelled seven miles to obtain relief; 'the officer told him he had not time to enter his name on the book, and he was sent away in that condition'. Nicholson encounters the man some days later 'creeping slowly in a bending posture upon the road'. He had once again been sent away empty-handed; 'What his future destiny was I never knew; but the Relieving Officer expressed no feelings of compunction when told of it some time after, nor did he know whether he had applied again.'[62] Although many of Nicholson's contemporaries offer political analysis of famine's causation, with both similarities and marked differences to her views, the immediacy and force with which her narrative moves from cause to terrible effect stand apart.

Nicholson's singular 'looking into' the lives of the poor, ironically, at first facilitated her entrance into upper-class society:

> The people of Dublin, among the comfortable classes, whatever hospitality they might manifest towards guests and visitors, had never troubled themselves by looking into the real *home* wants of the suffering poor. Enough they thought that societies of all kinds abounded, and a poor-house besides, were claims upon their purses to a full equivalent for all their consciences required, and to visit them was quite *un-lady-like*, if not dangerous. To many of those I had access as a matter of curiosity, to hear from me the tales of starvation, which they were now to have dealt out unsparingly; and so kind were the most of them that the interview generally ended by an invitation to eat, which was never refused when needed, and the meal thus saved was always given to the hungry.[63]

The tales provided by the 'un-lady-like' American thus afforded, to the 'comfortable classes', a certain voyeuristic pleasure;[64] more troubling is the extent to which this curiosity, even voyeurism, continues to be part of the reader's experience.

Her visits to the homes of the lower classes, however, were to render the American 'foreigner' increasingly suspicious to her contemporaries. Nicholson herself mimics the voices of her critics, such as the sceptical 'nominal professor': '"We do not understand your object, and do you go into the miserable cabins among the lower order".'[65] Furthermore, although Nicholson earlier states that the terrible events of 1846 onwards eliminated 'circuitous ceremony' and thus facilitated her access 'from mud cabin to estated gentleman's abode',[66] the later chapters suggest that her entry into Irish homes, particularly the homes of the poor, was made increasingly difficult by famine. *Ireland's Welcome to the Stranger*, Nicholson's first work, includes many accounts of staying overnight in cabins, with detailed descriptions of cabin interiors and bedding arrangements; significantly fewer of these are to be found in her famine work. On a number of occasions, the author admits her reluctance

to enter cabins. Of her visit to Arranmore, Co. Donegal, she writes:
'We went from cabin to cabin till I begged the curate to show me
no more.' At these moments, the famine discourse displays a
marked struggle to find adequate language, sometimes bordering on
animalistic terms and labouring to retain a humanized perspective:

> they stood up before us in a speechless, vacant, staring, stupid, yet
> most eloquent posture, mutely *graphically* saying, 'Here we are, your
> bone and your flesh, made in God's image like you. *Look at us!* What
> brought us here?' . . . they saluted us by crawling on all fours
> towards us, and trying to give some token of welcome.[67]

Famine narratives demonstrate a continual risk that the depictions of
famine victims will move outside the boundaries of human identity,
and hence beyond the possibility of identification, into subhuman
or superhuman terms. Vividly apparent in Nicholson's text are the
author's efforts to keep the narrative's focus, or gaze, on the victims
as 'bone and flesh', 'like you'.

In some of the most moving scenes in Nicholson's sketch of
famine, those seeking relief press against windows and doors, the
threshold between the woman observer and famine victims now
increasingly difficult to cross. At the home of the Hewitson family
in Derry, 'the lower window-frame in the kitchen was of board
instead of glass, this all having been broken by the pressure of faces
continually there'; in Newport,

> the door and window of the kind Mrs Arthur wore a spectacle of
> distress indescribable; naked, cold and dying, standing like petrified
> statues at the window, or imploring, for God's sake, a little food,
> till I almost wished that I might flee into the wilderness, far, far
> from the abode of any living creature.[68]

Soon afterwards, Nicholson is at dinner with a company of ministers during which she criticizes their luxurious fare, in particular
their taking of alcohol, citing the suffering of the people; in reply,
her companions cite the Marriage of Cana. Nicholson's account
continues:

When in an hour after dinner the tea was served, as is the custom in Ireland, one of the daughters of the family passing a window, looked down upon the pavement and saw a corpse with a blanket spread over it, lying upon the walk beneath the window. It was a mother and infant, dead, and a daughter of sixteen had brought and laid her there, hoping to induce the people to put her in a coffin; and as if she had been listening to the conversation at the dinner of the want of coffins, she had placed her mother under the very window and eye, where those wine-bibing ministers might apply the lesson. All was hushed, the blinds were down, and a few six-pences were quite unostentatiously sent out to the poor girl, as a beginning, to procure a coffin. The lesson ended here.[69]

The episode is an interesting one for a number of reasons; clearly displayed, along with Nicholson's strong objections to alcohol, are her alienation from most of the company inside and her imaginative sympathy with the girl outside which extends to some knowledge of the girl's age and purpose. One of the most moving themes throughout the narrative is also visible here: the desperate efforts of the poor to ensure a proper burial for their dead.[70]

By early 1847, during her travels in Connacht, the overwhel-ming nature of what Nicholson has witnessed becomes clear:

A cabin was seen closed one day a little out of the town, when a man had the curiosity to open it, and in a dark corner he found a family of the father, mother, and two children, lying in close compact. The father was considerably decomposed; the mother, it appeared, had died last, and probably fastened the door, which was always the custom when all hope was extinguished, to get into the darkest corner and die, where passers-by could not see them. Such *family* scenes were quite common, and the cabin was generally pulled down upon them for a grave. The man called, begging me to look in. *I did not*, and *could not* endure, as the famine progressed, such sights, as well as at the first, they were too *real*, and these reali-ties became a dread. In all my former walks over the island, by day or night, no shrinking or fear of danger ever retarded in the least my progress; but now, the horror of meeting living walking ghosts, or stumbling upon the dead in my path at night, inclined me to keep within when necessity did not call.[71]

In what are now familiar terms in Nicholson's writing, the horror of the family's death is expressed in terms of 'inside' and 'outside', of uncrossed thresholds. The mother has fastened the door so that others may not enter; Nicholson is, by now, unable to even 'look in' and, in stark contrast to her earlier 'excursions', increasingly stays at home.

In a letter to the *Cork Examiner* published in August 1848, William O'Connor described his encounter with Nicholson in the following words:

> It is a singular spectacle to witness – a lady gently nurtured and brought up, giving up, for a time, home and country and kindred – visiting a land stricken with famine – traversing on foot that land from boundary to boundary, making her way over solitary mountains and treading through remote glens, where scarcely the steps of civilization have reached, sharing the scanty potato of the poor but hospitable people, and lying down after a day of toil, in the miserable but secure cabin of a Kerry or Connaught peasant.[72]

To her later readers, the 'American stranger' continues to present a 'singular' and memorable 'spectacle'. Much of this distinctive quality comes from the character of the author and the negotiations which she personally attempted, across geographical and class boundaries. In that regard, the increasing physical and emotional difficulties which she experienced convey, vividly, the growing force of famine as well as the limitations of her position. Her account of famine is clearly mediated by her own political and personal perspectives, while benefiting from her identity as 'foreign' female. Yet the resulting narrative still remains a powerful testimony to the 'realities, and many of them fearful ones' of famine *and* its causation.

WOMEN'S PHILANTHROPY

Up to this, the discussion has centred on representations of famine victims and the construction of a female spectacle, in the writings of male and female authors. Women's famine narratives also, however, display a very different type of 'feminization of famine' through their interest in the philanthropic actions of upper and middle-class women. From these stories of women's famine philanthropy, recurring characterizations emerge: the 'ministering angel', or angel of mercy, and the self-sacrificing donor, figures strikingly familiar some one hundred and fifty years later.[73]

Nineteenth-century depictions of the plight of the poor, as the previous discussion has shown, highlight women's moral character, distinguished in times of famine by heroic or monstrous manifestations. In the discourse of philanthropy, however, the moral virtue of womanhood acquires a further meaning: justifying a particular, if limited, form of female agency for the upper classes. Studies of gender ideology during this period, most notably the work of Mary Poovey, have shown how Victorian concepts of 'maternal love' and 'maternal instinct' credited women not only with a nurturing instinct but also a particular 'moral influence'.[74] The following observation, first published in 1833 and reproduced by Poovey, provides a useful summary of what was, by the middle of the nineteenth century, a prevailing doctrine:

> The moral influence of woman upon man's character and domestic happiness, is mainly attributable to her natural and instinctive habits. Her love, her tenderness, her affectionate solicitude for his comfort and enjoyment, her devotedness, her unwearying care, her maternal fondness, her conjugal attractions, exercise a most ennobling impression upon his nature, and do more towards making him a good husband, a good father, and a useful citizen, than all the dogmas of political economy.[75]

Central to contemporary discourses on philanthropy was a similar emphasis on females' moral influence and domestic role;[76] a certain palliative was thus offered to women to compensate them for their separation from the public sphere and also to reinforce that separation. The occurrence of widespread famine, however, meant the convergence of domestic *and* public crises, and, consequently, an immense challenge to established systems, both in political and ideological terms. In this context, the status and significance accorded to women's famine philanthropy by contemporary commentators, particularly by female writers, deserve attention.

Until recently, information regarding Irish women's philanthropy was scarce, with attention focused largely on Britain and the United States;[77] the work of historians such as Maria Luddy, however, has now made available much-needed information regarding women's charitable endeavours.[78] Luddy's study, *Women and Philanthropy in Nineteenth-Century Ireland*, published in 1995, examines various types of charitable activities by Protestant and Catholic women: through benevolent societies and institutions, with prostitutes and children, in prison reform and in temperance movements. Details of women's famine-work, cited by Luddy, include the setting up of soup kitchens, the development of cottage industries, the nursing and visiting of famine victims, and women's involvement in various relief societies. A contemporary account by Catherine O'Connell, detailing her visits to Ireland between 1844 and 1850, also describes the operations of women's relief societies, particularly their visiting of the poor and encouragement of industry.[79] Some women's famine societies, as research by Helen Hatton and Rob Goodbody indicates, were subcommittees of the Society of Friends, with many others receiving financial support from the 'Friends'. The Ladies' Industrial Society of Dublin, one of whose activities was the training of young women in the making of lace, and the Dublin Ladies' Relief Association were among those supported by Quaker funds.[80]

One of the best-known relief societies at the time, cited in many contemporary testimonies, was the Belfast Ladies' Relief Association.[81] Its activities included the establishment of knitting and weaving workshops not only in Belfast but also, through the Belfast Ladies' Relief Association for Connaught, in the west of the country, aimed 'to improve, by industry, the temporal condition of the poor females of Connaught and their spiritual by the truth of the Bible'. By 1851, the society claimed that it had provided employment and education to over 2,000 poor girls and women, with fifty-four teachers sent to Connaught and 'remunerative industry' established in seventy districts, securing to 'poor females, who formerly earned nothing, wages to the amount of £5,000 a year'.[82] Samples of the society's work were included in the Great Exhibition at Crystal Palace in London in 1851. A number of visitors to Ireland commented on the work of the Belfast Association; writing of his encounter with the Connaught committee in March 1847, William Bennett noted, approvingly, the long-term nature of their programme: '[they] have looked beyond the present emergency; and propose rendering themselves permanent for educational and industrial objects'.[83] Asenath Nicholson also praised their work, both in Belfast and in Connaught; in *Lights and Shades of Ireland*, she declares that 'The Belfast Ladies' Association embraced an object which *lives* and *tells*, and will continue to do so, when they who formed it shall be no more on earth.'[84] Yet the history of this association also reveals interesting divisions between private and public intervention at this time; when in autumn 1847, having temporarily exhausted their funds, its Belfast committee applied to the British Treasury for financial assistance, they were informed that such intervention lay outside the scope of the government.[85]

Many contributions to Irish famine relief came from similar female societies in Britain. In 1847, the London Ladies' Irish Clothing Society forwarded cash and bales of clothing to Ireland; in order to encourage local industry, material or fabric rather than ready-made clothing was preferred.[86] The sister of William Bennett, to whom he addresses his account of his six-week journey around Ireland, was a working member of this committee; in addition to his mission to supply seed to remote districts, Bennett was charged with the distribution of £50 and three large bales of clothing from the Ladies' Irish Clothing Committee.[87] His narrative refers, on many occasions, to female acts of benevolence, detailing the distribution of clothing by women, many of whom were the wives, sisters or daughters of ministers, their administration of soup kitchens and the instruction of poor women in the manufacture of cheap clothing.

This 'promotion of female industry' among lower-class women by their upper-class 'sisters', it was hoped, would continue to deliver beneficial consequences when the immediate crisis had passed. Yet, as Bennett and many other Quaker visitors to Ireland including William Forster and R. Barclay Fox recognized, it faced a large obstacle: the securing of markets for the objects manufactured. Markets, both overseas and local, were vital in order that 'charitable contributions' would be replaced by 'healthy and permanent' trade.[88] Some contemporary observers suggested that women in England be asked to donate money to purchase goods which could then be distributed among the needy; this, according to William Forster, had the double advantage of clothing the poor and of supplying employment which would relieve poor women 'from the necessity of going on the public works to obtain bread'.[89] In such a scheme, English upper-class women would, through their Irish counterparts, finance both the manufacture and sale of articles by poor Irish women – hardly the most self-sustaining of markets. An alternative system, proposed by R. Barclay Fox, involved self-reliance to the extreme: some of the garments made by 'the peasants' could be purchased by the makers themselves with the wages earned.[90]

In 1865, Susanna Meredith, recounting the history of the Irish lace-making industry, recalls women's famine work in expansive terms: 'When famine ravaged Ireland in 1847, women were found inspired with an energy to work that was truly surprising. Wherever there was a female hand, it was set in motion, and, generally, it seized a needle, and wielded it vigorously for bread.'[91] Like many of her contemporaries, Meredith stresses the benefits of this work for women of all classes, but also, more rarely and quite intriguingly, she outlines the challenge thus delivered to the conventional order:

> Women of the upper ranks developed an extraordinary skill in needlework, and, also, a great commercial aptitude to turn it to a profitable account. The repose of aristocratic society, and the leisure of the cloister were disturbed. Ladies burst the bounds of conventionalisms, and went regularly into business, to procure remunerative occupation for the destitute of their own sex.[92]

Yet, although some records survive from better-known societies like the Belfast Association, much remains unknown and unexplored in the area of women's famine relief. Helen Hatton, in her detailed study of the history of the Society of Friends, acknowledges that information regarding the famine activities of female' members, women 'who laboured long and hard at soup kitchens, clothing distribution and industrial work', is conspicuously absent. Where 'glimpses' exist, for example in letters appealing for grants, 'too often women report they are trying to carry on alone because relief committees have broken down'.[93] A large part of famine relief, as Maria Luddy notes, was in fact performed by women on an individual basis, rather than through a charitable society.[94] The individual and localized nature of these relief-schemes helps to explain the scarcity of information regarding their scale and efficacy. Although historical studies show that women and children were 'the primary recipients of a charity which came increasingly to be provided by other women'[95] – 'the delicate touch of the peeress assisting the rough fingers of the peasant',[96] in Susanna Meredith's flowery terms – even fewer details survive as to the recipients of relief.

Memoirs and letters by women offer some significant additional insights into the operations of private charity. The diaries of Elizabeth Smith, for example, reveal the duties of a landowner's wife during the famine; these included, in Smith's case, the provision of soup and clothing to tenants, visiting their homes and the administration of a school for local children.[97] Maria Edgeworth's correspondence documents her requests for and receipt of assistance, on behalf of her tenants, from the Dublin Central Committee of the Society of Friends, in 1847.[98] This aid consisted of money and clothing, leather to make shoes for labourers, and £10 with the 'especial object of promoting female employment', for which a committee including Edgeworth was later formed.[99] The accompanying instructions from Dublin included the requirement that the distributing committee should 'go to the houses of the poor and actually *see* before they distribute and give to the most destitute and deserving'.[100] The fame of Edgeworth's name was itself sufficient to generate other donations, with contributions from relief committees in England and the United States including 'the ladies of New York', and a subscription by Boston children, allowing the purchase of one hundred and fifty pounds of flour and rice, which was memorably inscribed 'To Miss Edgeworth, for her poor'.[101] Yet, other than brief references to individuals like Smith, Edgeworth or Mary Letitia Martin, 'the Princess of Connemara', famine historiography has largely ignored the question of women's philanthropy.[102] This neglect extends to the wider issue of private relief and its role during the famine, questions raised to some extent by historians such as Cecil Woodham-Smith and Christine Kinealy but which still await a detailed study.[103]

The obscurity which now marks women's famine philanthropy is strikingly at odds with the significance with which it is accredited by many contemporary writers. In 1850, Sidney Godolphin Osborne, visiting workhouses in the west of Ireland, stated his relief at learning that in towns like Westport, Castlebar and Ballina industrial societies were providing employment for women, 'the profits of which may enable them, by gaining the bread of independence, to avoid the evils of workhouse association'.[104] For Osborne, such philanthropic work performed a vital economic and moral role. Earlier he had castigated the idleness of women in workhouses, made particularly regretful in his eyes because of its negation of employment opportunities elsewhere: 'the rearing of these thousands of workhouse mermaids, who live this mere hair-combing life, is just the thing which makes them most unfit for service or matrimony in the colonies'.[105] Welcoming the efforts of societies to turn these 'immense consumers' – a term used with a striking absence of irony – into 'producers', he concludes:

> It is only to those who have studied the nature of that social crisis, in which the west of Ireland is involved, that the great value of this impetus to native industry will come home. No step, however small, which can turn the hand-power of the women to account – to real fair profit, can be overvalued.[106]

Similarly, Maria Edgeworth, writing to Dr Joshua Harvey, member of the Society of Friends, in February 1847, emphasized the positive moral consequences of women's work.

> If we could be aided by a small sum to buy materials and to pay for women's work, we would set them to such needle work, knitting &c as would be in some degree profitable in a pecuniary point of view, and in a much greater degree useful both now and hereafter in preventing them from losing the proper sense of shame, or

becoming mere beggars and paupers, and sinking into idleness and consequent vice.[107]

Women's industry through knitting, spinning or weaving was thus to be encouraged in preventing the loss of shame or other 'consequent vice' seen to result from idleness. Interestingly, as the observations of William Bennett and William Forster show, a further evil to be avoided was the 'degrading' employment of women on public works.[108]

Although contemporary commentators such as Osborne record the significance of women's charitable activities in expansive terms, philanthropy has been dismissed by many historians as the leisure-pursuits of idle women and of little lasting consequence. Trollope's novel, *Castle Richmond*, illustrates this patronizing attitude, to some extent; in the scene in which Clara and the Fitzgerald sisters sell food to the hungry poor, the 'delicate touch of the peeress assisting the rough fingers of the peasant' is certainly seen. Yet the narrative's references to philanthropy also serve to cover over more troubling aspects of power and responsibility. In this regard, Trollope's narrative reinforces Mary Poovey's argument that, with the increasing articulation of virtue through gender in the late eighteenth and early nineteenth centuries, a depoliticization of virtue was made possible:

> virtue was depoliticized, moralized, and associated with the domestic sphere, which was being abstracted at the same time – both rhetorically, and, to a certain extent, materially – from the so-called public sphere of competition, self-interest, and economic aggression.[109]

This separation, however, emerges in famine narratives as an aim more desired than achieved, with the depiction of famine victims in a novel like *Castle Richmond* continually threatening to undo such 'abstractions'. Neither does the depoliticization of virtue occur without complication in women's famine writings of the period. While underlining the moral significance of women's work, usually embodied in local and individual acts of benevolence, many writers also explore its contribution to the public sphere, the intersections between private charity and political economy. As a result, they throw an interesting light on the increasingly vexed question of the location of female activity in private or public spheres.[110]

The writings of Maria Edgeworth and Asenath Nicholson, in particular, directly engage with contemporary political and economic debate, not only concerning the causation of famine but also the significance of relief, official and private. Both writers underline the willingness to work of poor women whom they have encountered. In the above-mentioned letter to Harvey, Edgeworth states:

> We find among the poorest women and children, even in their present distressed condition, sparks of this same principle of independence. A poor woman the other day in thanking our vicar for the assistance he gave in employing men and boys, according to the government arrangements, regretted that when so much was done for men, nothing has been thought of for women and children, who are, as she said, also willing to work, if they could be employed and paid, they would work to their utmost.[111]

Nicholson, also noting the desire to work among poor women, vehemently censures the contrasting idleness and ignorance of the 'genteel' woman:

> She looks pretty, walks genteelly, and talks sometimes quite enchantingly; but with all these appurtenances, the inquiry must and does arise – 'What are you good for?' The little common necessary daily duties which belong to woman are unheeded; and when any exigencies fall upon her she has no alternative.[112]

Acknowledging that this may appear a 'trifling' deficiency, she insists that its consequences, in times of famine, are disastrous:

> Now, as trifling as these things appear to many, yet Ireland has suffered, and is still doomed to suffer deeply, on these accounts. Many of these genteel ones are reduced to the last extremity, the mistresses not being able to give even the 10s. per quarter to a servant. She knows not how economically to prepare the scanty food which her husband may provide; and multitudes of this class are either in the walls of the union, or hovering about its precincts.[113]

The apathy or idleness of the Irish as cause of the famine is more usually, among contemporary writers, made the preserve of the lower orders; very rarely is its possession by genteel ladies considered relevant to the event. Nicholson's views on the role played by upper-class women thus differ strikingly from Trollope's indulgence of the 'little quota of work' performed by these 'delicate' women. Their influence and example, she insists, are vital in the context of famine food and the difficulties experienced in cooking Indian meal. She concludes: 'Had the women of the higher classes known how to prepare these articles in a proper manner, much money might have been saved, and many lives rescued, which are now lost.'[114] Although Nicholson characterizes women's work as largely hidden and domestic, its repercussions are of large, public significance; the failure of genteel women to be trained in domestic duties and their resulting ignorance in the preparation of food carry direct responsibility for others' hunger.

Many of the famine novels and stories written by women also deal with the subject of philanthropy; in 1875, one critic noted that a recurring theme in the many stories of the 1840s was the 'splendid unselfishness on the part of Irish ladies – the best type of whom can be surpassed by the women of no other race'.[115] References occur in Emily Fox's 1880 novel *Rose O'Connor*[116] and Louise Field's *Denis* (1896), with more detailed treatments in Elizabeth Hely Walshe's *Golden Hills* (1865), Annie Keary's *Castle Daly* (1875), as well as Mary Anne Hoare's collection of stories. The characterization of the young philanthropist in *Golden Hills* is quite typical: the daughter of a landowner seeks a 'purpose', being a little inclined 'to envy the stronger sex for their fixity of employment and reality of purpose'. She turns to charitable work, establishing a Sunday-school, together with a sewing-class for older girls; the project eventually succeeds, securing a market in England for the articles manufactured. The 'money-getting power, producing power' thus obtained proves crucial to withstanding famine; in Walshe's words, 'The sole support of many a poor family in the bitter winter following was from the labour of the daughters' thus employed.'[117]

The theme of women's moral responsibility and its economic significance receives most attention in the work of Hoare and

Keary. Mary Anne Hoare's story, 'The Knitted Collar', a short didactic tale, depicts the famine-related destitution of an urban family and the benevolent aid earned by their daughter Mary.[118] Employing the conventional theme of the deserving and undeserving poor, Hoare explains that the family's destitution is related not only to famine but to the drinking of the father, formerly a journeyman shoemaker; this, according to the author, justly renders them ineligible for the limited famine relief available. In contrast, the daughter Mary is distinguished by her industry and seeks to support her family through the sale of knitting and embroidery. The story centres on Mary's encounter with two sisters, one a fashionably-dressed lady who bargains with Mary for the purchase of the collar, the other marked by her 'benevolence of spirit' who rewards Mary for her honesty and later rescues her from starvation.

The dualistic and didactic quality of Hoare's tale is clear – woman as exploiter and as benefactor; though simply told, the story includes an interesting engagement with questions of political and moral economy. Challenged by her husband for taking 'the fruit' of another's industry for 'one-fifth of its value', the purchaser initially responds – with the full force of the free market behind her – '"why should it not be honest to purchase an article for the price at which its owner is willing to sell it?" '.[119] The closing moral of the tale provides a curious definition of true domestic economy: the woman must learn, in Hoare's words, to be 'thrifty, as a housewife should be, in buying from rich tradespeople' without cheapening 'the work of the poor'.[120]

The most engaging fictional philanthropist appears in Annie Keary's *Castle Daly* in the character of Anne O'Flaherty, landowner of Good People's Hollow and perpetual reformer. Anne's improving schemes include draining lands, wearing clothes of native manufacture, building new cabins and constructing workrooms for her tenants. As representative of an older, feudal order, she is drawn into conflict with John Thornley, an Englishman, a modern reformer who represents law and rational theory. To Anne, Thornley personifies 'a huge, crushing, iron monster called Political Economy . . . before whose Juggernaut wheels the prosperity of her populous little valley must inevitably be ground to powder some day'.[121] What makes Keary's novel particularly interesting is her determination to complicate easy dualisms; the dialogue between Anne as the voice of personal experience and passion and Thornley's cold 'monster' is also that of an older pragmatic woman and an idealistic young man. The novel includes a similar conflict between Ellen, Anne's niece and heir, and Bride, Thornley's sister, regarding famine relief. While Bride embodies a pragmatic philosophy which is firmly against waste and seeks to identify solid benefit, however harsh, Ellen favours a 'warm-hearted impulsiveness' as more appropriate to the Irish, arguing, in a passage popular among reviewers of the novel, that 'English or Scotch people may be reasonable enough to thrive on solid food, given with heart-wounds and stabs to their pride along with it, but we can't'.[122]

Keary's own position regarding this confrontation between the old 'clan feeling' and modern 'hard individualism' is difficult to assess. Writing to a relative in answer to some criticisms of the novel, the author explained that her aim was to make Anne of central importance, as 'influencer, not a repressor':

> for I do so wish to make Anne express my thoughts about the best sort of Irish people. I mean the Thornleys to be the strong-willed people: Ellen and Anne the sympathetic people, who *alter* those they live near not by subduing, but by permeating them with influence; and I want to show how much more powerful that way is, though the people who use it often look weak to observers who do not see far enough.[123]

What Keary sees as a distinctive Irish quality – altering through influence – is perhaps more familiar to us as a gendered type and throughout the nineteenth century was seen as the particular potential of female philanthropy. Anne, as philanthropist, thus serves to embody the power of influence and sympathy, a force greater than repression. The outcome of the novel, however, is less clear. On the one hand, Anne's influence on Thornley is visible, modifying his original beliefs; yet the course of the narrative, in particular the crisis of famine, also suggests that Anne and the world of Good People's Hollow represent an old, increasingly anachronistic order. Whether the end of the novel, with John's marriage to Ellen, Anne's heir, marks the triumph of her influence or its end remains an open question – fitting, perhaps, in light of the novel's dialogic structure. Yet, in its creation of characters such as Anne and John, and in the construction of their encounters, Keary's novel is a highly significant text for its time, resisting 'depoliticization' of virtue and its abstraction from the public sphere.

A discussion of women's philanthropy, however, risks over-estimating the resistance posed by these texts. Depictions of women's benevolence usually serve to reinforce class differences, while disguising them in moral terms. Though charitable actions by privileged women towards poor women may assert a solidarity between 'peeress' and 'peasant', it is of a temporary and limited nature, and generally closer to an expression of pity than a redefinition of social relations.

Yet, as many famine commentators attest, charity also could possess quite troubling political and social implications, endangering the existing social and economic order through the operations of what Trollope memorably termed 'promiscuous charity'. A vivid illustration of the varying reactions to private relief, among female observers of the time, is provided by a comparison of the writings of Asenath Nicholson and Maria Edgeworth. Nicholson, clearly engaging with contemporary debates, forcefully defends the giving of gratuitous relief: 'what was to be done must be done quickly, and in the kindly feeling which promptly lighted up, the givers would naturally and properly throw promiscuously whatever relief could be gathered by any hands that would offer'.[124] As her narrative continues, the subject of female philanthropy becomes part of a larger argument concerning government and voluntary famine relief in which the author strongly criticizes 'hireling' officials for waste and delay and praises the 'self-moved or heavenly-moved donor'.[125] Nicholson's narrative emerges as one of the most politicized treatments of philanthropy, welcoming its political implications and its potential undoing of the legacy and stereotypes of 'oppression': 'now that an industry, founded on righteous principles, was springing up – an industry that not only rewarded but elevated – the convenient term, "lazy Irish", was hiding its slanderous head'.[126]

'Promiscuous charity' was viewed far less favourably by Nicholson's peer, Maria Edgeworth, whose letters express a keen anxiety regarding its consequences. In 1847 and 1848, Edgeworth corresponded with members of the Society of Friends in Dublin and with her friend, the economist, Richard Jones; these letters display her deep interest in contemporary discourses of political economy and in the challenges posed to such orthodoxies by recent events. Again and again, Edgeworth stresses the importance of providing relief in the form of employment, rather than 'gratis feeding'. Writing to Dr Harvey on 1 February 1847, she reports: 'We are particularly anxious to enable the poor to work for themselves, wherever health and strength permit, that they may preserve some sense of self respect, and some spirit of independence and industry.'[127] From the early 1830s, Edgeworth had been in correspondence with Jones, professor of political economy in Haileybury, whom she described as the 'Voltaire of Political Economists'.[128] Her accounts to him of conditions in Edgeworthstown in 1847 vividly demonstrate her struggles to reconcile the reality and urgency of distress with long-held political and economic beliefs. Strongly opposed to the giving of gratuitous relief, she acknowledges that the present times allow some exceptions, yet greatly fears their consequences:

> How shall we get the people who have been fed gratis to believe that the government and their landlords are not bound to feed them always? They evidently have formed this idea. It was impolitic in the past circumstances to adhere strictly to the wholesome maxim: 'They who do not work shall not eat.' There were such numbers who had no *work* – who could not work from extenuation, disease, etc. Humanity could not leave these to perish from hunger – or if humanity had been out of the question fear could not have ventured it. The character of Paddy knows well how to take advantage of his own misfortunes and of all fears and blunders.[129]

Edgeworth's attitude here is difficult to locate precisely, the tone of the extract oscillating between compassion and censure. Intervention on behalf of those near-perishing from hunger is required by 'humanity' – but also by 'fear'. While her writing conveys some sympathy towards those who genuinely cannot work, it also betrays a deep, and troublingly familiar, distrust of the poor – the undisciplined yet cunning 'Paddy' ready and able to exploit 'his own misfortunes'.

In conclusion, women's nineteenth-century famine writings share many of the fears and dilemmas expressed by their male contemporaries regarding the operations of charity, the role of private relief, whether 'gratuitous' or earned, and its relation to official relief-systems – concerns and debates with marked relevance to our times. The following extract from the diary of Elizabeth Smith, written 21 January 1849, provides a type of postscript. In 1849, the famine is officially 'over', yet the author daily encounters people suffering from hunger and disease. As she writes, Smith recites justifications against intervention which are only too familiar: the danger of supporting those 'who have no claim . . . who little deserve help . . . who would not be really benefited . . . resulting in no good':

> If I could manage to give a bit of bread daily to each pauper child, but we have no money, much more than we can afford is spent on labour, the best kind of charity, leaving little for ought else, people not being quixotic enough to deny themselves the decencies they have been accustomed to for the support of those who have no claim upon them, who little deserve help and who would not be really benefited by it, only a temporary assistance it would be resulting in no good. These philosophick views are right doubtless, yet when I see hungry children I long to give them food.[130]

In these lines, a recurring strain in famine narratives is finally acknowledged – the disjunction between 'philosophick' views and the reality of people's hunger.

NOTES AND REFERENCES

1. References to famine also occur in Catherine M. O'Connell, *Excursions in Ireland during 1844 and 1850* (London, 1852), chapters 25 to 28, and, briefly, in Frances Power Cobbe, *Life of Frances Power Cobbe By Herself* (2 vols; London, 1894).

2. Laura Mulvey, 'Visual Pleasure and Narrative Cinema', *Screen*, 16, 3 (1975), pp. 6–18.

3. See Linda Williams, 'When the Woman Looks', in Mary Ann Doane, Patricia Mellencamp and Linda Williams (eds.), *Re-Vision: Essays in Feminist Film Criticism* (Maryland and Los Angeles, 1984), pp. 83–99; Lorraine Gamman and Margaret Marshment, *The Female Gaze* (London, 1988); E. Ann Kaplan, *Women and Film: Both Sides of the Camera* (London, 1983); and Judith Mayne, 'The Woman at the Keyhole: Women's Cinema and Feminist Criticism', in *New German Critique*, 23 (1981), pp. 27–43, republished in Doane et al., *Re-Vision*, pp. 49–66.

4. Mayne, 'The Woman at the Keyhole', pp. 54–55.

5. Stephen J. Brown's *Ireland in Fiction* ([1915]; second edition 1919, reprinted Shannon, 1968) is a useful guide to novels written during this period. Novels by male authors, besides those of Carleton and Trollope, which contain famine material, include David Power Conyngham's *Frank O'Donnell: A Tale of Irish Life* (Dublin, 1861), reprinted in America as *The O'Donnells of Glen Cottage* (New York, 1874), and, in the early twentieth century, Louis Walsh's *The Next Time: A Story of Forty-Eight* (Dublin, 1919).

6. Mary Anne Hoare, *Shamrock Leaves; or, Tales and Sketches of Ireland* (Dublin and London, 1851). Mary Anne Hoare (*c.* 1818–1872) was the wife of William Barry Hoare, a solicitor and attorney in Monkstown, Co. Cork, and is credited by the *Wellesley Index of Victorian Periodicals* with authorship of a short story 'The Mysterious Sketch', published in *Temple Bar XXXIV* (1872), pp. 212–24. For further information see Edward Hoare, *Some account of the early history and genealogy with pedigrees from 1330, unbroken to the present time, of the families of Hore and Hoare, with all their branches* (London, 1883).

7. Hoare, 'A Sketch of Famine', *Shamrock Leaves*, pp. 205–06.

8. Ibid., p. 213.

9. Mary Anne Sadlier, *New Lights; or, Life in Galway* (New York, 1853). Mary Anne Madden (1820–1903) was born in Cavan in 1820 and emigrated to Canada in 1844; in Montreal she married the publisher James Sadlier and the couple later moved to New York. Author of a large number of novels, and specializing in historical fiction with Catholic themes, she was one of the best-known Irish-American writers of her day.

10. Elizabeth Hely Walshe, *Golden Hills: A Tale of the Irish Famine* (London, 1865). Walshe (1835–68) was born and lived in Limerick, and was the author of a number of novels, including *The Manuscript Man; or, The Bible in*

Ireland (London, 1869) and *Golden Hills*, published by the Religious Tract Society of London. In a preface to one of her novels, she wrote that her writings aimed 'to produce a faithful, and in no wise [*sic*] exaggerated picture of the religious state of my poor country people'; Walshe died of consumption at the age of thirty-three.

11. Margaret (M. W.) Brew, *The Chronicles of Castle Cloyne; or, Pictures of the Munster People* ([1884]; 1885 edition reprinted in the Garland Series, New York and London, 1979), iii, p. 163. Brew was born in Clare and appears to have been the daughter of a well-to-do Catholic family. She was the author of one other novel, *The Burtons of Dunroe* (3 vols; [1880]; New York, 1979), and some stories and poems, published in the *Irish Monthly*.

12. Louise (E. M.) Field, *Denis: A Study in Black and White* (London, 1896). Louise Frances Story was born in Cavan in 1856; little is known of her life except for her authorship of a number of novels, including stories for girls, such as *Bryda: A Story of the Indian Mutiny* (London, 1888) and *Ethne* (London, 1887), a historical fiction concerning Cromwell's settlement of Ireland.

13. *Castle Daly: The Story of an Irish Home Thirty Years Ago* was first published in *Macmillan's Magazine XXIX-XXXII* (1874–75); the three-volume edition (London, 1875) was republished in Robert Lee Wolff's Garland Series (New York and London, 1979). Keary (1825–79) was born in Yorkshire, the daughter of an Irish-born clergyman. She published a number of novels and children's stories, many anonymously, *Castle Daly* being her most acclaimed novel. Charles Read's *Cabinet of Irish Literature* called it 'the best Irish story of the present generation'.

14. 'Biograms', *Irish Monthly XIV* (1886), p. 201. Keary based her novel largely on readings in Irish history and on her father's recollections of his childhood in Ireland. In her memoir of her sister, Eliza Keary records that Annie paid her 'first and only visit to Ireland' – a visit of some two weeks in the west of Ireland – while writing *Castle Daly*; see *Memoir of Annie Keary by her Sister* (London, 1882), p. 150, also cited in Robert Lee Wolff's introduction to the 1979 reprint of *Castle Daly*.

15. See reviews in *Saturday Review*, 9 October 1875, and *Graphic*, 21 August 1875.

16. *Graphic*, 21 August 1875.

17. See, for example, the *Athenaeum*, 27 June 1885 (p. 821) which highly praises the 'touching' and 'amusing' novel by 'Mr. Brew'.

18. See Stanley Lane-Poole's article on Annie Keary in *Macmillan's Magazine XLII* (1880), pp. 259–67.

19. Keary, *Castle Daly*, iii, chapter one.

20. Brew, *Chronicles of Castle Cloyne*, ii, p. 286.

21. Hoare, 'A Sketch of Famine', pp. 205–06.

22. Ibid., pp. 208–13.

23. Hoare, 'The Brethren of the Pups', p. 198.

24. Ibid., p. 199; this passage anticipates a similar moment in Canon John O'Rourke's *The History of the Great Irish Famine of 1847, with notices of earlier Irish famines* (Dublin, 1875), discussed in chapter one.

25. Hoare, 'The Brethren of the Pups', p. 199.

26. Walshe, *Golden Hills*, pp. 203–04.

27. Ibid.

28. See Christine Gledhill, 'Developments in Feminist Film Criticism', *Quarterly Review of Film Studies*, 3, 4 (1978), reproduced in Doane et al., *Re-Vision*, pp. 18–48. Similarly, Julia Kristeva asks: 'What is there, in the portrayal of the Maternal in general and particularly in its Christian, virginal one, that reduces social anguish and gratifies a male being; what is there that also satisfies a woman so that a commonality of the sexes is set up, beyond and in spite of their glaring incompatibility and permanent warfare?'; see 'Stabat Mater' (1977), reprinted and translated in Toril Moi (ed.), *The Kristeva Reader* (Oxford, 1986), p. 163.

29. See Gledhill, 'Developments', pp. 21, 37.

30. Kristeva, 'Stabat Mater', p. 176.

31. Ibid., p. 163; see note 28 above.

32. Field, *Denis*, pp. 291–92.

33. Ibid., p. 392.

34. 'The Famine of 1847, '48 and '49' was first published in London in 1850 as the third part of Nicholson's historical work, *Lights and Shades of Ireland*. The following year, the famine section was published in New York as a separate volume, entitled *Annals of the Famine in Ireland in 1847, 1848 and 1849*. Extracts from Nicholson's famine account are contained in Seamus Deane (ed.), *The Field Day Anthology of Irish Writing* (Derry, 1991), ii, pp. 133–45. For references to Nicholson, see also Frank O'Connor's *A Short History of Irish Literature: A Backward Look* (New York, 1967), pp. 134–39, and Christopher Woods, 'American Travellers in Ireland before and during the Great Famine: A Case of Culture-Shock', in H. Kosok (ed.), *Literary Interrelations: Ireland, England and the World* (Tübingen, 1987), iii, pp. 77–84.

35. Mayne, 'The Woman at the Keyhole', pp. 54–55.

36. Nicholson's age is difficult to identify precisely; in 1847, she was described by her contemporary, Elizabeth Smith, as being fifty years of age (see note 42 below).

37. J. L., introduction to Asenath Nicholson, *Annals of the Famine in Ireland, in 1847, 1848, and 1849* (New York, 1851).

38. Asenath Nicholson, *Ireland's Welcome to the Stranger; or, Excursions through Ireland in 1844, and 1845, for the purpose of personally investigating the condition of the poor* (London, 1847), preface.

39. Most commentators on Nicholson's work distinguish it from proselytism; for example, Helen Hatton, author of *The Largest Amount of Good: Quaker Relief in Ireland, 1654–1921* (Kingston and Montreal, 1993), writes, 'Full of blunt, outspoken Yankee common sense, Nicholson was not a ranter, and

did not approach her task from a "missionary" frame, as did some of the relief officers of the evangelically based agencies' (p. 136). From her narrative, it would appear that the physical destitution of the poor was her main concern.

40. Alfred T. Sheppard, introduction to Asenath Nicholson, *The Bible in Ireland* (abridged version of *Ireland's Welcome*; London, 1926). Similarly, in *Lights and Shades of Ireland*, Nicholson gives a detailed account of the various denominations existing in Ireland such as Presbyterians, the Society of Friends, Methodists and others, and describes herself as 'a listener who belongs to no one of them' (p. 419).

41. *The Achill Missionary Herald and Western Witness*, 25 June 1845, p. 65.

42. William Bennett, *Narrative of a recent journey of six weeks in Ireland in connexion with the subject of supplying small seed to some of the remoter districts* (London and Dublin, 1847), p. 96; *Howitt's Journal*, 28 August 1847, p. 141. Another reader of *Ireland's Welcome* was less complimentary: in November 1847, Elizabeth Smith commented in her diary that its author 'is not quite mad – only an enthusiast, and too imaginative, too quick, to be quite correct in her facts or her inferences'; cited in Elizabeth (Smith) Grant, *The Highland Lady in Ireland, Journals 1840–1850*, (eds.) Patricia Pelly and Andrew Tod (Edinburgh, 1991), pp. 354–55.

43. *Howitt's Journal*, 28 August 1847, p. 141; this article included a review of *Ireland's Welcome* together with a letter from Nicholson, dated 3 August, describing famine conditions in Donegal. The issue of 27 November 1847 published another letter by Nicholson, dated 30 October and written in Belmullet, as part of a long article entitled 'Frightful Condition and Prospects of Ireland'; both of these letters were later incorporated into *Lights and Shades*.

44. One reason for her return was to work on the proofs for *Ireland's Welcome*; Nicholson was to use the royalties from that volume for famine relief.

45. Hatton, in her history of Quaker relief, describes Nicholson as the 'field agent of the New York Irish Relief Society'; though not a Quaker agent, her supplies and funds were channelled through the Central Relief Committee (*The Largest Amount of Good*, pp. 50, 257).

46. Bennett, *Six Weeks in Ireland*, pp. 96–97.

47. J. L., introduction to Nicholson, *Annals of the Famine*.

48. Nicholson, *Lights and Shades of Ireland* (London, 1850), preface.

49. Ibid., pp. 8, 10, 229.

50. Ibid., p. 233.

51. Ibid., p. 224.

52. Ibid., pp. 224–25.

53. Ibid., p. 230.

54. Ibid., pp. 231–32.

55. Ibid., p. 237.

56. Ibid., p. 301.

57. Ibid., p. 408.

58. Ibid., pp. 308–09.
59. Ibid., pp. 237–39.
60. Ibid., p. 239.
61. Ibid., p. 439.
62. Ibid., p. 441.
63. Ibid., p. 234.
64. Linda Williams defines voyeurism as affording 'the impression of looking in on a private world unaware of the spectator's own existence' ('When the Woman Looks', p. 83).
65. Nicholson, *Lights and Shades of Ireland*, p. 429.
66. Ibid., p. 246.
67. Ibid., pp. 271–72.
68. Ibid., pp. 256, 284.
69. Ibid., p. 294.
70. Nicholson's narrative includes many harrowing examples of this theme, including a reference to a girl's body eaten by dogs (p. 290) and the story of 'Abraham and Sara' (pp. 287–91).
71. Nicholson, *Lights and Shades of Ireland*, p. 330.
72. William O'Connor, letter to *Cork Examiner*, 31 August 1848, quoted in Nicholson, *Lights and Shades*, p. 385.
73. See, for example, Andy Storey, 'Who tells us what about the "Third World"?', *Irish Times*, 14 February 1996, p. 21.
74. Mary Poovey, *Uneven Developments: The Ideological Work of Gender in Mid-Victorian England* (Chicago, 1988), pp. 7–8.
75. Peter Gaskell, *The Manufacturing Population of England* ([1833]; New York, 1972), cited in Poovey, *Uneven Developments*, p. 8
76. Thus, the *Cork Examiner* of 1 January 1847, describing relief work in Dungarvan, praised woman's 'more refined and subtle perception, that heart touching sensibility so peculiarly her own'; reproduced in Maria Luddy, *Women in Ireland, 1800–1918: A Documentary History* (Cork, 1995), pp. 52–53.
77. Important studies include Lori D. Ginzberg, *Women and the Work of Benevolence: Morality, Politics, and Class in the Nineteenth-Century United States* (New Haven and London, 1990); F. K. Prochaska, *Women and Philanthropy in Nineteenth-Century England* (Oxford, 1980); Anne Summers, 'A Home from Home – Women's Philanthropic Work in the Nineteenth Century', in Sandra Burman (ed.), *Fit Work for Women* (London, 1979), pp. 33–63, and Jessica Gerard, 'Lady Bountiful: Women of the Landed Classes and Rural Philanthropy', in *Victorian Studies*, 30 (1987), pp. 183–210.
78. See Maria Luddy, *Women and Philanthropy in Nineteenth-Century Ireland* (Cambridge, 1995) and Margaret H. Preston, 'Lay Women and Philanthropy in Dublin, 1860–1880', in *Éire-Ireland*, 28, 4 (1993), pp. 74–85. Luddy's *Women in Ireland* also reproduces some contemporary documents relating to women's relief activities, including an extract from Elizabeth Smith's diary (pp. 50–54). An interesting contemporary account of the Cork Ladies' Relief

Society is provided by Catherine M. O'Connell in her *Excursions in Ireland*, pp. 248–51.

79. In chapter twenty-eight of her narrative, entitled 'Union of Charity' and written in 1847, O'Connell describes in detail the operations of a visiting relief society 'comprising all the ladies of the town and immediate neighbourhood . . . under the guardianship of the clergymen of both religions', in the 'small country town of G—' (pp. 269–81).

80. See Hatton, *The Largest Amount of Good*, p. 186, and Roy Goodbody, *A Suitable Channel: Quaker Relief in the Great Famine* (Bray, 1995), pp. 45, 68. Hatton also notes that 'substantial loans' from the Cork Committee went to a committee in Ballycotton providing 'Reproductive Relief' and employing women (p. 186).

81. See Christine Kinealy, *This Great Calamity: The Irish Famine, 1845–1852* (Dublin, 1994), pp. 165–66; Luddy, *Women and Philanthropy*, pp. 187–88; Hatton, *The Largest Amount of Good*, p. 186, and John Edgar, *The Women of the West: Ireland Helped to Help Herself* (Belfast, 1849).

82. See Appendix XXI to Society of Friends, *Transactions of the Central Relief Committee of the Society of Friends during the famine in Ireland, in 1846 and 1847* (Dublin, 1852), pp. 436–38, in which details from John Edgar, regarding the operations of the 'Belfast Ladies' Industrial Association for Connaught', are reproduced.

83. Bennett, *Six Weeks in Ireland*, p. 92.

84. Nicholson, *Lights and Shades*, pp. 249–51.

85. Kinealy, *This Great Calamity*, p. 166.

86. Goodbody, *A Suitable Channel*, p. 43.

87. Bennett, *Six Weeks in Ireland*, pp. 92–95, 136.

88. R. Barclay Fox, *Narrative of a Visit to some parts of Ireland* (London, 1847), pp. 1, 5. Helen Hatton also notes that a general meeting of the Friends was held in London on 3 June 1847 to deal with the question of a market for the goods manufactured by destitute women (*The Largest Amount of Good*, p. 176).

89. See James Hack Tuke's *Narrative of the Second, Third and Fourth weeks of William Forster's visit to some of the Distressed Districts in Ireland* (London, 1847), p. 10.

90. Fox, *Narrative*, pp. 2–3.

91. Susanna Meredith, *The Lacemakers: Sketches of Irish Character with Some Account of the Effort to Establish Lace-Making in Ireland* (London, 1865), p. 5.

92. Ibid., p. 6.

93. Hatton, *The Largest Amount of Good*, p. 259.

94. Luddy, *Women and Philanthropy*, p. 188.

95. Ibid., p. 19; documents relating to the operations of the Cork Ladies' Relief Society, reproduced by Luddy in *Women in Ireland, 1800–1918*, include a list of queries to be addressed to applicants for relief, one being 'What is the state of the females, widows etc., as regards sickness, poverty, age and infirmity, and how many are unable to work for their own support?' (p. 54).

96. Meredith, *The Lacemakers*, p. 2.

97. Elizabeth Smith (born Elizabeth Grant) moved from Scotland to Ireland in 1830; her husband Colonel Henry Smith was a small landowner in Baltiboys, Co. Wicklow. Two editions of Smith's diaries are available: Patricia Pelly and Andrew Tod (eds.), *The Highland Lady in Ireland: Elizabeth Grant of Rothiemurchus* (Edinburgh, 1991), and David Thomson and Moyra McGusty (eds.), *The Irish Journals of Elizabeth Smith: 1840–1850* (Oxford, 1980). For a discussion of Smith's diaries, see Janet K. TeBrake, 'Personal Narratives as Historical Sources: the Journal of Elizabeth Smith', in *History Ireland*, 3, 1 (1995), pp. 51–56.

98. Selections of Edgeworth's famine correspondence are available in Frances Edgeworth, *A Memoir of Maria Edgeworth with A Selection from Her Letters* (3 vols; London, 1867), iii, pp. 249–55, and Augustus J. C. Hare, *The Life and Letters of Maria Edgeworth* (2 vols; London, 1894), ii, pp. 323–28. For correspondence between Edgeworth and the Central Relief Committee, Dublin, 1847–48, see National Library, Dublin, Ms. 989; letters from Edgeworth to Joshua Harvey and others, written January to February 1847, regarding the benevolence of the Society of Friends, are also included in the Ballitore papers (National Library, Dublin). A useful discussion of this topic is Michael Hurst's *Maria Edgeworth and the Public Scene: Intellect, Fine Feeling and Landlordism in the Age of Reform* (London, 1969), pp. 155–68.

99. See Maria Edgeworth's correspondence with the Dublin Central Relief Committee of the Society of Friends, Ms. 989; Hurst, *Maria Edgeworth*, pp. 155–56; Hare, *Life and Letters*, ii, pp. 323–24; Frances Edgeworth, *Maria Edgeworth*, iii, p. 250.

100. Maria Edgeworth's letter to Fanny Edgeworth, 9 March 1847, quoted in Hurst, *Maria Edgeworth*, p. 157 [emphasis in original].

101. Hurst, *Maria Edgeworth*, pp. 161–62; Hare, *Life and Letters*, ii, pp. 324, 328; Frances Edgeworth, *Maria Edgeworth*, iii, pp. 251–53, 290. Additional funds for relief were generated by Edgeworth's writing of *Orlandino*, her last work. In a story often recited by Edgeworth's biographers, the porters who carried the American provisions refused to accept payment; later each received a woollen comforter knitted by Edgeworth herself, in the last year of her life; see Frances Edgeworth, *Maria Edgeworth*, iii, p. 290.

102. Mary Letitia Martin, the 'Princess of Connemara', was the granddaughter of Richard 'Humanity Dick' Martin of Ballinahinch, Co. Galway. She inherited her family's heavily-mortgaged estates and this debt, together with the sums she spent on famine relief for her tenants, resulted in her estate being one of the first sold under the Encumbered Estates Act.

103. See Kinealy, *This Great Calamity*, pp. 157–67, and Cecil Woodham-Smith, *The Great Hunger* ([1962]; London, 1987), pp. 241–46.

104. Sidney Godolphin Osborne, *Gleanings in the West of Ireland* (London, 1850), p. 99.

105. Ibid., p. 55.

106. Ibid., p. 102.
107. Maria Edgeworth to Dr Joshua Harvey, Central Relief Committee, 1 February 1847, in Ms. 989.
108. See Bennett, *Six Weeks in Ireland*, p. 20, and Tuke's *Narrative*, p. 10.
109. Poovey, *Uneven Developments*, p. 9.
110. For a succinct summary of a parallel debate in American women's history, see Nancy A. Hewitt, 'Beyond the Search for Sisterhood: American Women's History in the 1980s', in *Social History*, 10, 3 (1985), pp. 299–319.
111. Edgeworth to Harvey, 1 February 1847.
112. Nicholson, *Lights and Shades*, p. 218.
113. Ibid.
114. Ibid., p. 220.
115. *Saturday Review*, 40 (1875), pp. 470–71.
116. *Rose O'Connor* by Emily Fox was first published in Chicago in 1880, under the pseudonym of Toler King, and concerns the later famine of 1879–90. This famine was also the subject of Louise Berens' *Steadfast unto Death: A Tale of the Irish Famine of Today* (London, 1880), a highly sensationalized famine story.
117. Walshe, *Golden Hills*, pp. 122, 216.
118. Mary Anne Hoare, 'The Knitted Collar', in *Shamrock Leaves*, pp. 57–67.
119. Ibid., p. 63.
120. Ibid., p. 67.
121. Keary, *Castle Daly*, i, p. 151.
122. Ibid., ii, p. 196.
123. Quoted in Eliza Keary, *Memoir*, pp. 153–54; also cited in Robert Lee Wolff, introduction to Garland reprint of *Castle Daly*.
124. Asenath Nicholson, *Lights and Shades*, p. 407.
125. Ibid., pp. 253–55, 438–41.
126. Ibid., p. 251.
127. Edgeworth to Harvey, 1 February 1847.
128. Richard Jones (1790–1855) was a highly prominent political economist of the time, professor of Political Economy in King's College London from 1833 to 1835, and Malthus' successor as chair at East India College at Haileybury where he remained from 1835 until his death. Edgeworth and Jones's correspondence covered a variety of topics, and frequently concerned their mutual love of rose-growing. The manuscripts of many of their letters, from 1833 to 1849, are to be found in the Edgeworth Papers (National Library, Dublin), Ms. 22, 822. Extracts are also included in Hurst, *Maria Edgeworth*, pp. 164–68.
129. Edgeworth to Jones, 14 June 1847, Ms. 22, 822; also cited in Hurst, *Maria Edgeworth*, p. 167.
130. Diary entry for 21 January 1849; reproduced in *The Highland Lady*, p. 211.

— 3 —

Impersonating the Past:
Twentieth-Century Irish Famine Literature

As soon as a story is well known – and such is the case with most traditional and popular narratives as well as with the national chronicles of the founding events of a given community – retelling takes the place of telling.

Paul Ricoeur[1]

Very aged men and women, who can remember the famine, still look back across it as we all look back across some personal grief, some catastrophe which has shattered our lives and made havoc of everything we cared for. We, too, go on again after a while as if nothing had happened, yet we know all the while that matters are not in the least as they were before, that on the contrary they never can or will be.

Emily Lawless[2]

Twentieth-century Irish literature includes a significant number of famine narratives – some famous, others less well known. Yet many of these texts have had a key role in constructing and preserving a memory of famine, retelling the 'story' of the 1840s as a central event in 'the national chronicle' for generations of readers both within Ireland and outside. The silence which has surrounded famine in much of Irish historiography, the 'striking paucity' of reference highlighted by Cormac Ó Gráda, Terry Eagleton and others,[3] gives literature of this period an additional significance; shaping readers' awareness and interpretation of the events of the past, famine literature has, to some extent, fulfilled the role of history.[4]

Beginning with the literature of the revival, this chapter will explore representations of famine from the end of the nineteenth century to the present. The relations between the literary and the historical imagination continue to be of interest throughout twentieth-century famine writing, each generation producing distinctive versions. In 1937, itself an important date in national chronology, Liam O'Flaherty's novel *Famine* appeared and quickly became one of the most important of all Irish famine narratives. O'Flaherty's novel remains a moving depiction of famine, his characters arguably the most memorable of all fictional victims. In 1962, the publication of Cecil Woodham-Smith's *The Great Hunger* sparked controversy, on one hand, and large book sales on the other; her history was also to have a considerable influence on the famine literature produced later that decade by poet Seamus Heaney and playwright Tom Murphy. The 1990s sees the emergence of another generation of famine writing, and unprecedented levels of interest evident among historians and other writers.

With literature playing the role of history and history, on occasion, deemed fiction,[5] the relation of past and present also increases in complexity. Reviewing Woodham-Smith's history, the critic Steven Marcus has emphasized its 'peculiar historical relevance', in which the past is revealed 'as a genuine mode of the present'.[6] Thus, Marcus argues, 'on a strict definition, history can only be a study of the present, the past itself being in fact one mode which the present takes'.[7] The presence of the past in contemporary Ireland, famine's enduring legacy, has received much comment; in the lines from Heaney's poem, 'where potato diggers are/you still smell the running sore'.[8] Yet the implications of Marcus's comments go further; if 'the past retains its vitality in so far as it impersonates the present, either in its aversions or ideals',[9] the act of remembering and retelling the past is shaped by its relevance to our present – be it the closing pages of Liam O'Flaherty's novel or the recent famine poems of Eavan Boland. Literature's special power to present the past, to make it imaginatively real, takes on another meaning: the past as an image and revelation of the present.

As twentieth-century literature continues its efforts to imagine what may have been, female figures perform important roles. Recurring characterizations emerge: the famine mother, the ministering angel, the sacrificial victim. In some of the most moving representations, writers confront the various strategies employed in order to survive, the heroic and also the disturbing manifestations of 'mother love'. In one recent example, Eavan Boland's poem, 'The Making of an Irish Goddess', the speaker attempts

> an accurate inscription
> of that agony:
> the failed harvests,
> the fields rotting to horizon,
> the children devoured by their mothers
> whose souls, they would have said,
> went straight to hell,
> followed by their own.[10]

Demeter's love for Persephone finds a tragic parallel in the actions of these Irish women; in the time of famine, the mother's mythical search in the underworld and her resurrection of her daughter are also dreadfully reversed. The mothers' 'devouring' of their children further echoes the actions of Kali, Hindu goddess of death and destruction. From myth through history, the speaker, herself a mother, seeks to re-embody the past, to physically 'inscribe' it into the present. This ambition has for Boland, as for many other writers, a double quality: tracing the past through its manifestations in the present, and recognizing ourselves in the events of history. A critical role in this configuring of past and present develops for the female figure in much twentieth-century famine literature. Her sacrificial actions increase in symbolic significance and are appropriated for different versions of the 'national chronicle': for some writers, they constitute the means, perhaps disturbingly so, of a community's survival; for others, they form part of a story of resistance and impending freedom; and for others still, the sign of a heroic past now cast into oblivion.

FAMINE AND THE REVIVAL

In February 1892, on a lecture tour in France, Maud Gonne spoke to an audience at the Catholic University of Cercle du Luxembourg of 'the famine of '48' and its legacy for the present. The force of her oration is still palpable:

> The Middle Ages in the most sombre period of their history never beheld such misery. Men and women ate the dogs, the rats, and the grass of the field, and some even, when all food was gone, ate the dead bodies. Those who died were cast into great ditches so hurriedly opened and badly closed again that the pestilential odors helped to make death travel more rapidly. They were called the pits of the famine, for into them the famine cast all its harvest. Ireland was heroic in her suffering. Whole families, when they had eaten their last crust, and understood that they had to die, looked once upon the sun and then closed up the doors of their cabins with stones, that no one might look upon their last agony. Weeks afterwards men would find their skeletons gathered round the extinguished hearth. I do not exaggerate, gentlemen. I have added nothing to the mournful reality. If you come to my country, every stone will repeat to us this tragic history. It was only fifty years ago. It still lives in thousands of memories. I have been told it by women who have heard the last sigh of their children without being able to lessen their agony with one drop of milk. It has seemed to me at evening on those mountains of Ireland, so full of savage majesty when the wind sighed over the pits of the famine where the thousands of dead enrich the harvests of the future, it has seemed to me that I heard an avenging voice calling down on our oppressors the execration of men and the justice of God.[11]

Gonne's lecture captures and expands what were, by the turn of the century, some of the central motifs used in 'retelling' the horrors of the Great Famine: women without milk for their children; families who 'closed up the doors of their cabins with stones, that no one might look upon their last agony'; adults and children driven by hunger to eating grass, dogs, even dead bodies. Some months later, extracts from the speech were made available to American readers in a letter to the *Boston Pilot* written by W. B.

Yeats. Commenting on the eloquence of this 'new Speranza', Yeats located precisely the source of Gonne's oratorical power:

> with rare mastery over the picturesque it unrolls incidents that compel attention and burn themselves into the memory. A man or woman trained on the political platforms of the day would have given figures and arguments and have been forgotten ten minutes after. But many who heard this passage will never forget as long as they live the skeletons huddled by the extinguished hearths and the great pits where lie thousands who make fertile the harvests of the future.[12]

Intriguingly, he remarked that it was

> the kind of speech, both in its limitations and in its triumphs, which could only be made by a woman. From first to last it is emotional and even poignant, and has that curious power of unconsciously seizing salient incidents which is so distinguishing a mark of the novel writing of women. Its logic is none the less irresistible because it is the logic of the heart.[13]

Whatever its 'logic', Gonne's oration, delivered less than fifty years after the events she describes, is a fiery assertion of the continuing memory of the past and its crucial role in the politics of the present.

On the other hand, the view that historical and literary representations are mostly silent about famine has become quite a commonplace assertion. In support of his argument that a 'repression or evasion' of famine has been 'at work in Irish literary culture', Terry Eagleton has specifically queried: 'Where is the Famine in the literature of the Revival?'[14] Explicit mention is indeed strikingly absent from the work of Joyce, and the event of famine carefully distanced into medieval times, and thus removed from its recent occurrence, in Yeats's *The Countess Cathleen*. Yet, apart from the more oblique references to famine which can be identified in these authors' works, the literature of the Irish revival, contrary to Eagleton's implication, includes many vivid and significant engagements with the subject of famine.[15] In the English language, these occur in the fictional writing of Rosa Mulholland, the historical essays of Emily Lawless, and in both the journalistic and literary works of Maud Gonne. With regard to Irish-language treatments, the moving references to famine given by Peadar Ua Laoghaire in his autobiography are quite frequently cited, and deservedly so; less well known are other famine texts such as the plays by lexicographer and critic Patrick Dinneen.[16]

For many authors working in the last years of the nineteenth century and early years of the twentieth, traces of the 'Great Famine' were still visible on the Irish landscape and stories of its horrors to be heard from survivors. In Emily Lawless's essay, 'Famine Roads and Famine Memories', first published in 1897, the author testifies to the 'poor perishing memorials' to the 'great Irish Famine' which linger in the west: 'wrecks of cabins . . . the last trace of what was once a populous village' and the 'famine road'.[17] Of this, the Irish landscape's most evocative 'trace' of famine, Lawless writes:

> Certain words and certain combinations of words seem to need an eminently local education in order adequately to appreciate them. These two words, 'Famine road,' are amongst the number. To other, larger minds than ours they are probably without any particular meaning or inwardness. To the home-staying Irishman or Irishwoman they mean only too much. To hear them casually uttered is to be penetrated by a sense of something at once familiar and terrible. The entire history of two of the most appalling years that any country has ever been called upon to pass through seems to be summed up, and compendiously packed into them.[18]

The immediacy and relevance of famine for those writing in the last years of the nineteenth century was further underlined by the recurrence of hunger, disease and starvation in the years after the 1840s. In the second half of the nineteenth century, a number of minor famines occurred, with significant distress between 1859 and 1864 and, more famously, from 1879 to 1880. No less than three minor famines occurred in the 1890s, with blight returning in 1890 and 1894, and widespread crop failure in 1897.[19]

The famine of 1879–80 forms the subject of a number of contemporary fictional works, some written by non-Irish authors, with the theme of famine usually providing 'local colour' for sentimental fictions.[20] A more interesting literary treatment is Rosa Mulholland's story, 'The Hungry Death', set in Inisbofin, a small island off the coast of Mayo.[21] The year in which 'The Hungry Death' takes place is not identified but details in the story suggest that it is based on a period of distress experienced by the inhabitants of Inisbofin in 1886. The political and economic causes of hardship receive little attention beyond reference to the absence 'of even the rudest piers' and a defence of the 'good landlord'. Instead famine is attributed, primarily, to the harsh climate endured by the isolated island and is fought against by a local moral economy, 'so long as the monster can be beaten back by one neighbour from another neighbour's threshold'. In this particular year, the excessive rain leads to unparalleled scarcity and distress, both on the island and on the mainland:

> It is hard for any one who has never witnessed such a state of things to imagine the condition of ten or twelve hundred living creatures on a barren island girded round with angry breakers; the strong arms around them paralysed, first by the storms that dash their boats to pieces, and rend and destroy their fishing gear, and the devastation of the earth that makes labor useless, and later by the faintness and sickness which comes from hunger long endured, and the cold from which they have no longer a defence . . . Troops of children that a few months ago were rosy and sturdy, sporting on the sea-shore, now stretched their emaciated limbs by the fireless hearths, and wasted to death before their maddened mothers' eyes. The old and ailing vanished like flax before a flame.[22]

The story's central character is Brigid Lavelle, whose father owns the 'finest house in Bofin', though Lavelle's prosperity is more a difference in degree rather than kind from his fellow-islanders. Brigid's love for Coll Prendergast is disguised by her proud scorning of his attentions; the resulting misunderstanding and separation form the first part of the story. Coll, soon after, falls in love with the young Moya Maillie, daughter of a poverty-stricken island widow. When the 'hungry death' appears, the Maillies are among the first to suffer, while Brigid becomes a 'benefactor', distributing her dead father's savings in charity among her neighbours. When Moya is near death from hunger, Coll turns to Brigid for help. At first, she refuses, then, guilt-stricken, she gives her last meal to save Moya's life: '"There isn't enough for all of us," she said, "an' some of us be to die. It was always her or me; an' now it'll be me."'[23]

The exchange which takes place between the two women, in which Brigid gives her life for her rival, taking Moya's place as famine victim, echoes the love-plot in another famine story, Carleton's *The Black Prophet*. In Mulholland's narrative, however, the act gains a number of symbolic dimensions. Arriving at Moya's home, Brigid is the ministering angel, 'an angel of light upon the threshold'; benefactor, she also becomes famine victim. Her act of self-sacrifice is explicitly linked to that of Christ, with the sight of 'the thorn-crowned face' upon a cross prompting her to action. The closing lines of the story reinforce the parallel: Moya and Coll emigrate to America, there 'they pray together for the soul of Brigid Lavelle, who, when in this world, had loved one of them too well, and died to save the life of the other'.[24] The figure of the ministering angel, as discussed in chapter two, is present in earlier famine narratives; what is significant, in Mulholland's story, is the extension of her self-sacrificing character. As benefactor, Brigid gives not only food but also her life, a sacrificial act which will safeguard others' survival. In the stories of famine which follow 'The Hungry Death', the symbolic appropriation of philanthropy develops, with implications for the survival of not only another individual but of a whole community.

One year after Mulholland's story, the 'ministering angel' received her most famous literary incarnation in W. B. Yeats's *The Countess Cathleen*.[25] This play, the first version of which appeared in 1892, presents the story of a woman who, in a time of famine, sells her soul to the devil in order to save her people from hunger; she is saved from damnation since 'The Light of Lights/Looks always on the motive, not the deed/The Shadow of Shadows on the deed alone.'[26] Originally set in the sixteenth century, later versions of the play indicate a vaguer location, 'in Ireland and in old times', suggesting Yeats's deliberate distancing of the play from

well-known historical events. This, in turn, has led some critics to
argue that the starvation represented by the play is more symbolic
than actual.[27] On closer reading, however, the play contains a
number of echoes of 1840s accounts, with references to 'walking'
graves, to those who store up grain 'to prosper on the hunger of
the poor'.[28] The early scenes of the play convey the anger and
bitterness of those who are starving; in scene five, the bargains
made with the devils by the poor take place against the backdrop
of a dead body, that of Mary who tried to live on 'nettles, dock
and dandelion'.[29] More ironic allusions come from the devils who
have learned, in Trollope's words, 'deep lessons of political economy' and argue against 'the evils of mere charity' to the undeserving
poor. The political perspective which they mimic is challenged by
the following memorable rejoinder from Mary, one of the few
peasants to refuse the devils' bargain and who dies as a result:

> Those scruples may befit a common time.
> I had thought there was a pushing to and fro,
> At times like this, that overset the scale
> And trampled measure down.[30]

With this background of hunger and the desperation of those who
are starving, the central focus of the play becomes the character of
Cathleen, doubly 'uncommon' in the heroism of her spirit and the
nobility of her birth:

>   I have sworn,
> By her whose heart the seven sorrows have pierced,
> To pray before this altar until my heart
> Has grown to Heaven like a tree, and there
> Rustled its leaves, till Heaven has saved my people.[31]

Like Mulholland's story, the act of self-sacrifice is explicitly linked
to the Christian tradition in which Cathleen emerges as both the
suffering mother and the crucified figure, benefactor and sacrificial
victim.

Yeats's relationship with Maud Gonne was a central influence,
both on the inception and the many revisions of the play. His

original source was a fable which he included in *Fairy and Folk Tales of the Irish Peasantry*, published in 1888.[32] On meeting Maud Gonne, the following year, the story gained a new life; through her,

> he understood the story of the Countess selling her soul to save her starving people as a symbol of all souls who lose their peace or their fineness of soul or the beauty of their spirit in political service, and as a symbol of her soul which seemed to him incapable of rest.[33]

The first edition of the play was thus dedicated 'to my friend, Miss Maud Gonne, at whose suggestion it was planned out and begun some three years ago'. Aspects of Cathleen's character may also derive from accounts of Gonne's visits to Donegal between 1888 and 1890 when her campaigns against evictions earned her the title of 'Woman of the Sidhe'.[34] The play was itself to prove strikingly prophetic of Gonne's extensive famine activities later in the decade, with Cathleen's reminder that 'A learned theologian has laid down/ That starving men may take what's necessary,/And yet be sinless', anticipating Gonne and Connolly's use of this argument in their 1898 pamphlet, *The Right to Life and the Rights of Property*.[35] Events in Yeats's relationship with Gonne continued to shape the play, demonstrated by the expansion, in later versions, of the character of Aleel, the poet whose love Cathleen refuses. And, with life imitating art, Gonne came more and more to play the part Yeats had written for her.

The life and writings of Maud Gonne include some of the most significant discourses on famine of the period. Early in 1898, almost ten years after her campaigns against evictions in Donegal, Gonne travelled to the west of Ireland where heavy rain, crop failure and a fall in prices had once again caused significant distress. On her return to Dublin she collaborated with Connolly to produce the pamphlet *The Right to Life and the Rights of Property* in which quotations from Pope Clement I, Pope Gregory the Great, Thomas Aquinas and Cardinal Manning were used to encourage starving tenants to learn from the past:

> In the year 1847 our people died in thousands of starvation, although every ship leaving an Irish port was laden with food in

abundance. The Irish people in that awful year might have seized that food, cattle, corn, and all manner of provisions before it reached the seaports, have prevented the famine, and saved their country from ruin, but did not do so, believing such action to be sinful, and dreading to peril their souls to save their bodies. But in this belief, we now know, they were entirely mistaken. The very highest authorities on the doctrines of the Church agree that no *human* law can stand between starving people and their RIGHT TO FOOD, including the right to take that food whenever they can find it, openly or secretly, with or without the owner's permission.[36]

Gonne returned to Mayo in late February and spent most of the following month observing and reporting the extent of famine as well as pursuing actions for immediate relief. As her autobiography records, and as the newspaper articles which she wrote at the time also attest, she visited those suffering from hunger and disease and organized the cooking and distribution of food as well as the nursing of fever patients. Her reports, published in the *Freeman's Journal* in Dublin, in the New York *Irish World* and in other papers, were influential in generating interest in and financial donations towards the conditions in Mayo.[37] Gonne's work also included vigorous campaigns for better employment conditions on the relief works and for the establishment of a fish-curing station. In Belmullet, working with Monsignor Hewson, she organized a large public demonstration to coincide with a meeting of the Board of Governors. Gonne's threat of violence proved successful in persuading the Board to agree to a number of demands, including the raising of relief rates and support for the planting of new crops. Recalling the event in her autobiography, *A Servant of the Queen*, she recounts her conversation with the officials, as 'Outside, through the open window, we could hear the confused murmur of that great throng and the strange soft sound of thousands of bare feet beating on the hard earth.'[38] As Margaret Ward, Gonne's biographer, notes, this 'eerie' description 'has an undeniably authentic ring'.[39]

Vivid testimony to the suffering of the poor appears in Gonne's correspondence to newspapers in the spring of 1898; many of their details would reappear in her later famine play. Two lengthy letters from Gonne were published in the *Freeman's Journal*; the first, written from Belmullet, was published on 9 March, the second, written on her return to Dublin, on the thirtieth. Her visit to one family, in which five of the seven children had already died, 'owing to want of proper food', is simply and directly described:

> By the turf fire sat the mother, a woman who had been once beautiful, tears trickling slowly and silently down her hollow cheeks on to the golden hair of the child she held tightly in her arms. Death had already set its stamp upon that little one also . . . 'Don't you think he will get better?' she asked, but there was no hope in her dark eyes, only a terrible fear . . . She stretched out her arm and clutched the other child, a boy of eight years, to her. His little legs seen through his ragged trousers were indescribably thin. I turned away, I could not bear to look at that group, for I felt that that woman would soon be childless . . .[40]

Gonne notes that the father was absent, working on the relief works for three shillings a week, with the price of a hundred-weight of Indian meal then five shillings. Both letters contain a fierce and detailed castigation of existing systems of relief: 'a more shocking or miserable sight I never witnessed. If they were designed with the object of doing harm instead of doing good, they could not have succeeded better'.[41] Such controversies regarding employment and methods of payment of relief are painfully familiar. Emphasized, in particular, is the inadequacy and inefficacy of the 'pittance' paid to people who are taken away from their own holdings at a crucial time, in contrast to the 'intelligent' administration of private relief to support the draining and replanting of land.

Her 9 March letter includes a lengthy description of what was, to Gonne, an especially disturbing sight:

> What shocked me the most on the relief works was that women should be engaged on them. There they were: old, bent, women of sixty; young, slight girls of sixteen working away with pickaxes and spades under the pouring rain, or worse, carrying great stones or sods of turf on their backs.[42]

Questioning a number of women, the narrator discovers that one 'delicate-looking girl of about sixteen' must walk 'twelve miles a day – seventy-two miles a week – and to do work which would be hard for a man during eight hours, to keep her mother and younger sisters, and all she gets to eat is a piece of Indian corn bread twice a day. She had no boots on, and one foot was bleeding.' Under the rules of the time that heads of households alone be employed, women either widowed or deserted could work on public relief; the refusal to allow grown sons take their place struck Gonne as one of the most unjust aspects of the relief system. Her condemnation of this practice echoes earlier commentators like William Bennett, with an insistence, however, on the physical rather than moral dangers of such work.

> If there are women who read this article, in the name of our common womanhood let them raise a protest against this shameful cruelty. Women are physically unfitted for this work; nature intended them to be mothers, and exertion of this kind is calculated to do them serious, and permanent injury . . . Oh, my sisters, women of Ireland, it is time we shake off our indifference and realize that we have duties of solidarity to each other. It is a slight to all of us that it should be possible to treat any Irish women as these helpless, uncomplaining, starving peasant women of Erris are being treated.[43]

Her letters end with ringing appeals for solidarity from women, of higher class and from other regions, towards the 'starving peasant women of Erris'.

Gonne's writings demonstrate her keen awareness of the rhetorical power of this type of 'feminization' of famine. The sufferings of poor women are highlighted, together with the injustices they endure, while a special appeal for intervention is directed towards other women, 'in name of our common womanhood'. Gonne's reiteration of the 'solidarity' of women differs significantly from the rhetorical address employed in the pamphlet, *The Right to Life and the Rights of Property*, produced that same year, in which 'fellow countrymen' are summoned to perform their duty 'whether as fathers or sons, as husbands or as Irishmen'. In a later newspaper article, she continues her emphasis on the female character of famine, in this case underlining the failures of a 'common

womanhood' and the responsibility held by one woman for the
suffering of 'countless Irish mothers' and 'poor Irish emigrant girls'.
The visit of Queen Victoria to Ireland, in April 1900, led Gonne
to write an impassioned article in *L'Irlande Libre*, the newspaper she
had launched in Paris in 1897:

> And in truth for Victoria, in the decrepitude of her 81 years, to
> have decided after an absence of half a century to revisit the
> country she hates and whose inhabitants are the victims of the
> criminal policy of her reign, the survivors of 60 years of organized
> famine, the political necessity must have been terribly strong; for
> after all she is a woman, and however vile and selfish and pitiless
> her soul may be, she must sometimes tremble as death approaches
> when she thinks of the countless Irish mothers who, shelterless
> under the cloudy Irish sky, watching their starving little ones, have
> cursed her before they died.
>
> Every eviction during 63 years has been carried out in Victoria's
> name, and if there is a Justice in Heaven, the shame of these poor
> Irish emigrant girls, whose very innocence makes them an easy prey
> and who have been overcome in the terrible struggle for existence
> on a foreign shore, will fall on this woman, whose bourgeoise virtue
> is so boasted, and in whose name their houses were destroyed.[44]

Given the force of Gonne's rhetoric, it is not surprising that the
appearance of a translation of this article, entitled 'The Famine
Queen', in the *United Irishman* of 7 April 1900, led to an order for
the seizure of all copies of the newspaper.[45]

By now stories of Victoria's meanness during the famine, no less
powerful for their historical inaccuracy, were well established. In
similar fashion to Gonne's piece, a contemporary poem, Anna
Parnell's 'To the Memory of Commandant Scheepers', denounces
the 'Famine Queen' and the events occurring during her reign.[46]
Victoria's identity as mother and Queen are contrasted bitterly
with the plight of Irish mothers:

> What though famished women
> Are eating their babes to-day,
> Under the Empress-Queen,
> That England may feast and play,

When all is clear, all serene,
In English eyes
And English skies?
It matters naught to those who've taught,
Her soldiers to slay
As lawful prey,
Young children in a mother's name.

The horrors of famine extend, in Parnell's retelling, beyond the eating of dead bodies which were cited in Gonne's 1892 oration, to the cannibalistic acts of 'famished' mothers. This image in turn echoes the anonymously-published 'Thanatos, 1849', a poem which appeared in the *Irishman*, 5 May 1849, and in which 'mother-love' is grotesquely challenged:

A mother's heart was marble-clad, her eye was fierce and wild –
A hungry Demon lurked therein, while gazing on her child.
The mother-love was warm and true; the Want was long with-
  stood –
Strength failed at last; she gorged the flesh – the offspring of her
  blood.⁴⁷

While the nationalistic tone of 'Thanatos' is clear, the denunci-atory force of Parnell and Gonne's writings gathers further power from the feminization of famine's cause as well as its horrific consequence: deeds originating in another 'mother's name'. Thus the *L'Irlande Libre* article, as Elizabeth Coxhead mentions, was accompanied by 'a front-page cartoon of the Queen in a shamrock gown, gazing on the dead who rose from their graves and pointed accusing fingers at her, the roofless walls of what had been their houses behind them'.⁴⁸

With all their rhetorical flourishes and excesses, Maud Gonne's famine writings display the actions of a pragmatic and politically astute woman, an aspect of her personality frequently obscured by the more mythical dimension of Gonne as Cathleen, whether Countess or Ní Houlihan. Irish cultural history has produced two Maud Gonnes, the first an activist whose words, until recently, could contribute to the banning of a television programme,⁴⁹ the

other the legendary love object of Yeats's poetry. The creation of
a mythical Gonne was not alone the work of Yeats, however. In *A
Servant of the Queen*, Gonne carefully recounts the legendary status
given her by the people of Donegal and Mayo. Her work against
evictions in Donegal had earned her the title, 'Woman of the
Sidhe'; later, campaigning in Mayo in 1898, she heard of the
prophecy of Brian Ruadh: 'That there would be a famine and that
a woman dressed in green would come and preach the revolt.'[50]
The foreword to her autobiography, entitled 'I Saw the Queen' –
with ironic echoes of Victoria – offers a vivid example of Maud's
own myth-making power. The volume begins with references
to famine and resistance: 'I was returning from Mayo triumphant.
I had stopped a famine and saved many lives by making the people
share my own belief that courage and will are unconquerable and,
where allied to the mysterious forces of the land, can accomplish
anything.' Gonne describes looking out of the window of the train
and seeing 'a tall, beautiful woman with dark hair blown on the
wind and I knew it was Cathleen Ní Houlihan . . . I heard a
voice say: "You are one of the little stones on which the feet of
the Queen have rested on her way to Freedom".'[51] Yet *A Servant
of the Queen* also reveals the pragmatic politician, always aware of
the potential of her own mythic status: 'In Donegal, being the
woman of the Sidhe had helped me to put evicted families back in
their homes and release prisoners. I hoped that being the woman
of the prophecies in Mayo would help me to stop the famine.'[52]

Gonne's play *Dawn*, first printed in October 1904 in Griffith's
United Irishman, continues the myth-making activity.[53] The play
contains many echoes of the author's travels in Donegal and in
Mayo, with references to evictions, the neglect of children due
to the employment of female heads of families on the roads and
reminders of Brian Ruadh's prophecy. Within the first 'tableau' is
staged the death of Michael who 'fainted at the works'; his death
marks Bride's movement from individual to symbolic figure. At
first, Bride, 'a woman of about forty, who is evicted', appears as
one among many famine characters; her husband has been killed
trying to resist eviction, one son is in jail, another has joined the
soldiers. As the play progresses, her character becomes increasingly

allegorical: 'Bride of the Sorrows' for whom the people will fight, driving out 'the Stranger' from 'the land', providing the 'stones' on which her foot will rest on the walk 'to Freedom'. The death of Brideen, Bride's daughter, is the spur to action, the call to vengeance: 'The dead are speaking to us. They are telling us we have endured too long; that the day of waiting is over, and the day for deeds has come. By dead Brideen, we swear we will make Bride of the Sorrows Bride of the Victories.'[54] As patriotic drama and with obvious echoes of *Cathleen Ní Houlihan*, *Dawn* performs a direct appropriation of famine to the story of nationalism. Using the symbol of woman-as-nation, Gonne expands the maternal aspects of this figure: the death of the daughter sparks the move-ment to liberate the mother's land. The woman's death is thus the spur to others' resistance, and famine the mark of a martyred motherland.

A striking aspect of revival literature is the choice of drama, by a number of writers, as the genre in which to represent famine: Yeats's *Countess Cathleen*, Maud Gonne's *Dawn*, as well as plays written and produced in Irish, such as Patrick Dinneen's *Creideamh agus Gorta* and *Teachtaire Ó Dhia*. More generally, Stephen Watt has highlighted the oblique presence of famine in melodrama of the period, staged both in Ireland and in London's East End.[55] The existence of such a variety of famine drama has implications which remain to be fully explored. With specific reference to the writers of the literary revival, one of the explanations which has been offered for the supposed scarcity of famine representations is the 'politics of form'; thus Eagleton argues that since much of the revival writing 'is programmatically non-representational', it is 'no fit medium for historical realism, if indeed any fit medium for such subject matter is conceivable'.[56] Yet the work of Yeats, Dinneen and others indicates a number of attempts to stage the subject of famine, to make the spectacle of hunger present and recognizable, embodied through individual characters. A recurring representational strategy evident in their work, illustrative of the difficulties but also of the choices of representation, is a movement of the theme of hunger from the actual towards the symbolic sphere; thus stories of heroic self-sacrifice and service to an ideal come to dominate the dramatic action. Yet, if the audience is to understand and be involved by this action, the heroic deeds must also be seen to emerge from people's suffering, from the visible desperation of hunger.

Yeats's *Countess Cathleen* received many productions after its first staging in 1892, including, as the author himself noted, many performances by amateurs in England and America.[57] Patrick Dinneen's play, *Creideamh agus Gorta* (Faith and Famine), also appears to have been frequently performed in the early years of the century, by Gaelic League groups around the country.[58] Dinneen's play involves a particular symbolic appropriation of the story of famine, in this case for 'Mother Church'. In a preface to the text, first published by the Gaelic League in 1901, the author explains that his play is based on a 'well-authenticated incident of the Famine period' and provides evidence of the 'nefarious system of souperism as it existed in the Famine years'.[59] Its representation of a famine mother echoes the concern with 'primal shelter' expressed in nineteenth-century narratives, and anticipates her symbolic role throughout the following century. Yet the characterization offered by Dinneen is especially troubling. The dramatic action can be briefly summarized: Cáit, the mother, seeing her three children close to death from hunger, asks one son, and then another, to present himself at the home of the 'souper', or Protestant minister, in the hope that the sight of his suffering will move the minister to charity. Her sons refuse even to approach his door; in their words, 'Death is better, Mother.' They are soon rewarded for their heroism, and angels welcome them to heaven. Meanwhile Cáit must spend the rest of her life grieving 'for the temptation she offered'; as the angels instruct her:

> you must carry yourself from this on through your life
> full of sorrow, your hard heart tormented
> the black clouds closing over you
> in sorrow and longing, without relief, as long as you live.[60]

At the end of this life of torment, she will be redeemed by her sons.

Cáit's final speech is suitably resigned; she celebrates her sons' departure, 'your souls safe from the stain of Eve', and praises the

God who 'left you finally without the food of the day/suckling my breast – great praises to his holy will'.[61] The tone of the play makes it extremely unlikely that any irony or protest is intended. Instead Cáit's actions are presented as the well-intentioned but ultimately sinful deeds of a daughter of Eve. Although a 'resisting' reader may yearn for alternative or wider standards of judgement of a mother's role, Dinneen offers no further exploration. In the closing lines, Cáit proclaims her sorrowful fate:

> now there is before me only a fog in this life
> my heart forever torn by sorrow
> walking the earth with a tormented mind
> evidently dying since the light of the day left me.
>
> the earth and the sky darkened by cloud
> sorrow the only sound to be heard
> a cold wind blowing down from above
> and mental anguish lasting through my life.[62]

The themes of sacrifice and renunciation, central to the famine texts of the period, thus continue in Dinneen's play; in this version, however, the female character must await the redemption offered by her sons, having herself fallen short of the ideal. The anxiety inherent in the maternal figure reappears in an interesting way in *Creideamh agus Gorta*; the 'lack' which she represents is no longer simply that of food or nourishment but more a spiritual deprivation. The concern with spiritual welfare also possesses a nationalist dimension; in this regard, Dinneen's text illustrates a contemporary obsession with women's role in preserving the religious and, hence, national character. Parallels with the discourse on nationalism and gender employed elsewhere in the twentieth century – in famine-stricken Bengal – will be explored in the succeeding chapter. What is clear in the literature of Irish revival, specifically in its attempts to stage the themes of hunger and starvation, is a concern with the symbolic significance of famine deaths and the implications, occasionally even more fearful, of survival.

THE MEMORIES OF AN 'OUTCAST' CLASS

As the twentieth century progresses, the figure of 'the ministering angel' acquires a special significance within literary representations of the Irish 'Big House'. Authors such as Edith Somerville and William Trevor present famine as a central event in their characters' family history, its implications extending to the fate of the wider Ascendancy class. In these chronicles, the 1840s famine is recalled as both a glorious and sorrowful event, a time in which representatives of the family, usually women, sacrificed their lives in order to feed the starving. The glory and martyrdom of the past, of ruined fortunes and lost lives, have a crucial role in the present: faced with exclusion from the developing Irish state, inhabitants of the 'Big House' emphasize their identity as fellow-victims of famine.

In June 1925, Edith Somerville finished writing *The Big House of Inver*. The original inspiration for the novel came in 1912, when Violet Martin (Ross), Somerville's cousin and partner, wrote to her of an empty house she had seen; at the door of the house stood the daughter of the last owner who, 'since her people died', would not enter. Ross's letter ended: 'If we dared to write up that subject – !'[63] Thirteen years later, ten years after the death of Ross, Edith Somerville published her story of the decline of the Prendeville family. The novel's central theme is the doomed attempt by Shibby, illegitimate daughter of the Prendevilles, to restore the family fortunes, recently gained by the middle-class Westons. It ends with the burning of the Big House, now owned and insured by John Weldon.

Reference to famine occurs briefly and early in the narrative, as part of the history of the Prendevilles; the family genealogy includes an ancestor who died because of her work during the 1840s famine.[64] The narrator compares the woman's famine work to the colonial service of her son in India, and firmly values the woman's labour as 'fought against heavier odds than her son had to face'.[65] Her labours include the setting up of a soup kitchen, the waiving of rents, the killing of her animals for soup, the writing of begging letters to England and America and the procuring of a cargo of American meal. Tragically, her death occurs when the worst of the famine is over, as Somerville records in the following short but lyrical eulogy:

> In the end of the trouble, when the storm had to some extent died down and the shadow was lifting a little, she, who had come safe through the worst of the bad times, went down with the famine-fever that still loitered on in 'backwards places'. A beggar-woman brought it in her rags to Inver, and Madam Prendeville died of it, with the tears wet on her cheeks for the son whom she would not see again.[66]

The political significance of Madam Prendeville's death is made immediately explicit: it attests to the suffering of 'people of all classes during the years of the famine of 1845', in particular by the owners of 'ancient properties' or Big Houses to whom 'swarming families of the people' looked for help.[67] The narrator notes that 'the martyrdoms, and the heroisms, and the devotion' of the time 'have passed into oblivion', yet reflects that this neglect is

> better so, perhaps, when it is remembered how a not extravagant exercise of political foresight might have saved the martyrdoms. As for the other matters, it might only intensify the embittering of a now outcast class to be reminded of what things it suffered and sacrificed doing what it held to be its duty.[68]

Somerville's reference to the embitterment of a 'now outcast class' signals the position of the Ascendancy in the years following the War of Independence and the creation of the Irish Free State. In spite of the narrator's suggestion that what was 'suffered and sacrificed' by landlords during the famine is best forgotten, the novel itself seeks to undo this oblivion through the story of Madam Prendeville's death. Two of the titles considered by Somerville for the novel, 'A Victim of the Past' and 'Restoration', illustrate the narrative's wider purpose of restoring the past to the present.

The depiction of the actions of the Prendevilles during the famine is drawn largely from the biography of the Martin family. In her memoir, 'The Martins of Ross', Martin recounts her parents' establishment of a soup kitchen during the famine, their 'rapid pens' sending 'the story far'; her aunt also performed philanthropic work, contracting fever from her work 'in a school that she had got together on the estate, where she herself taught little girls to read and write and knit, and kept them alive with breakfasts of oatmeal porridge'.[69] Her essay outlines the sacrifices made by the landlord class, quoting from A. M. Sullivan to support its argument: 'No adequate tribute has ever been paid to those Irish landlords – and they were men of every party and creed – who perished, martyrs to duty, in that awful time; who did not fly the plague-reeking workhouse, or fever-tainted court.'[70] In *The Big House of Inver*, Stephen Gwynn's *History of Ireland* is used as a similar, corroborating source, testifying to the heroism of those who 'distinguished themselves by a self-sacrificing devotion', in particular one man, Richard Martin of Ballynahinch, a distant kinsman of Violet Martin, who flung 'all that was left of his fortune and health into an effort to save his poor, and died in the effort'.[71]

The question of the role of landlords during the famine has, from the 1840s to today, been a controversial topic in famine historiography; as early as 1847, Maria Edgeworth insisted that

> The cry against Irish landlords, which has been unjust, will be completely put down by the humanity and most active exertions of the landed proprietors during the distress in Ireland . . . I could name at least ten or twelve great landed proprietors who have this season and last year lost their lives from overexertion and from fever caught in attending their tenants and the poor.[72]

The famine philanthropy of the landed classes and its personal and economic toll are central concerns in much nineteenth-century fiction, as the previous chapters have shown. Similarly, in her history of Ireland, first published in 1887, Emily Lawless pays tribute to the 'untiring energy and the most absolute self-devotedness' shown by men and women, especially 'strong men, heads of houses'.[73] The overwhelming psychological impact of famine is vividly conveyed; acknowledging that these men were themselves 'out of reach of actual hunger', Lawless attributes their deaths to 'sheer distress of mind, and the effort to cope with what was beyond the power of any human being to cope with'. Fictional versions of the self-sacrificing benefactor, however, tend to characterize the famine ancestor more often as female.[74] In crisis representations such as famine literature, concepts of 'maternal instinct' and the related emphasis on women's special moral influence become especially prominent. Some of the difficulties involved in assessing this work, and the significance attributed to it by contemporary commentators, have been discussed in chapter two. In 'Big House' narratives, the treatment of female philanthropy and self-sacrifice is especially revealing, less for its account of the famine ancestor and more for what it says about the fate of her descendants, those who 'retell' the story of famine.

An exchange, similar to that represented in Somerville and Ross's *The Big House of Inver*, in which the woman gives food and receives death in return, occurs in John Hewitt's 1971 poem, 'The Scar'.[75] The 'sick man', 'tapping upon my great-grandmother's shutter/and begging, I was told, a piece of bread' brings infection

> rank from the cabins of the stricken west,
> the spores from black potato-stalks, the spittle
> mottled with poison in his rattling chest;
> and she, who, by her nature, quickly answered,
> accepted in return the famine-fever;
> and that chance meeting, that brief confrontation,
> conscribed me of the Irishry for ever.

Hewitt interprets the encounter as a crucial determinant of his own identity, but with a marked ambivalence, evident in the word 'conscribed'. The speaker's relationship with 'the Irishry' – interestingly 'Irishry' rather than 'Irish' – is a troubled one. Yet, the death of the female ancestor, a shared loss in the past, remains the means of asserting a commonality in the present:

> Though much I cherish is outside their vision,
> and much they prize I have no claim to share,
> yet in that woman's death I found my nation:
> the old wound aches and shows its fellow-scar.

The 'woman's death' is thus the means through which her descendants' 'nation' is established and defended.

The crucial relevance of the past to a community's identity in
the present continues as a theme in William Trevor's writings; the
past revealed, in Steven Marcus's words, as 'a genuine mode of the
present'.[76] The 1840s famine and the Irish War of Independence
continue to be key events in what is now, in the late twentieth
century, a lengthier chronology. Trevor's interpretation of the role
of the Ascendancy class, however, gains in ambivalence through his
writings, from *Fools of Fortune* (1983) to the story 'The News from
Ireland' (1986) to his novel *The Silence in the Garden* (1988).[77] In *Fools
of Fortune*, the memory of a famine ancestor haunts the narrative:

> Anna Quinton had travelled the neighbourhood during the Famine
> of 1846, doing what she could for the starving and the dying, her
> carriage so heavy with grain and flour that once its axle broke in
> half. *The meat goes bad in the heat* she wrote, *but even so they grab it from*
> *my hands.* When she died of famine fever her dog-faced husband
> shut himself into Kilneagh for eleven years, not seeing anyone. It
> was said that she haunted him: looking from his bedroom window
> one morning he saw her on a distant hill – an apparition like the
> Virgin Mary. She told him that he must give away the greater part
> of his estate to those who had suffered loss and deprivation in the
> Famine, and in his continuing love of her he did so.[78]

As a schoolboy, Willy learns that Anna's agitation for the famine
poor alienated her both from her family in England and her Irish
neighbours; now, seventy years later, his father's friendship with
Michael Collins makes them 'outcasts' within their own class and
leads to the burning of the house by the Black and Tans. As the
flames destroy the house, leading to the death of Willy's father and
sisters, the famine ancestors return: 'Through the fever of this
nightmare floated the two portraits in the drawing-room, my dog-
faced great-grandfather and plain, merciful Anna Quinton.'[79] Both
generations become part of a history of 'massacres and martyrs';[80]
from each, a sacrificial victim is demanded.

In Trevor's later famine narratives, the relationship of the
Ascendancy family to the Irish population is more ambiguous. His
short story 'The News from Ireland', first published in 1986, is set
in 1847 and told from the point of view of Anna Maria Heddoe,

the newly-arrived governess, 'a young woman of principle and sensibility, stranger and visitor to Ireland'.[81] Anna's attitude towards famine victims wavers between horror and sympathy: as an outsider, she is repelled by reports of cannibalism and the possible infliction on a child of stigmata, wounds considered by the local people to be miraculously conferred.[82] Yet her diary also records her growing sympathy, a sympathy extending to those who may have inflicted the wounds on their child: 'it was related to the desperation of survival, to an act so barbarous that one could not pass it by'.[83]

Although similar in name, Anna differs greatly from her namesake in *Fools of Fortune*. The last words of the story suggest that she will remain in Ireland, reaching an uneasy accommodation: 'stranger and visitor, she has learnt to live with things'.[84] The relationship of the Pulvertaft family to the Irish population is also very different to the intimacy which characterized the Quinton family. Mrs Pulvertaft's dream of running naked through an unfamiliar landscape expresses the precarious position of her family; her husband's dedication to the building of a famine road is both well-intentioned and 'absurd'. While Anna sees the road as 'an act of charity' which 'in years to come' would 'stand as a memorial to this awful time', the future, as dreamt by Fogarty, the butler, takes a very different form:

> He told me of a dream he'd had the night before or last week, I was too upset to note which. The descendants of the people who had been hungry were in the dream, and the son of George Arthur Pulvertaft was shot in the hall of the house, and no Pulvertaft lived in the place again. The road that had been laid in charity was overgrown through neglect, and the gardens were as they had been at the time of old Hugh Pulvertaft, their beauty strangled as they returned to wildness. Fogarty's voice quivered as his rigmarole ridiculously rambled on; an institution for corrected girls the house became, without carpets on the floors. The bones of the dogs that generations of Pulvertafts had buried in the grounds were dug up by the corrected girls when they were ordered by a Mother Superior to make vegetable beds. They threw the bones about, pretending to be frightened of them, pretending they were the bones of people.[85]

The journey into the past, performed by 'News from Ireland', uncovers a troubling future, realized in Trevor's later novel *The Silence in the Garden*. Here, some of the events in Fogarty's dream have taken place: attacks on the Rolleston family during the War of Independence, their house now fallen into ruin. The Rollestons receive a double legacy from the past. Their ancestors include the 'Famine Rollestons' who 'waived their rents and their tithes' – monies never collected since – but also Cromwellian planters. Such dark origins continue to trouble the present: 'Time had tamed the Rollestons, who had come to the island with slaughter in their wake, but time could not be trusted.'[86] By the end of the novel, specific historical episodes have faded into a type of metahistory: time 'never just passes . . . It is always on one side or the other. Women huddled in their corners, children begged, men disappeared. Would their time ever come? How could it come? And yet it did'.[87] Underlying the ambivalent history of this landed family, the stories of past benevolence and slaughter, is the knowledge that its chronicle is ending, soon to be 'silent'.

Within the genre of Big House writing and its representations of famine recurs a striking motif: the encounter between upper-class woman and poor peasant in which food is exchanged for disease. The giver of fever, the 'other' from whom contagion is received, is cast in shadow; the heroic ancestor is named and remembered. Troubling questions remain as to the role and function of this symbolic encounter: does the ancestor personify or disguise notions of responsibility, confront or disguise inequalities of power? The narrative clearly seeks to assert the shared experience of victimization, but, in highlighting this theme, also risks portraying famine as a self-reflexive or enclosed event, a circle of victimization in which individuals swop places.

The recalling and retelling of past acts of generosity is ultimately of most meaning in the present. Sacrifices made by ancestors, their cost in financial and personal terms, serve to challenge the isolation and alienation experienced by their descendants. The death of the famine ancestor thus emerges as strangely necessary for the future of her community, her martyrdom constituting her descendants' strongest claim to an Irish identity. Sacrificial victim, she embodies the ravages of famine in the past but also a means of survival for her descendants in the future.

A MOTHER'S 'NATURE': O'FLAHERTY AND MURPHY

Thirty years separates the first appearances of the twentieth-century's most famous famine texts: Liam O'Flaherty's novel, *Famine*, first published in 1937, and Tom Murphy's similarly-titled play, first staged in Dublin's Peacock theatre in 1968. Both works are distinguished by a detailed and moving exploration of the means used by people to withstand famine, physically and psychologically; more than any other famine representation, they compel readers and audiences to imagine what people did to survive. Their literary achievement involves rendering the 'actuality' of hunger and starvation, but with a keen eye on its later significance. As the desperation of hunger and of resistance become prominent, survival and its cost emerge as the central themes. Thus, in making present the adaptive strategies employed by people in the past, O'Flaherty and Murphy also raise in complex ways the relationship of their audiences to what is represented – as descendants and also as outsiders.

Liam O'Flaherty's novel, *Famine*, remains one of the best-selling Irish novels. First published in 1937, it emerged while the new state was still in the process of self-definition; the Irish Constitution, another version of the 'national chronicle', was first published that same year.[88] In one of the earliest reviews of the novel, Seán O'Faolain declared: 'It is tremendous. It is biblical. It is the best Irish historical novel to date', while another reviewer characterized O'Flaherty's writing of the novel in more mythical terms: 'It seems indeed as though the memory of this great tragedy had seized upon the writer rather than that he had merely chosen it as a subject, as though he had in some sort fulfilled a destiny by writing this book.'[89] From its first publication, *Famine* had a significant role in shaping readers' knowledge and understanding of the past. One interesting indication of this is provided by school textbooks of the time: although the events of the 1840s were discussed in history books such as Mary Hayden's *A Short History of the People of Ireland* or James Carty's *A Classbook of Irish History*, famine was conspicuously absent from a text such as *Ireland in Prose and Poetry*, published in 1930.⁹⁰ The contents of this book, a literary reader designed for use in the senior cycle, include references to O'Connell, the Young Irelanders, Mitchel's trial (without reference to famine), emigration and the Fenians, represented in extracts from the works of Canon Sheehan, Justin McCarthy and others. Thus, in this particular version, the national story emerges as one of continuing, heroic resistance, and one in which the experience of famine is not to be mentioned.

O'Flaherty's novel, in turn, employed a variety of historical sources. Much of its political detail is drawn from Canon John O'Rourke's *The History of the Great Irish Famine of 1847 with notices of earlier Irish famines*, first published in 1875.⁹¹ O'Rourke's work had employed a considerable amount of contemporary testimony, including conversations with famine survivors and details from query-sheets sent to various clergymen and doctors around the country. Other aspects of *Famine*, such as the description of the coming of the blight, echo folklore accounts; it seems likely that O'Flaherty was drawing from local tradition in Aran and, as Roger McHugh has noted, the novel has itself some of the simple and forceful qualities of an oral narrative.⁹² In his discussion of O'Flaherty's novel, Patrick Sheeran has highlighted a further influence, James Connolly's discussion of the famine in *Labour in Irish History*, in which Connolly forcefully argues that the central responsibility for famine lay in the social rather than the political system: 'No man who accepts capitalistic society and the laws thereof can logically find fault with the statesmen of England for their acts in that awful period.'⁹³ Finally, in its study of the relationship between the individual and what seem to be inexorable forces, and in its depiction of the conflict between tradition and innovation, *Famine* has much to do with the 1930s world in which it was written.

The novel's powerful immediacy, from the detailed opening chapters to the quiet tragedy of Brian Kilmartin's death, helps to explain its continuing popularity. Its analysis of the causes underlying famine, however, is often unwieldy, awkwardly combining aspects of both O'Rourke and Connolly's arguments. Through the character of the curate, Gellan, O'Flaherty delivers a strong indictment of British rule; on the other hand, the 'gombeen' Hynes family demonstrates the role of the capitalistic, social order. The convergence of multiple factors in producing famine – political oppression, social injustice and providential disaster – is acknowledged in the following passage, delivered at the beginning of chapter forty-three:

> When government is an expression of the people's will, a menace to any section of the community rouses the authorities to protective action. Under a tyranny, the only active forces of government are those of coercion. Unless the interests of the ruling class are threatened, authority remains indifferent. We have seen how the feudal government acted with brutal force when the interests of the landowner were threatened, even to the extent of plundering the poor people's property. Now it remains to be seen what that same government did when those poor lost, by the act of God, all that was left to them by the police and Mr. Chadwick – the potato crop which they had sown.[94]

At this moment, the challenge faced by O'Flaherty is one common to novelists of famine: the difficulties of integrating historical explanation within the famine story. The result, in the case of *Famine*, can be awkward, with clumsy generalizations given at the beginning of chapters, as in the example above. These framing passages remain at a remove from the rest of the story; the occasional use of the first person – either an authorial 'we' or an even more intrusive 'I' – further complicates the narrative.

As the narrative progresses, O'Flaherty turns to a number of female characters to indicate the horrors of famine and, specifically, the dilemmas and actions involved in the attempt to survive. The novel's heroine is Mary Kilmartin, whose beauty and innovative instincts single her out from her fellow-peasants. Earlier in the narrative there is some suggestion that Mary's character possesses an allegorical function; as 'beautiful creature, with the gracious dignity of a queen', she briefly personifies, for Doctor Hynes, love for an 'Irish earth . . . your real mother'.[95] Yet this analogy remains undeveloped, even contradicted by another detail concerning Mary's ancestry. Since Mary's mother is the daughter of an English sailor, she inherits a different 'racial strain'⁹⁶ – and there is a curious implication that this accounts for her distinctive, reforming qualities. A more coherent, if predictable, symbolic pattern is produced through the contrast between Mary and her sister, Ellie, as images of the condition of the wider political body. In a familiar stereotype, Mary's beauty is contrasted with the 'coarse and sensual' attractions of her sister who is involved in an 'unnatural' liaison with Chadwick, the local agent. O'Flaherty signals the degenerate nature of English rule through Chadwick's impotence, his exploitation of Ellie and his attempted assault on Mary. Similarly, the position of Doctor Hynes, the classic 'middleman', torn between his aspirations to an upper class and the influence of the 'subject race' of his birth, is made apparent through his relationship with the sisters. Mary and Ellie become double objects of fantasy for Hynes, the one symbolizing 'Ireland as mother', the other offering an 'intoxication' of the flesh.⁹⁷

O'Flaherty is more convincing when he turns away from such clumsy allegory and towards, in his own words, the 'evaporation' of 'the urge towards the ideal'.⁹⁸ This process is firstly associated with Doctor Hynes; immediately following the curate's instructions to him to 'learn to love this Irish earth, as your real mother', Hynes encounters the 'actuality' of a 'starving mother and child'.⁹⁹ The inadequacy of the ideal is made even clearer later in the narrative when the doctor encounters the grotesque, diseased body of a woman, 'in an advanced state of corruption'.¹⁰⁰ To underline, if labour, the point, Hynes himself contracts the plague from this encounter. It is, however, through the changes evident in Mary that the reality of hunger and its 'evaporation of the ideal' are presented most forcefully. As she struggles to resist despair, her body comes to bear the traces of famine:

> Now she looked quite a virago. The imminence of famine had wrought a marked change in her countenance. She bore a strange resemblance to Kitty Hernon. There was no similarity of features and her beauty was still as radiant as ever. But there was a similarity of the mouth and of the eyes. Her mouth had gathered together, somehow, like the first movement of the mouth of a person going

to whistle. Her eyes seemed to be searching for something. They were never still. They were fierce, on the alert, suspicious. Her hands, too, were shifty, and it was pitiful the way she now grabbed at her food, tore it greedily with her teeth and looked around in an uncouth fashion while she ate; just like the old man. Formerly, she used to be so dainty and so restful, as if she were in a delicious swoon of passion.[101]

Mary's determination to survive, culminating in her decision to emigrate, is crucially related to her identity as mother. Through her character and those of two other women, Kitty Hernon, Mary's sister-in-law, and Sally O'Hanlon, O'Flaherty produces his most memorable images of famine's consequence: the dilemmas endured by mothers who seek to protect their children and the desperate strategies to which they are driven.

The story of Kitty Hernon, daughter of Brian Kilmartin, is told in some detail. Her husband, Patch Hernon, has gone mad and is eventually incarcerated, leaving her to fend for their seven children. Two of her children are sent with her sister to America; in chapter twenty-seven of the novel, she offers her 'two babies' to the Protestant clergyman, Mr Coburn. Kitty's lengthy appeal to Coburn, the mother's lament, forms one of the most moving passages in the novel.

> Who can tell it better than a poor mother? Answer me that. I can't ask you for the love of God to take them, sir, and I knowing it will damn their souls. All the same, take them, put them in a home, even if they are brought up as Protestants. I struggled all winter, sir, yes, ma'am, I struggled through the snow and the hailstones, but now it's beyond me. I tried the workhouse as well. It's full to the doors and a poor place it is to find shelter, with the creatures lying sick in their own dirt. Where could a poor mother go? God is against us, so let the devil have his due . . . Sure, I went dry, saving your presence, sir, I went dry with the worry about the rent that we owed . . . Let people say what they like, but it's the nature of a mother to feed her children, even if she has to walk the fiery roads of Hell for it . . . God gave them to me but hunger took them away.[102]

Kitty's words provide a striking contrast to another dramatization of the 'nature of a mother', Dinneen's Cáit. O'Flaherty's depiction is more detailed and more sympathetic, exploring the mother's motivation and the conflict which she suffers between religious belief and love for her children. Yet, as the episode closes and as Kitty leaves the village, Coburn having refused to accept the children, a certain distancing occurs: 'They gaped at her in wonder, as she sat there in the parson's gig, gaunt and wild-eyed, gap-toothed, in her ragged, black shawl, with her ragged children within the fold of her gaunt arms, like starved chicks under the out-stretched wings of their dam.'[103] The final image of Kitty is thus of a hag-like 'crazy woman'.

The suggestion of madness also gathers around the novel's other famine mother, Sally, who is Mary's neighbour. At the beginning of the novel, Sally and her husband are squatters, having been evicted from their land; when famine comes, they receive relief from the public works, then the work is suddenly ended and Sally's husband dies soon after. The novel traces Sally's decline, her loss of 'courage and resourcefulness': 'in her eyes was that dreadful famine look; the scared stare of an animal'.[104] In an episode near to the end of the novel, references to Sally's pale face, her fierce, 'glittering' eyes and 'ludicrous grin' gradually convey, to Mary and the reader, the dreadful fact that Sally has killed her children:

> 'I had a right to put them out of their suffering,' Sally cried, 'and I'll bury them, too, when I have done my share of looking at their little faces. God gave them to me. I couldn't let them lie there screeching with the pain and nobody to help them. Is it with the meat of a dog I would go on filling their mouths and it only making them screech with the pain?'[105]

Throughout famine narratives, infanticide represents one of the most 'unspeakable' of horrors, its narration an especially difficult task. Towards the end of the episode, O'Flaherty warns, though somewhat heavyhandedly, of the difficulties of judgement, employing the alternative viewpoints of the policeman and sanitary officer. The policeman, an Ulster Protestant, refuses to believe the woman is mad, arguing instead that 'she wanted to get into jail, where she would be better fed. Sure, these people are half cannibals. They are no better than Hottentots, same as I saw written in a newspaper.' Simms, the sanitary officer, deemed by O'Flaherty to be a Protestant 'of Southern English descent and therefore more civilized in his prejudices', strongly rejects the argument 'that an Irish mother, papish or not papish, would kill her own children in the hope of getting a bite of food'.[106] For Mary, Sally's action spells deepest despair:

> There was no God for her or the other poor people, who were starving to death. God belonged to the rich, among whom there was no hunger and no understanding of hunger. To be afflicted with hunger was considered, in the world of the rich, a crime which placed the sufferers outside the bounds of humanity.[107]

Yet O'Flaherty's representation of the horror of infanticide does itself perform a certain dehumanizing of Sally: her actions are those of a 'scared' 'animal', her 'ludicrous grin' further establishes her insanity. That a woman, driven mad, should kill her children is the most shocking of famine episodes; that it should be the action of a sane woman appears, for most authors, almost unthinkable.[108]

Famine's female characterizations possess dimensions rare in famine narratives: unlike the superficial depictions of female victims to be found elsewhere, O'Flaherty explores women's motivations, allows each character a voice and foregrounds the dangers and difficulties of judgement. Kitty's speech to Coburn and Mary's gradual comprehension of what Sally has done are among the most affecting representations of famine. Within these episodes, however, O'Flaherty's own struggles to render these horrors, to establish and maintain their nearness to the reader, are apparent. The ambivalent presentation of Sally, 'savage' or 'good mother', and Kitty's identity as eloquent hag, demonstrate the difficulties faced by the author in retaining their characters within, in Mary's words, the 'bounds of humanity'. As a result, the characterizations move into a moral register; the moral complexities of the women's actions come to dominate the discourse: troubling questions of a mother's 'nature' and 'right'. Once again, the extremities of famine appear as a crisis in maternity. Torn between the demands of God and the exigencies of hunger, mothers seek to protect their children; in Kitty's words, 'God gave them to me but hunger took them away.'[109] The consequence for O'Flaherty's novel is a curious disjunction between famine's economic and political nature and the moral character of its consequences.

The difficulties of representation and O'Flaherty's particular successes may also be seen in *Famine*'s final chapter, which tells of the death of Brian Kilmartin in quiet yet piercing detail:

> He clutched the handle of the spade, leaned forward, threatened the frosty earth with the point, and raised his foot. There was a deep, gurgling sound in his throat and he fell forward headlong. The spade skidded away over the frost and rolled into a hollow. The old man lay still with his arms stretched out.
>
> The dog became silent and lay down on his belly. Then he raised his snout and sniffed the air. He shuddered. Then he dragged himself along the ground until he came to the old man's naked foot. He smelt it. He rose slowly to his feet, raised his mane slightly, and advanced, an inch at a time, smelling along the old man's naked shins and thighs . . .
>
> Suddenly he raised his snout, sat back on his haunches, and uttered a long howl. Then he lay down on his side and nestled against the old man's shoulder.[110]

Reading these lines, one can understand why an early reviewer said of the novel that 'there are moments in it that have the heroic quality of sudden piercing lines in an old saga'.[111] It unforgettably captures the importance of burial, the threat posed by famine to custom and human decencies. These themes are some of the most frequent and vivid in famine representations, extending back to Asenath Nicholson's travel narrative and, nearer to O'Flaherty's time and a probable influence on his novel, Seosamh MacGrianna's short story 'Ar an Trá Fholamh' (On the empty shore).[112] The story ends as Cathal, having carried his relative's body on his back for some miles, finally reaches the graveyard by the shore:

He set to work, and dug a yard deep. He had not the courage to go down further. He took up the corpse that was like a bit of a stick, and laid it in the grave. It was very hard to throw a spadeful of clay on an uncovered corpse. It was hard to put the clay over that face, into the nostrils, through the beard. It was like killing someone. Slowly the trunk went out of sight. For a long time the knees, which were drawn up a little, were visible above the sand, and the beard kept sticking up. It disappeared. The grave was filled, until it was a little mound like the other graves around it.

Cathal cast the spade from him, and flung himself down on the grave, with his two arms bent under his face, his body fixed to the ground in his agony.

A white seagull sailed on its wings above his head, crying and crying piteously. The sun came out from behind a cloud, and spread a weak watery light, that was like the spirit of fire and the spirit of frost commingled. It spread around over the covering of the dead, over fields of undug potatoes, over roads that were lonely, over houses where silence reigned.[113]

MacGrianna's final perspective, strongly reminiscent of Joyce's 'The Dead', moves over the whole landscape, 'over roads that were lonely, over houses where silence reigned'. Some forty years later, an almost microscopic focus would be adopted in the twentieth century's other great famine story, 'Gorta' (Famine), by Máirtín Ó Cadhain.[114] A man lies dying, with a rotting potato in his hand; in the course of the story, the various insects and birds of prey which approach his body are minutely examined. Ó Cadhain's deliberate omission of historical reference or any biographical detail gives the story a timeless and almost apocalyptic quality.

The closing lines of O'Flaherty's novel and MacGrianna's story rank among the realistic narrative's most successful representations of famine, Ó Cadhain's narrative more surreal in style. Yet the symbolic dimensions signalled by the conclusion to O'Flaherty's novel also deserve comment. As a confrontation between the individual and inexorable circumstance, Brian's death is tragic; this tragedy, however, occurs as a force associated more with Nature and the inevitable than the politics of starvation. The novel's political comment is to be found instead in the context of its other ending, in its representation of survival and survivors. As Mary and Martin depart for America, the narrative describes, in an image repeated throughout nationalist historiography, sacks of grain being exported to England as ships are loaded with people bound for America. Many critics have criticized this ending as 'improbable' and artistically inappropriate.[115] Whatever the cost to the credibility of the plot, the message directed to the novel's readers is clear. The reference to emigrants' 'cries for future vengeance' invokes events in Irish history from the story's end in 1847 to the time of its publication in 1937. In particular, it gestures to Irish-American readers, a community for whom the 1840s famine had become a charter-myth, and who, from the novel's first publication, represented a significant part of O'Flaherty's audience.[116] Hopes for the future are embodied in the survivors who emigrate, in particular through Michael, Mary and Martin's child; the novel thus ends with both a cyclical time of birth and renewal, what might be termed 'women's time', as well as the linear history concluded with Brian's death.

In 1945, less than ten years after O'Flaherty's novel first appeared, commemorations of the hundred-year anniversary of the beginning of the Great Famine included the production of a famine play, Gerard Healy's *The Black Stranger*.[117] In Healy's play, famine's relationship to the story of emigration is viewed in a strikingly different way. The dramatic action is centred on the experiences of one family: Michael, one son, is killed in an attempt at physical resistance; Bart, the remaining son, is about to emigrate to America, the only place 'where there's freedom'. At the last moment, he changes his mind:

> Bridie: So you didn't go after all, Bart.
> Bart: No.
> Bridie: Why not?
> Bart: I don't know. I just came back.[118]

Bart's return also vindicates his father Patrick's argument that leaving Ireland will make the famine 'matter', since no-one will be left to carry on. One of Patrick's lines resonates through the play: 'What does it matter about the famine if you can manage to live through it?'[119] Interestingly, this dramatization of famine, while commemorating others' heroic though futile efforts at resistance, is ultimately a celebration, and congratulation, of those who have survived, who 'manage to live through' the famine *and* remain in Ireland.

As part of its story of survival, Healy's play also depicts an adaptive strategy rarely discussed in famine writings and scarcely represented in Irish famine literature – women's prostitution.[120] In the second act of *The Black Stranger*, reference is made to a conversation overheard between two sailors: 'They said women was always scarce here before, but they were cheap now, an' young an' plentiful.'[121] Soon afterwards Bridie, a local girl to whom both brothers are suitors, is discovered to have procured meal through prostituting her body. The scene in which the others discover the truth and in which Bridie defends what she has done – her purpose being to feed a pregnant woman – is one of the most powerful in the play:

> Bridie: I don't care, so I don't. It was a harder thing to do than just sit be the fire. I don't care. The meal is there for you now, Mag. It'll make a cake or two an' you needn't be cryin' to yourself all the night because you've no food for the baby. What I did doesn't matther now. I'm glad it's over, but it doesn't matther to me. I'll put it out of me mind, the same as it never happened. It wouldn't matther t' any of you aither, if you didn't know about it.
>
> Mag [rising and lifting the bag of meal and going to Bridie]: It matthers to me. I won't forget it as long as I live, an' when the baby comes, I'll name it after you – I'll teach you to love it as much it'll love me – it'll be your child as much as mine. There's nothing to be sorry about. I'd do the same meself. What's a little thing like that, or the sins of the whole world, compared to the life of my baby, that's harmless an' helpless an' never asked to be brought here an' that'll begin life in cold an' misery an' hunger when it does come?[122]

The remainder of the play outlines a further sense in which Bridie's actions 'matther'. She herself recognizes that Michael's anxiety to leave, to pursue a doomed attempt at resistance, is linked to her 'visit to the town':

Michael: No, that doesn't matther. You had to do that.
Bridie: You're as bad a liar as meself, Michael. Go on so an' get it over with.[123]

On the one hand, Healy's play bravely engages with the untold and hidden stories of survival; yet women's prostitution is ultimately secondary to, and redeemed by, the heroic resistance of men. At the end of the play, Mag and her child have died; her husband recalls his wife 'stone cold by the fire and the baby still trying to suck milk from her breast' and reveals that he smothered the child.[124] The future of the family will be safeguarded through Bridie's marriage to Bart; through this marriage, as Bridie emphasizes, she will have 'Michael's son', ensuring that Michael is thus remembered.

The theme of survival, its complex and challenging manifestations, is central to twentieth-century 'retellings' of famine, not just as part of what may have happened in the past but also in the relationship of the audience or readers to what is presented. Writing of the genesis of his famine play, Tom Murphy has described how 'consciously or unconsciously, rightly or wrongly, another thought/ feeling was emerging: Was I, in what I shall call my times, the mid-twentieth century, a student or a victim of the Famine?'[125] A sense of famine's enduring legacy underlies the work of some of the most famous poets of the twentieth century: in Patrick Kavanagh's portrait of sexual repression and deprivation, *The Great Hunger* (1942), or, more explicitly, in Seamus Heaney's poem, 'At a Potato Digging'.[126] The 'live skulls, blind-eyed' of the past are still to be read from the contemporary scene: 'where potato diggers are/you still smell the running sore'.[127] In recent years, however, and especially in the context of the one hundred and fiftieth anniversary of the 'Great Famine', the relation between past and present has become a more complex question, the direct lineage between famine victim and descendant increasingly suspect. Characterizations of the Irish today as descendants of famine victims have produced some gross simplifications, and risk producing a complacency about the past and present. An alternative tendency is to insist that the contemporary Irish are instead the descendants of survivors; yet this argument, countering martyrdom with guilt, can yield equally generalized and sterile results.

In this context, many of the questions raised by Tom Murphy's play remain acutely relevant. Commenting on the play's origins, in an introduction to his collected plays, Murphy stresses its autobiographical and historical character: 'Consciously and unconsciously, in the writing of the play, while aware of the public event that was the Irish Famine in the 1840s, I was drawing on the private well and recreating moods and events, apprehensions of myself and my own times.'[128] 'Famine,' he argues, is a 'racial memory', a 'debilitating history' which has left its 'mark' – a point to be emphasized but not exaggerated:

> it would be foolish to suggest that the moodiness of the Irish personality that is commented on – we blow hot, we blow cold, swing from light to black, black to jet black – stems solely from the Famine, as it would be foolish to suggest that the Irish race was a singularly, warm, wild and happy one in pre-Famine times.[129]

Famine owes much of its historical detail to Cecil Woodham-Smith's history, first published in 1962.[130] Other sources include histories, memoirs and accounts of the Irish famine, particularly the fictional writings of Carleton and O'Flaherty, as well as contemporary media accounts and depictions of starvation. In Murphy's words, 'three broad approaches' exist from which *Famine* can be viewed: historical, autobiographical and dramatic; 'It has, as a play, a life of its own and, tired of history, tired of me, it continues its own process of discovery to its own conclusions.'[131]

Productions of the play, however, can leave one with the sense of a 'discovery' as yet unaccomplished. In 1993, in a preview to Garry Hynes' anniversary production of Murphy's play at the Abbey, Fintan O'Toole correctly noted that 'on the landscape of contemporary Irish theatre, *Famine* juts up as an awesome if somewhat forbidding peak, one that has been climbed but never conquered'.[132] One of the reasons for this, according to O'Toole, is the 'epic scale' of the piece, its need for a 'grand public space'. Other features of the play, such as its multiplicity of scenes and the resulting fragmentary quality, pose additional challenges to production. But the questions generated by a production of Murphy's play go further, raising again the difficulties of attempting to represent the events and horrors of famine. Is the audience ever more than a spectator to actions both historically and psychologically distant? Does the play succeed in offering, as O'Toole argues it does, a 'representation of hunger that is about "us" not "them"'?[133]

Famine is a play with great potential power, much of which comes from Murphy's refusal to present either a simplistic chronicle of resistance, a tempting but erroneous version of famine, or the alternative, a one-dimensional representation of a series of passive victims. Significantly, as Murphy himself explains, he chose to end the play in spring 1847, when the 'historical worst' was yet to come, since 'I don't think that a play can do "justice" to the actuality of famine'.[134] Instead the play explores the strategies being employed by famine characters to survive, and their price. Men recall, in conversation, stories from earlier famines, of children 'green from eating the grass', of 'a child under a bush, eating its mother's breast' – poignantly prophetic, as the audience is aware, of the characters' own fates in the months to come. Meanwhile, they attempt to survive in various ways, through emigration, employment from the agent, spite, physical resistance, or even just by talk; as Murphy says of the character Dan, 'he is alive as long as he can hear himself talking'.[135]

The central conflict in the play occurs between John Connor and his wife. John, in his attempt to understand what is happening and to do what is 'right', surrounds himself with increasingly abstract political definitions. The force of his character lies in its ambivalence; his actions are both heroic and futile, questioning and questionable.[136] His wife, 'Mother', on the other hand, is pragmatic – in many ways, disturbingly so. She favours emigration, is willing to renounce her religion for food, suggests making coffins since 'they'll be in demand' and steals turf from others in order to save her family. John's assertion, 'it's only by right that we can hope at all now',[137] is challenged by her powerful questions:

'What's right? What's right in a country when the land goes sour? Where is a woman with childre when nature lets her down?'[138]

The character of 'Mother', pragmatic provider for her family and eloquent opponent of men's futile actions, is a type familiar in Irish writing, with strong echoes of Sean O'Casey's Juno:

> Right. Our noble men can afford what's right. Will I keep stealing from the dying . . . No rights or wrongs or ráiméis talks, but bread, bread, bread. From where, but myself – Not him, not You – but always the slave, slave of the slave, day after day, to keep us alive, for another famine . . . Jesus Christ above, what's wrong at all, and all the clever persons in the world? Biteens of bread are needen only.[139]

In critical readings, the pragmatism and anti-idealism of this character-type are usually welcomed, along with her resistance to political rhetoric. Yet a troubling stereotype underlies such figures: the perspective which they are made to represent is not simply apolitical but forcefully 'anti-political'; access to political action or to men's political discourse is thus denied, both to Juno and to the famine-mother. A separation of spheres emerges in which women's realm is that of children, the family and 'nature', in isolation from the political, even human realm.[140] Murphy's construction of the characters of John and 'Mother' risks reinforcing this separation: woman's sphere is 'nature', John's that of complex political abstraction. The implications of this extend, however, beyond unappealing gender stereotypes, and critically shape an audience's very understanding of famine. The mother's appeals, with all their dramatic force – 'Where is a woman with childre when nature lets her down?' – risk reinforcing equations of famine and natural disaster, an interpretation clearly not part of the author's intention. A striking paradox results whereby the mother, in opposing John's efforts to find what is 'right', embodies famine's wrongs, but also the impossibility of their definition.

The ambivalences generated by such a reading continue in the play's final scenes. John's instinct for survival emerges as a dominant force; as he declares, 'I don't understand it myself, but I have to live. Someone has to live.'[141] And yet, in the most troubling moment of the play, his continued living is possible only through killing his wife and his son. The mother's existence is, however, the one deemed parasitical; in her words, 'I can only attack your strength to withhold myself a while longer from their last whim.'[142] Against this, John 'protects himself' and his daughter through an action which is also termed the *mother's* moment of freedom, the final protection of her 'right'. A troubling result of Murphy's less complex and stereotypical characterization of the mother is thus apparent: her death can more easily appear a necessary, if dreadful, action.

On the other hand, this episode is also one of the most moving and harrowing representations, compelling us to imagine what famine may mean, the appalling choices to be made. Within the community of those who are starving, the survival of one may require another's death. To a twentieth-century audience, seeking to comprehend the events of the past, Murphy's play remains one of the most significant depictions of the strategies and price of survival. In the process, the long line of sacrificial victims which emerges from twentieth-century famine literature, ancestral mothers whose deaths are made necessary to survival, receives another member.

Finally, one of the most interesting of all twentieth-century treatments of famine is to be found in *Birchwood*, John Banville's 1973 novel.[143] In this parodic version of the 'Big House' story, the narrative begins with the familiar summary of family genealogy, moving forward to the present. Book two dramatically reverses this sequential plot, as references to hunger and starvation, stories of coffins with sliding tops and of people eating grass, signal a return to the past, in particular to the events of the 1840s. Most ominously, an 'eerie, malevolent silence' pervades; as Gabriel, narrator and central character, notes: 'For all their laughter and their shrieks, the silence was still there beneath all, the anguish and the dumb longing of those whose absence sat beside us like an implacable black bird in this house of the dead. It was not hunger that was killing us, but the famine itself.'[144] By now, 'famine' has become a 'thought' in itself, an example of what Paul Ricoeur calls a 'colligatory word' through which we can 'apprehend a set of historical events under a common denominator', a 'well-known story' in which 'retelling takes the place of telling'.[145]

Banville's novel, more than any other famine narrative, displays a compelling self-consciousness about the manner of its own 'retelling'. Within the famine story, efforts by the characters to keep 'reality at bay' through exaggeration fail to succeed; their 'tall stories' are surpassed by the dreadful truth: 'Reality was hunger, and there was no gainsaying that.'[146] One example of this 'reality' is the experience of Ida, raped and killed by soldiers. Gabriel meditates, in some detail, on the meaning and significance of her death:

> Odd, but I can remember no tears. Lamentations seemed somehow superfluous. If one stopped and thought for a moment about her death one said *yes, really, it's logical enough*, and it was, with the grotesque logic of the times. When we looked back now we saw that it was for this death we had waited, suspended up here in the mountains, as though a sacrifice were necessary before we could move on, and the sacrifice of course was the slaughter of innocence. Or is all that too subtle, too neat?[147]

Readers of famine literature, who have encountered over and over again the 'slaughter' or 'sacrifice' of female 'innocence' as sign of famine's horror, might well answer 'yes' to Banville's questions. The sacrificial death of a female famine victim is, as this chapter has shown, one of the most frequent motifs in twentieth-century representations, her death deemed necessary for the survival of the community. Yet to what extent this sacrifice is 'necessary' or 'logical', with the 'grotesque logic of the times', deserves some further exploration.

Women's experience is the site of many of famine's worst horrors, from the writing of the 1840s through to the present. As cited earlier the anonymous author of 'Thanatos', in 1849, imaged the catastrophe through the breakdown of the relationship between mother and child; almost one hundred and fifty years later, Eavan Boland's 'The Making of an Irish Goddess' would recall

> the failed harvests,
> the fields rotting to the horizon,
> the children devoured by their mothers
> whose souls, they would have said,

> went straight to hell,
> followed by their own.[148]

Over and over again, the extremity of the times appears as a crisis in maternity, tragically, sometimes horrifically, transformed into the source of death rather than life. The mother's power may thus, as Julia Kristeva observes, be 'baleful' as well as positive, since 'the mother gives us life, but not infinity'.[149] Yet, in a related theme which gathers in force through the twentieth century, women give life, and a form of social infinity, through their own deaths. The female figure emerges as the guarantee of society's continuance; her sacrificial death safeguards the fate of her descendants.

The famine narrative usually seeks to secure the reader's recognition of the 'logic' of this representation; yet Banville's novel also suggests a means of resistance. As famine progresses, Gabriel notes a change in the face of Sybil, one of his travelling-companions, 'a minute but devastating change': 'Her left eye seemed to droop a fraction lower than the right, and this imbalance gave to what had been her cool measured gaze a querulous, faintly crazed cast.'[150] This trace of famine brings us back some hundred and thirty years to another woman's face, depicted by James Mahony in the *Illustrated London News* of February 1847.[151] Banville's sibyl, female voice of prophecy or revelation, links present and past, and is the means through which insight is delivered:

> I hardly dare to voice the notion which, if it did not come to me then comes to me now, the insane notion that perhaps it was on her, on Sybil, our bright bitch, that the sorrow of the country, of those baffled people in the rotting fields, of the stricken eyes staring out of hovels, was visited against her will and even without her knowledge so that tears might be shed and the inexpressible expressed. Does that seem a ridiculous suggestion? But I do not suggest, I only wonder.[152]

Through Gabriel's perspective, the very basis of female representations is uncovered. The figure of woman is the means through which the 'sorrow of the country' is given form, its pain and horror communicated. Thus 'tears' are shed, and 'the inexpressible expressed'. An 'accurate inscription'[153] of the horror of the past must remain, despite the best efforts of authors such as O'Flaherty, Murphy and Boland, an aspiration. Instead what emerges clearly from all of these texts is a recurring strategy of representation: the choice of female images, not simply as an expression of 'the grotesque logic of the times', but to enable famine's narration.

NOTES AND REFERENCES

1. Paul Ricoeur, 'Narrative Time', in *Critical Inquiry*, 7, 1 (1980), p. 179.
2. Emily Lawless, *Ireland* ([1887]; London, 1912), p. 400. Lawless dedicated this history of Ireland to the Earl of Dufferin, then (in 1887) Viceroy of India, and, in his youth, the author of *Narrative of a Journey from Oxford to Skibbereen during the Year of the Irish Famine* (Oxford, 1847).
3. See Cormac Ó Gráda, *Ireland Before and After the Famine: Explorations in Economic History, 1800–1930* ([1988]; Manchester, 1993), pp. 98–101; Terry Eagleton, *Heathcliff and the Great Hunger: Studies in Irish Culture* (London, 1995), p. 12.
4. In 1910, the Sussex-born novelist, Mildred Darby, writing under the pseudonym 'Andrew Merry', emphasized, in an introduction to her famine novel, *The Hunger* (London, 1910), that 'Few people of the present generation know more of the appalling catastrophe than its broad outlines, gathered from some attenuated volume of Irish History'; to compensate for this, Darby quotes in detail from the reminiscences of survivors and from testimonies written during the famine.
5. One striking example, cited by Ó Gráda in *The Great Irish Famine* (London, 1989), p. 11, is the essay topic set for University College Dublin students in 1963: '*The Great Hunger* is a great novel'.
6. Steven Marcus, 'Hunger and Ideology', in *Representations: Essays on Literature and Society* ([1975]; New York, 1990), p. 7.
7. Ibid., p. 7.
8. Seamus Heaney, 'At a Potato Digging', from *Death of a Naturalist* (London, 1966), pp. 31–33.
9. Philip Rahv, cited in Marcus, 'Hunger and Ideology', p. 7.
10. Eavan Boland, 'The Making of an Irish Goddess', from *Outside History* (Manchester, 1990), pp. 31–32.
11. Gonne's lecture was delivered to the Cercle Catholique des Étudiants du Luxembourg de Paris on 20 February 1892; see her description in Maud Gonne MacBride, *A Servant of the Queen: Reminiscences* (London, 1938), pp. 153–56.
12. W. B. Yeats, 'The New "Speranza"', *Boston Pilot*, 30 July 1892; reproduced in George Bornstein and Hugh Witemeyer (eds.), *Letters to the New Island*:

Collected Works of W. B. Yeats, Volume VII ([1934]; New York, 1989), pp. 61–63.

13. Ibid., p. 62. Some months earlier, on 16 Jan 1892, Yeats published a letter in *United Ireland*, also praising 'the new "Speranza"' for her efforts to keep 'France informed of the true state of the Irish Question'; see John Frayne, *The Uncollected Prose of W. B. Yeats* (London, 1970), i, pp. 212–14.

14. Eagleton, *Heathcliff and the Great Hunger*, p. 13.

15. As mentioned in the introduction, broader definitions of what constitutes 'famine' material have produced interesting rereadings, in particular Mary Lowe-Evans' reading of Joyce in *Crimes Against Fecundity: Joyce and Population Control* (New York, 1989), pp. 5–29.

16. An tAthair Peadar Ua Laoghaire's *Mo Sgéal (Scéal) Féin* (My own story) was first published in 1915. Father Patrick Dinneen (Pádraig Ua Duinnín) was the author of two famine plays: *Creideamh agus Gorta* (Faith and famine), first published in 1901, and *Teachtaire Ó Dhia* (A messenger from God), written in 1922. For a recent discussion of these famine writings, see Máirín Nic Eoin's study of twentieth-century Irish-language famine literature in Cathal Póirtéir (ed.), *Gnéithe den Ghorta* (Dublin, 1995), pp. 107–30. See also Philip O'Leary's *The Prose Literature of the Gaelic Revival, 1881–1921: Ideology and Innovation* (Pennsylvania, 1994), pp. 195–96.

17. Emily Lawless, 'Famine Roads and Memories', in *Traits and Confidences* ([1897]; reprinted in Garland Series, New York and London, 1979), pp. 142– 62. *Traits and Confidences* also includes a love story set during the famine, recalled in 'After the Famine'. A further link between Lawless and a tradition of famine representations, extending back to the writings of Edmund Spenser and others, is suggested by a scene in *With Essex in Ireland* ([1890]; reprinted New York and London, 1979), set during the Desmond wars of 1579–83, in which the ghosts of the 'walking dead', those 'slain or died of famine' (pp. 142–48), are seen.

18. Lawless, 'Famine Roads', pp. 150–51. A century after Lawless's essay, famine roads remain one of the most significant traces of the 1840s, commemorated with 'famine walks' in many localities. See also Eavan Boland's poem, 'That the Science of Cartography is Limited', from *In a Time of Violence* (Manchester, 1994), p. 5:

> the line which says woodland and cries hunger
> and gives out among sweet pine and cypress
> and finds no horizon.

19. See Tim P. O'Neill, 'The Persistence of Famine in Ireland', in Cathal Póirtéir (ed.), *The Great Irish Famine* (Dublin, 1995), pp. 204–18.

20. For example, Louise Berens' *Steadfast unto Death* (London, 1880) and Emily Fox's *Rose O'Connor* (Chicago, 1880). References to the famine of 1879–80 are also to be found in the historical and autobiographical writings of Mary Frances Cusack, including *The Nun of Kenmare: An Autobiography* (London, 1889) and *The Case of Ireland stated: a plea for my people and my race* (Dublin, 1881). Cusack also employed some references to famine in her anti-proselyte novel, *Tim O'Halloran's Choice; or, from Killarney to New York* (London, 1877).

21. First published in 1891, in Mulholland's collection, *The Haunted Organist of Hurly Burly and Other Stories*, 'The Hungry Death' was selected, that same year, by W. B. Yeats for publication in his anthology, *Representative Irish Tales*. Mulholland's story was the only work by a living writer included by Yeats; in his foreword, he declared Mulholland to be 'the novelist of contemporary Catholic Ireland'. The story was later republished in the *Irish Monthly*, XLII (1914).

22. Rosa Mulholland, 'The Hungry Death', in W. B. Yeats, *Representative Irish Tales* (New York and London, 1891), ii, pp. 313–14.

23. Ibid., p. 324.

24. Ibid., p. 327.

25. Yeats's play was first published in 1892 in *The Countess Kathleen and Various Legends and Lyrics*; many versions of the play, entitled *The Countess Cathleen*, followed. See M. J. Sidnell, 'Yeats's First Work for the Stage: The Earliest Versions of the *Countess Kathleen*', in Desmond E. Maxwell and S. B. Bushrui (eds.), *W. B.Yeats,1865–1965: Centenary Essays* (Ibadan, 1964), pp. 167–88, and A. Norman Jeffares and A. S. Knowland, *A Commentary on the Collected Plays of W. B. Yeats* (London, 1975), pp. 1–7.

26. *The Countess Cathleen*, in W. B. Yeats, *Collected Plays* ([1952]; London, 1982), scene v, p. 50.

27. See Jeffares and Knowland, *Commentary*, p. 7.

28. Yeats, *The Countess Cathleen*, scene i, p. 3; scene iii, p. 30.

29. Ibid., scene v, p. 38.

30. Ibid., scene i, p. 13.

31. Ibid., scene iii, p. 27.

32. In a note to the play, included in *Poems* (London, 1927), Yeats explained that he had found the story 'in what professed to be a collection of Irish folklore in an Irish newspaper', but learned some years later that the story was of a more recent origin, included in a French collection of tales, *Les Matinées de Timothée Trimm* by Léo Lespès, and concerning an Irish woman, 'Ketty O'Connor'; this note is reproduced in Jeffares and Knowland, *Commentary*, pp. 3–5.

33. See A. Norman Jeffares, *W. B. Yeats: A New Biography* (London, 1988), p. 65; also Joseph Hone, *W. B. Yeats, 1865–1939* (London, 1942), p. 87; also cited in Jeffares and Knowland, *Commentary*, p. 6.

34. See Nancy Cardozo, *Maud Gonne: Lucky Eyes and a High Heart* (London, 1978), p. 78, and Gonne, *A Servant of the Queen*, p. 241.

35. Yeats, *Countess Cathleen*, scene ii, pp. 20–21. The equivalent passage in the 1892 edition reads: 'Yet learned theologians have laid down/That he who has no food, offending no way,/May take his meat and bread from too-full larders'.

36. Maud Gonne and James Connolly, *The Right to Life and the Rights of Property* (privately published, 1898); extracts reproduced in Cardozo, *Maud Gonne*, pp. 144–45; Gonne, *A Servant of the Queen*, pp. 227–28, and Margaret Ward, *Maud Gonne: Ireland's Joan of Arc* (London, 1990), p. 49. See also C. Desmond Greaves, *The Life and Times of James Connolly* (London, 1961), p. 83.

37. Gonne, *A Servant of the Queen*, pp. 226–46; see also Anna MacBride White and A. Norman Jeffares (eds.), *The Gonne–Yeats letters, 1893–1938: 'Always your Friend'* (London, 1992), pp. 82–89.

38. Gonne, *A Servant of the Queen*, p. 243.

39. Ward, *Maud Gonne*, p. 51.

40. Maud Gonne, 'Relief Work in Erris', *Freeman's Journal*, 9 March 1898, and 'The Distress in the West', *Freeman's Journal*, 30 March 1898; cited in MacBride and Jeffares, *'Always your Friend'*, p. 469. Seven years earlier, in August 1891, Maud's one-year-old son, George, had died of meningitis.

41. Gonne, 'Relief Work in Erris'.

42. Ibid.

43. Ibid.

44. Gonne, 'Reine de la Disette', republished as 'The Famine Queen' in the *United Irishman*, 7 April 1900; quoted in Elizabeth Coxhead, *Daughters of Erin* (Gerrards Cross, 1965), pp. 45–46, and Ward, *Maud Gonne*, p. 61. Three years earlier, Gonne had been involved in protests held on the anniversary of Victoria's coronation, Jubilee Day, 22 June 1897, when she hung, in Dublin streets, flags illustrated with details of the famines and evictions which had occurred during Victoria's reign; see Ward, *Maud Gonne*, p. 45.

45. Ward, *Maud Gonne*, p. 62. On 21 April 1900, a letter by W. B. Yeats appeared in the *United Irishman* on the subject of Victoria's visit, entitled 'Noble and Ignoble Loyalties'; in the course of the letter, he refers to her visit in 1849, when 'we had the Great Famine to forget', and compares loyalty to Queen Victoria with Irish devotion to 'Kathleen Ny (*sic*) Hoolihan'.

46. Anna Parnell, 'To the Memory of Commandant Scheepers', in *Old Tales and New* (Dublin and London, 1905), pp. 60–66; one section of the poem is specifically directed towards Victoria's jubilee, entitled '22nd June 1897'.

47. 'Thanatos, 1849', *Irishman*, 5 May 1849, reproduced in Chris Morash (ed.), *The Hungry Voice* (Dublin, 1989), pp. 165–66.

48. Coxhead, *Daughters of Erin*, p. 45. During 1891 and 1894, Gonne also published articles on 'Le Martyre de l'Irlande', including the subject of famine, in the fortnightly *Journal des Voyages*; see C. L. Innes, *Woman and Nation in Irish Literature and Society: 1880–1935* (London, 1993), pp. 128–34.

49. *Mother Ireland,* researched and directed by Anne Crilly, and produced by Derry film and video in 1988, includes historical footage of Gonne speaking at a political rally, material deemed, when the film was first produced, to be in contravention of British broadcasting regulations.

50. Gonne, *A Servant of the Queen*, p. 240.

51. Ibid., p. vii.

52. Ibid., p. 241.

53. *Dawn* was first published in Griffith's *United Irishman*, 29 October 1904, and republished in Robert Hogan (ed.), *Lost Plays of the Irish Renaissance* (Dixon, Calif., 1970), pp. 73–84; as Hogan notes, no record of the play's production has, as yet, been discovered.

54. Gonne, *Dawn*, tableau 3, in Hogan, *Lost Plays*, p. 84.

55. See Julia Williams and Stephen Watt, 'Representing a "Great Distress": Melodrama, Gender and the Irish Famine', in Michael Hays and Anastasis Nikolopoulou (eds.), *Culture and Society in Twentieth-Century Melodrama* (New York, forthcoming 1996), a highly suggestive study of formulations of masculinity and femininity in famine melodrama. Dramatic texts discussed include the little-known *Emerald Heart* (186–), produced in London's East End, and Hubert O'Grady's *The Famine* (1886), produced in the Queen's Royal, Dublin, among other theatres, and republished in the *Journal of Irish Literature*, 19 (1985), pp.14–49.

56. Eagleton, *Heathcliff and the Great Hunger*, p. 13.

57. See Yeats's note to *The Countess Cathleen*, in *Poems* ([1895]; revised and reprinted, London, 1927), p. 315.

58. The Keating Branch of the Gaelic League presented *Creideamh agus Gorta* at the Abbey Theatre on 27 and 28 October 1905; see O'Leary, *Prose Literature of the Gaelic Revival*, pp. 195, 301–03, and Robert Hogan and James Kilroy, *The Abbey Theatre: The Years of Synge, 1905–1909* (Dublin, 1978), p. 45. Writing in the *Arrow*, on 1 June 1907, Lady Gregory observed, with admirable restraint: 'Protestant friends of mine have been able to admire, as I do, the spiritual beauty of Father Dinneen's *Faith and Famine*, though we believe its picture of Protestant bigotry to be not only a caricature but an impossibility' ('An Explanation', p. 5; also quoted by Hogan and Kilroy, *Abbey Theatre*, p. 157).

59. Patrick Dinneen, *Creideamh agus Gorta: traghidheacht bhaineas le haimsir an drochshaoghail* (Faith and Famine: a tragic drama relating to the famine) (Dublin, 1901), preface.

60. Ibid., scene v, p. 35 (my translation).

61. Ibid., scene v, pp. 35–36 (my translation).

62. Ibid., scene v, p. 36 (my translation).

63. See 'Extract from a Letter to Edith Somerville from Martin Ross', 18 March 1912, reproduced in Edith Somerville and Martin Ross, *The Big House of Inver* ([1925]; London, 1978), p. 313.

64. Somerville and Ross, *The Big House of Inver*, pp. 18–21.

65. Ibid., p. 18.

66. Ibid., pp. 20–21.

67. Ibid., p. 18.

68. Ibid., p. 19.

69. Martin Ross, 'The Martins of Ross', in Somerville and Ross, *Irish Memories* (London, 1917), pp. 16–17.

70. Ibid., p. 17.

71. Somerville and Ross, *The Big House of Inver*, p. 19. Gwynn confuses Richard Martin, (1754–1834), with his son Thomas, (d. 1847), father of 'the Princess of Connemara.'

72. Maria Edgeworth, letter to Richard Jones, 14 June 1847, in Edgeworth Papers, National Library, Dublin, Ms. 22, 822; also cited in Michael Hurst,

Maria Edgeworth and the Public Scene: Intellect, Fine Feeling and Landlordism in the Age of Reform (London, 1969), p. 166.

73. Lawless, *Ireland*, p. 400.

74. This noble woman-martyr also briefly appears in Walter Macken's *The Silent People* (London, 1962) and Elizabeth Byrd's *The Famished Land* (London, 1972). See also Michael Mullen, *The Hungry Land* (New York and London, 1986).

75. John Hewitt, 'The Scar', in *Out of My Time* (Belfast, 1974), p. 40.

76. Marcus, 'Hunger and Ideology', p. 7.

77. William Trevor, *Fools of Fortune* (New York, 1983), 'The News from Ireland' in *The News from Ireland and Other Stories* (London, 1986), and *The Silence in the Garden* (London, 1988).

78. Trevor, *Fools of Fortune*, p. 13.

79. Ibid., p. 52.

80. Ibid., p. 199.

81. Trevor, 'The News from Ireland', p. 9.

82. Ibid., p. 32.

83. Ibid.

84. Ibid., p. 46.

85. Ibid., p. 44.

86. Trevor, *The Silence in the Garden*, p. 188.

87. Ibid.

88. *Famine* quickly became a best-selling novel, popular with book clubs both in England and America; the many languages into which it has been translated include French, Spanish, Portuguese, Dutch and German.

89. Sean O'Faolain, review of *Famine*, in *Ireland Today*, II, 2 (1937), pp. 81–82; M. L., review of *Famine* in *Irish Book Lover*, XXV (1937), pp. 22–23.

90. Mary Hayden, *A Short History of the Irish People* (Dublin, 1921); James Carty, *A Class-book of Irish History* (Dublin, 1929); *Ireland in Prose and Poetry: Junior and Senior Books* (Dublin, 1930).

91. Canon John O'Rourke, *The History of the Great Irish Famine of 1847, with notices of earlier Irish famines* (Dublin, 1875).

92. Roger McHugh, 'The Famine in Irish Oral Tradition', in R. D. Edwards and T. D. Williams (eds.), *The Great Famine: Studies in Irish History* (Dublin, 1956), p. 436.

93. James Connolly, *Labour in Irish History* (Dublin, 1910), pp. 162–63; the chapter on famine is intriguingly entitled 'Our Irish Girondins sacrifice the Irish Peasantry upon the Altar of Private Property'. See also Patrick Sheeran, *The Novels of Liam O'Flaherty* (Dublin, 1976), p. 207.

94. Liam O'Flaherty, *Famine* ([1937]; Dublin, 1979), p. 324. For recent discussions of the novel, see John Hildebidle, *Five Irish Writers: The Errand of Keeping Alive* (Cambridge, Mass., 1989), pp. 22–23, and Julia Williams in Williams and Watt, 'Representing a "Great Distress"', pp. 22–34.

95. O'Flaherty, *Famine*, pp. 122–23.

96. Ibid., p. 62.

97. Ibid., pp. 47, 123, 134.
98. Ibid., p. 391.
99. Ibid., p. 124.
100. Ibid., pp. 315–16.
101. Ibid., p. 337.
102. Ibid., pp. 212–13.
103. Ibid., pp. 215–16.
104. Ibid., p. 339.
105. Ibid., p. 414.
106. Ibid., p. 418.
107. Ibid., p. 420.
108. Striking parallels exist between the difficulties experienced by O'Flaherty and those confronted by Toni Morrison in her 1987 novel, *Beloved* (New York, 1987), which tells the story of a woman's act of infanticide – where 'mother-love was a killer' (p. 132). To Paul D, Sethe's actions are those of an animal: '"You got two feet, Sethe, not four"' (p. 165); through Sethe, Morrison warns of the impossibility of ever reaching the centre of this subject: 'the circle she was making around the room, him, the subject, would remain one . . . she could never close in, pin it down for anyone who had to ask. If they didn't get it right off – she could never explain' (p. 163).
109. O'Flaherty, *Famine*, p. 213.
110. Ibid., p. 448. Any suggestion of sentimentality in O'Flaherty's narration is dispelled by the reader's recollection that Brian's dog, earlier in the story, has fed on the dead body of Thomsy. This detail in turn echoes many 1840s descriptions of corpses eaten by dogs and rats; see Asenath Nicholson, *Lights and Shades of Ireland* (London, 1850), p. 290.
111. M. L., review of *Famine* in *Irish Book Lover*, XXV (1937), pp. 22–23.
112. MacGrianna's story was first published in *An tUltach*, December 1925, and later in MacGrianna's collection of stories, *An Grá agus An Ghruaim* (Dublin, 1929). According to Séamus MacGrianna, the author's brother, the story is based on an incident which occurred in Donegal during the famine; see Nic Eoin, 'Ar an Trá Fholamh – an Gorta Mór in Litríocht Ghaeilge na hAoise seo', pp. 115–18. This story has been reproduced, in English and in Irish, in Seamus Deane (ed.), *The Field Day Anthology of Irish Writing* (Derry, 1991), iii, pp. 845–49.
113. MacGrianna, 'Ar an Trá Fholamh', in Deane (ed.), *Field Day Anthology*, iii, p. 849; translation by Séamus Ó Néill.
114. Ó Cadhain's story was first published in *Comhar*, May 1967, and included in the author's collection of stories, *An tSraith ar Lár*, that same year. No English translation exists. See Nic Eoin, 'Ar an Trá Fholamh – an Gorta Mór in Litríocht Ghaeilge na hAoise seo', pp. 123–25, and Gearóid Denvir, *Cadhan Aonair* (Dublin, 1987), pp. 255–57.
115. See Sheeran, *The Novels of Liam O'Flaherty*, p. 224, and Hildebidle, *Five Irish Writers*, p. 23.

116. O'Flaherty spent much of the 1930s in Hollywood; in 1935 his novel *The Informer* was released as a film, directed by John Ford, and won four academy awards. The cover note to the 1937 American edition of *Famine* declared that 'an imposing array of producers and stars is bidding for the privilege of screening *Famine* in the hope it may duplicate *The Informer*'s success'. With this hope in mind, perhaps, O'Flaherty had dedicated *Famine* to John Ford.

117. Gerald Healy (1918–63) was also the author of *Thy Dear Father* (1943) and an actor who had played in both the Gate and Abbey companies. *The Black Stranger* was performed by the Players' Theatre, first in Cork in February 1945, for over a week and in the Gate Theatre, Dublin, beginning 6 March, for a six-week run. See Robert Hogan, *After the Irish Renaissance: A Critical History of the Irish Drama since* The Plough and the Stars (London and Melbourne, 1968), pp. 224–26. Hogan praises the play as a 'leanly written, tightly structured piece of realism'. The text of *The Black Stranger* was published in Dublin in 1950.

118. Healy, *The Black Stranger*, act III, p. 53.

119. Ibid., act III, p. 49. The hundredth anniversary of the Great Famine, in 1945 onwards, is notable for the absence of official commemoration (see Mary Daly, 'Why the Great Famine got Forgotten in the Dark 1840s', *Sunday Tribune*, 22 January 1995). The popularity and warm reception of Healy's play, however, suggests a much greater level of popular interest.

120. Maria Luddy notes that records for arrests for prostitution in Dublin show that the greatest number of arrests occurred during the famine years; see her article 'Prostitution and Rescue Work in the Nineteenth Century', in Maria Luddy and Clíona Murphy (eds.), *Women Surviving: Studies in Irish Women's History in the Nineteenth and Twentieth Centuries* (Dublin, 1989), p. 56. As the next chapter will discuss in detail, the theme of prostitution as a strategy employed during famine is a central motif in literary representations of the 1940s Bengal famine, many of which are contemporaneous with Healy's play.

121. Healy, *The Black Stranger*, act II, p. 34.

122. Ibid., act II, p. 37. A very different opinion was expressed by A. J. Leventhal in his review of the Dublin production of *The Black Stranger* in the *Dublin Magazine*, XX (April 1945), p. 44. The scene in which Bridie's prostitution is revealed, exemplified, to Leventhal, the 'real weakness of the play': 'The author transfers his own broad humanity to the stage puppets. There is no horror, no moral indignation among these pious Catholic peasants. She is accepted as a good girl by all. Her lover is the only one to react with any violence, and he goes off to pike as many redcoats as he can, before meeting his own death at their hands.'

123. Healy, *The Black Stranger*, act II, p. 40.

124. Ibid., act III, p. 50.

125. Tom Murphy, 'Introduction' to *Plays: One* (London, 1992), xi. *Famine* was first produced in 1968 and published by the Gallery Press in 1977.

126. Patrick Kavanagh, *The Great Hunger* (Dublin, 1942); see also Kavanagh's portrait of a post-famine landscape in *Lough Derg* (Curragh, 1978).

127. Heaney, 'At a Potato Digging', p. 33.

128. Murphy, 'Introduction', xiv.

129. Ibid., p. xi.

130. Recalling its first appearance, Murphy writes: '*The Great Hunger* was a major event in the publishing world and I expected it to inspire a half-dozen plays on the subject of the Irish Famine. I'm still surprised that they did not materialise', in 'Introduction', p. x.

131. Ibid., p. ix.

132. Fintan O'Toole, 'Some Food for Thought', *Irish Times*, theatre guide, 1 October 1993, p. 4.

133. Ibid., p. 4.

134. Murphy, 'Introduction', p. xvii.

135. Ibid., p. xiv.

136. The stature of John's character, the combination of great bravery and error at a time of crisis and change, finds an interesting parallel with the tragic yet ambivalent heroes in the writings of the novelist Chinua Achebe, in particular the character of Ezeulu in *Arrow of God* (London, 1964).

137. Murphy, *Famine*, scene iii, p. 33.

138. Ibid.

139. Ibid., scene xi, p. 84.

140. See Jane Gallop, *Thinking through the Body* (New York, 1988), pp. 1–2; similarly Marina Warner warns that 'this conflation of woman and nature only continues the false perception that neither is inside culture, that women do not participate in it, let alone create it. The converse is true. Both – woman and nature – are essential parts of an indivisible civilization, which cannot continue without them', *Monuments and Maidens: The Allegory of the Female Form* (London, 1985), pp. 324–25. Warner also cites Theodor Adorno's provocative observation from *Minima Moralia* ([1951]; London, 1978): 'Whatever is in the context of bourgeois delusion called nature, is merely the scar of social mutilation' (p. 325).

141. Murphy, *Famine*, scene x, p. 81.

142. Ibid., scene xi, p. 85.

143. John Banville, *Birchwood* ([1973]; London, 1987).

144. Ibid., p. 153.

145. Ricoeur, 'Narrative Time', p. 179.

146. Banville, *Birchwood*, p. 144.

147. Ibid., p. 147.

148. Boland, 'The Making of an Irish Goddess'.

149. Julia Kristeva, *Powers of Horror: An Essay on Abjection* (1980), trans. Leon S. Roudiez (New York, 1982), p. 158.

150. Banville, *Birchwood*, p. 142.

151. See the discussion of this image in chapter 1, pp. 21–23.

152. Banville, *Birchwood*, p. 143.

153. Boland, 'The Making of an Irish Goddess'.

— 4 —

Literature of the Bengal Famine

In August [1943] I was travelling by rail from Madras to Calcutta, on some business not connected with the famine . . . I stepped cheerfully down from my compartment en route for a hearty meal. The whole platform was thronged with emaciated and ragged people, of all ages and sexes, many half-dead, hoping to board a train for Calcutta. What I particularly remember is a loud, bleating, wailing noise which the starving crowd made, a combination of begging and misery. When some years later I read accounts of the Irish famine at its height, by visitors to stricken areas in West Cork, I was reminded of the platform at Khargpur Junction.

Wallace Ruddell Aykroyd[1]

Between 1943 and 1944 (measured 1350 Bengali era), large-scale famine occurred in the province of Bengal, an area comprising the present-day Indian state of West Bengal and former East Bengal (later East Pakistan, and now Bangladesh). In contrast to the frequency of famines which had marked the second half of the nineteenth century, India had not experienced a major famine since 1908. Bengal itself, when ranked with other Indian provinces according to the historical incidence of disaster, displays a comparatively low occurrence of famine.[2] One famine commission, reporting in 1880, observed that 'the eastern districts of the province enjoy so ample and regular a rainfall and such abundant river inundation as to ensure the safety of the crops in the driest years'.[3]

The famine of 1943–44, however, was catastrophic in its effects. Historical and critical studies continue to emerge, while, as a living memory for many Bengalis, the 'famine of fifty' remains a measure of time and change.

THE HISTORICAL CONTEXT

The commencement and duration of the Bengal famine are difficult to identify precisely, given the official delay at the time in acknowledging famine's existence. Amartya Sen observes that, although the Indian Secretary of State eventually acknowledged the existence of famine in the British parliament in October 1943, 'one curious aspect of the Bengal famine was that it was never officially "declared" as a famine'.[4] Such an official recognition would, as Sen explains, 'have brought in an obligation to organize work programmes and relief operations specified by the "Famine Code", dating from 1883'.[5]

The first evidence of famine appeared in rural districts of Bengal early in 1943: in February, commissioners' and district officers' reports refer to 'indications of distress'; the following month, they note that 'acute distress prevails'.[6] Official indifference and propaganda policies of 'no shortage' were quickly challenged by the flood of rural destitutes into Calcutta during the summer months. In July and August, the English language newspaper, the *Statesman*, played a crucial role in breaking the official silence with forceful editorials condemning official inaction, accompanied by dramatic photographs of destitutes, despite the editor's initial reluctance to publish such news during a war situation.[7] Yet, even a year later, when the extent of the famine was clear and when some limited relief measures had been implemented, official evasion continued. Wallace Ruddell Aykroyd, a nutrition expert and member of the Famine Inquiry Commission which was appointed in 1944 to explore the causes of the Bengal famine, acknowledges the official preference for familiar euphemisms such as 'food shortage' and 'distress': 'famine was a bad word, and officially famine had been vanquished in the nineteenth century'.[8] Having delayed in its recognition of famine, the administration also prematurely declared famine's end. While Sen's study of mortality figures reveals that more than half of famine-related deaths occurred between 1943 and 1946, as epidemics spread throughout Bengal, the Famine Commission's estimate of deaths extended only to the first half of 1944.[9]

The historiography of the Bengal famine includes a complex debate on the question of famine's causation, both the specific occurrence in 1943 and with regard to famine in general. As early as 1945, the Famine Inquiry Commission attributed the disaster, primarily, to 'the serious shortage in the total supply of rice available for consumption in Bengal as compared with the total supply normally available'.[10] In his *Poverty and Famines*, Amartya Sen strongly challenges this previously standard interpretation. He argues that the crop availability in 1943, although representing a shortfall in food, was not necessarily disastrous; although five per cent lower than the average of the preceding five years, it was thirteen per cent higher than that of 1941, when no famine occurred.[11] What is significant, in Sen's interpretation, is that by the middle of 1943 'a moderate short-fall in *produc*tion had by then been translated into an exceptional short-fall in *market release*';[12] thus, rice was not available for purchase by the poorer and, in particular, the landless sections of the rural population. This analysis of what occurred in Bengal in the early 1940s is crucial to Sen's redefinition of the nature of famine itself; rather than a simple issue of shortage or 'food availability decline', famine involves a crucial change in people's access or 'entitlement' to food.

However, as David Arnold demonstrates, Sen's thesis is not in itself sufficient to explain how famine is caused:

> for all the unquestionable importance of his work, it must be doubted whether Sen has really provided a theory of famine *causation*, as he contends in challenging the 'food availability decline' argument, so much as given an explanation of how famines develop once they have (for whatever reason) been set in motion.[13]

The causes of the Bengal famine, the factors which set it in motion, are both long-term and immediate. More long-term factors, identified by Arnold, include the subdivision of holdings, 'the long-term decline of agriculture in the province, the growing pressure on the land and the peasants' increasing burden of debt', which, 'taken together, made some kind of crisis, if not inevitable, then at least highly likely and much harder to resist once it began'.[14] The particular vulnerability of much of Bengal's population is also clear from B. M. Bhatia's analysis of the pre-famine position:

> Apart from two million families of wage labourers who because of their poverty must have been stinting in their consumption of cereals, there were 5.5 million families of cultivators whose income was insufficient to afford them a life of 'reasonable comfort'. The income of these families permitted a bare subsistence in normal years.[15]

A contemporary memorandum similarly notes that 'so delicate was the balance between actual starvation and bare subsistence that the slightest tilting of the scales in the value and supply of food was enough to put it out of the reach of many and to bring large classes within the range of famine'.[16]

The immediate causes of starvation in 1940s Bengal were massive price rises which placed food out of the reach of landless people and smaller cultivators. In turn, this breakdown in the market and distribution of food largely resulted from war-related measures. Following its entry into the war in 1941, Japan conquered Burma in April and May of 1942, cutting off imports of Burmese rice into Bengal and creating a fear of invasion. This perceived threat led to a number of government measures such as the 'boat denial' policy under which government officials removed from coastal areas or destroyed some 66,000 boats, and thus the sole income of hundreds of thousands of peasants.[17] 'Military reasons' also dictated the forced movement of some 35,000 peasant households and led to the 'rice denial' scheme under which 40,000 tons of grain were forcibly purchased from local cultivators and made available, through subsidized distribution schemes, to urban military or industrial workers.[18] Although these measures were limited both in geographical scope and numerical significance, their psychological impact was immense. Huge increases in the price of rice and panic hoarding, what Bhatia calls a 'psychosis of shortage',[19] followed. Producers and traders withheld rice from markets for fear of invasion or official requisitioning, because of price controls or in the expectation of further increases. The wholesale price of rice, between nine and ten rupees per maund in November 1942, thus rose to over thirty rupees by May 1943, with unofficial reports of prices of over a hundred rupees in some districts later in the year.[20]

Much of the responsibility for the intensification of famine may thus be attributed to private speculators who purchased and hoarded large quantities of rice. Drawing from his experience as a member of the Famine Commission, Aykroyd quotes the indignation expressed by witnesses against 'profiteers, speculators and hoarders' who caused 'mass suffering and death': 'the Commission itself made what it called the "gruesome calculation" that for every death in the famine roughly a thousand rupees of excess profits were made'.[21] Many of the literary representations of famine similarly castigate the actions of hoarders and speculators. The complexities of this issue, however, and the general difficulty of determining who has 'gained' from famine, given the pervasiveness of actions which might be termed 'hoarding', are confronted by Paul Greenough, who argues that if the criterion for such an accusation is the 'mere possession of a stock of rice or paddy beyond immediate means', then 'millions of persons' would be termed guilty.[22] This argument has interesting parallels with efforts by Irish historians to establish the reality of 'hoarding', angrily associated with the 'gombeen man' in folk-memory of the 1840s famine.[23]

An alternative emphasis in Bengal famine historiography focuses on the inadequacies of the official administration, which failed to anticipate or prevent famine. Within the 'official' sphere, one may distinguish three different levels of government: the provincial government of Bengal, the central government of India, and the London India Office – 'Whitehall, New Delhi and Bengal'.[24] As Bhatia and Sen observe, the local Bengal government was distinguished by inexperience, indecision and delay; the failure of a number of its food procurement and price control schemes only added to the chaos.[25] The prohibition of exports from other provinces prevented the price decrease which imports to Bengal would have produced; while free trade in rice was introduced, in the Eastern region only, in May 1943, it was abandoned in July. With reference to the role of the central government, Bhatia writes:

> While Bengal tried frantically to secure supplies of foodgrains to meet the shortage, the Central Government went on preaching the gospel of plenty. At the Conference held in Calcutta in March 1943, when Bengal was in desperate need of supplies, the provincial government was roundly told by the representative of the Central Government, Mr. Sumner Butler, 'to put its own house in order' . . . The attitude of the Central Government till the end of the Viceroyalty of Lord Linlithgow [October 1943] was one of callous disregard for the misfortunes of Bengal.[26]

The adherence by the government of India to the concept of provincial responsibility crucially limited any relief measures, a policy sadly reminiscent of nineteenth-century notions of local responsibility regarding Ireland. A further level of indifference marked the London administration's attitude to India; one example was its refusal of contemporary calls for a re-allocation of shipping in order to bring imports into India. Even the newly appointed Viceroy, Lord Wavell, wrote to Winston Churchill, in October 1944, that 'the vital problems of India are being treated by His Majesty's Government with neglect, even sometimes with hostility and contempt'.[27] The extent of famine mortality was to fuel arguments for Indian independence and become a key argument against British rule; later Jawaharal Nehru, first prime minister of India, was to comment: 'Obviously, if a National Government had been formed in 1942 there would have been a great deal of co-operation with the people . . . I am quite convinced that the Bengal famine [could then either have] been avoided or at any rate very greatly minimized.'[28] Nehru's castigation of the international community, chiefly 'rich England and richer America', for its neglect of Bengal included interesting exceptions:

> But in spite of government obstruction and desire to minimize the overwhelming tragedy of Bengal, sensitive and warmhearted men and women in England and America and elsewhere came to our

help. Above all, the governments of China and Éire, poor in their own resources, full of their own difficulties, yet having had bitter experience themselves of famine and misery, and sensing what ailed the body and spirit of India, gave generous help. India has a long memory, but whatever else she remembers or forgets, she will not forget these gracious and friendly acts.[29]

Turning to the victims of the Bengal famine, various estimates have been made as to the number of people who died. In 1945, the official Famine Inquiry Commission set the death toll of the Bengal famine at 'about 1.5 million'; a figure later described as an underestimate by Aykroyd, one of its members.[30] Unlike contemporary estimates, such as that given by the Commission or the higher figure of 2.7 million suggested by K. P. Chattopadhyaya, which cover up to June 1944, Amartya Sen argues that famine-related mortality continued until 1946, at least, due to epidemics such as cholera, malaria and smallpox.[31] The resulting figures offered by Sen are of an excess mortality of over one million in 1943 and a total famine mortality of three million.[32] Significantly, in this calculation, while starvation deaths reached their peak in September and October 1943, the death rate, owing to famine-related disease, was to continue to rise after this period. Thus, as Sen stresses, the 'time pattern' of famine mortality is of particular importance: 'Very substantially more than half the deaths attributable to the famine of 1943 took place *after* 1943.'[33]

In terms of occupation, the most vulnerable sections of the population included agricultural labourers, fishermen, transport workers and craftsmen, i.e. waged labourers and sellers of commodities and services, with peasant cultivators and share-croppers, as direct producers of rice, least affected.[34] Whether or not male or female victims were disproportionately affected receives differing conclusions. Many contemporary observers claimed that a significant difference existed; Das, in his survey of destitutes in Calcutta in September 1943, observed that 'for every dead woman there were nearly two dead men'.[35] Both the Famine Inquiry Commission and the department of anthropology in Calcutta also claimed that there was a much higher death rate among adult men than adult women, the latter calling it 'a very sinister and significant feature of the mortality figures'.[36] More recently, Paul Greenough has also argued, on the basis of unpublished mortality data collected at the time of the famine, that a greater number of men died and that females, in most age categories, experienced smaller increases in mortality; these findings, Greenough argues, represent a significant change in previous patterns of deaths.[37] One significant exception to the overall pattern is demonstrated by men, aged between the ages of twenty and forty, who appear to have had a slightly greater 'advantage' than women. This bias, in Greenough's view, is to be understood, at least in part, as 'deliberated conduct', intended to assure the continuance of the patrilineage beyond the immediate crisis.[38]

Amartya Sen's findings conflict with those of Greenough in a number of ways. Sen argues that famine mortality, in terms both of sex and age, intensified normal patterns of mortality: 'While the proportion of men in excess mortality in 1943 [fifty-four per cent] is a bit higher than in the pre-famine average [fifty-two per cent], the difference is small, and over the larger period of famine mortality the proportionate breakdown of the excess [fifty-two per cent] is just the same as for the pre-famine average.'[39] Furthermore, as Sen demonstrates, the male population exceeded the female population in Bengal; thus the recorded death rate per unit of population was higher for women in every year of the decade 1941 to 1950.[40] The differences being so small, he concludes that, 'as far as the 1943 famine is concerned', there is 'little need for going into the rather contrived explanations that have been proposed to explain the supposed contrast of sex ratios'.[41] It would thus appear from Sen's figures that, in absolute terms, the consensus of contemporary commentators is correct and more men died during the famine; any attempt, however, to draw substantial conclusions from these figures is undermined both by the narrowness of the margin and by the reminder that, relative to their proportion of the population, women had a marginally higher death rate and thus a slightly lower chance of survival.

One crucial aspect of Greenough's work on the Bengal famine, beyond the contested question of famine mortality, is his focus on policies and decision-making regarding access to food, not only in the official sphere but within villages, communities and families.[42] The controversial issue of famine's 'man-made' character, hotly debated from the 1840s to the present in Irish historiography, and with obvious continuing relevance, thus receives a significant redefinition:

> A search for the man or men who 'made' the Bengal famine thus comes to little now when a wider perspective is adopted, while the strong political feelings at the time made suspect every contemporary exercise in assigning blame – including the 'Report on Bengal'. There is, however, an entirely different sense in which the famine can be said to have been 'man-made'. In the course of 1943, distinct patterns of victimization occurred in affected Bengal villages. Resource-controlling males – landlords, cultivators, heads of households – declared their inability to feed all those who habitually depended upon them for food and for protection from danger. Patterns of abandonment began to emerge, marked by the snapping of moral and economic bonds upon which rural society had hitherto been erected and leading inevitably to the starvation, sickness and the death of millions.[43]

Greenough's inspection of the processes of abandonment which occurred at the domestic level provides crucial insights into the experience of famine, beyond generalized and simplistic surveys of mortality figures. With reference to the Bengal famine, recurring events include the desertion of women by their husbands and the sale or abandonment of children by their parents. As Greenough argues, these 'clearly immoral' acts constituted a form of adaptation to crisis, through the 'often intentional exclusion of less-valued family members', under the threat of 'total familial extinction'.[44] Famine is crucially 'not only starvation but concerns the *meaning* of starvation and how a society chooses to distribute the social costs'.[45]

Literary representations of the Bengal famine, both contemporary and in the succeeding years, reveal an interesting ambivalence with regard to the question of women's supposed resilience to famine. On one hand, authors emphasize the special vulnerability of women, widowed or deserted by their husbands, unable to find employment, etc. The following comment by Ela Sen, a short-story writer, is quite representative:

Who suffered most? To answer that question briefly, one would have to say – they who were the weakest either physically or econo-mically. In this, to take a general census, one finds that the severest repercussions fell upon the women, who are in a body to-day faced with social disintegration. Next on the list one would place certain classes of men such as landless labourers, the weavers, the fishermen and the potters . . . The question of how vitally it affected the women is wider – because their suffering was from all sides, economic as well as moral. It is strange to relate that a far higher percentage of men and children perished during these times than women for somehow in spite of the odds against them they clung tenaciously to life and were not willing victims of demoralization.[46]

Yet, as this passage also demonstrates, an emphasis on women's vulnerability frequently co-exists with a belief in their tenaciousness and greater resistance. In this regard, many literary texts reinforce the assumption by contemporary observers that more men had died during the famine; in many of the stories, men are absent, having gone in search of work, been imprisoned or died from hunger or disease. What is once again striking about Bengali famine literature is how rarely these experiences, those of male suffering and victimization, are made the centre of the narrative. Instead, much of the detail of Bengali novels and stories, as will be shown, concerns the various survival strategies employed by women during famine, their occasional success and their dreadful failure. Throughout these narratives, much attention is given to the conse-quences of these desperate strategies, not just for the individual woman but for society in general. The collapse of family ties, chiefly that between mother and child, signals, most dramatically, famine's threat to a social order. In addition, as the next section will explore, the increasing appropriation of famine as part of a story of oppression and resistance gives women an even greater symbolic role, embodying the victimized and threatened nation.

LITERARY REPRESENTATIONS OF FAMINE

> Still fresh in memory's eye the scene I view,
> The shrivelled limbs, sunk eyes, the lifeless hue;

> Still hear the mother's shrieks and infant's moans,
> Cries of despair and agonising groans.
> In wild confusion dead and dying lie:
> Hark to the jackal's yell and vulture's cry,
> The dog's fell howl, as midst the glare of day
> They riot unmolested on their prey!
> Dire scenes of horror, which no pen can trace,
> Nor rolling years from memory's page efface.
>
> Sir John Shore, 1770

In 1944, this depiction by John Shore of scenes of famine in 1770 Bengal was reproduced by Kali Charan Ghosh as a vivid epigraph to his account of the famine then occurring.[47] Ghosh, in a chapter entitled 'Dire Scenes of Horror', quotes in detail from contemporary eye-witness accounts and newspaper reports, repeating graphic and terrible descriptions of unburied corpses, bodies 'devoured' by vultures and dogs, and jackals attacking even those who had not yet died.[48] Similar reports appeared throughout newspapers in the second half of 1943, in the *Statesman*, the *Hindusthan Standard* and other journals, accompanied by illustrations of the plight of city destitutes. These photographs showed dead bodies lying on the pavements, women attempting, in vain, to find food for their children, children ransacking dustbins to find morsels of food, others abandoned by their parents, and pictures of 'the lucky few' who became recipients of relief.[49]

Yet, as Sen and others have demonstrated, the Bengal famine was 'essentially a rural phenomenon', with the rural population producing by far the greater number of victims.[50] Insulated by subsidized food distribution schemes, the population of Calcutta experienced famine largely through the flood of destitutes who came to the city from the countryside; hence 'most people who died in Calcutta from starvation and from related diseases in the famine year were destitutes who had moved to Calcutta in search of food'.[51] One of the most striking features of the Bengal famine is the extent of such migration;[52] this exodus also becomes one of the central motifs in representations of the famine, whether in non-fictional or fictional form. The urban emphasis which generally characterizes Bengali famine literature differentiates it from other representations, in particular from Irish literature of famine. Most frequently, as the following texts demonstrate, the famine story tells of the movement of country-folk to Calcutta and their plight there, rarely with a possibility of return.

The Bengal famine is the subject of a significant number of literary texts, with novels written by Bhabani Bhattacharya and Tarasankar Bandyopadhyay, and many short stories, including works by Ela Sen, Krishan Chandar and Manik Bandyopadhyay.[53] Many of these narratives, such as Tarasankar's novel and Manik's story, were written in Bengali, or, in the case of Krishan Chandar's stories, Urdu; English translations of all three texts are now available. Others, such as Bhabani Bhattacharya's two famine novels and Ela Sen's collection of short stories, were written in English. The general nature of these literary representations of famine will be explored in this section; the significance and the specific forms of their 'feminization of famine' constitute the subject of the remainder of the chapter.

The three texts first to be discussed were published in the immediate aftermath of famine; the first, Krishan Chandar's *Ann Dātā*, underlines famine's existence, thus challenging the evasion and denial practised both by outsiders and men of power within Bengal. Tarasankar's novel, *Manwantar*, deals with the prelude to famine, while famine's aftermath provides the subject of Ela Sen's collection of stories, *Darkening Days*. In the years after, the 'famine of fifty' continued to provide the subject for fiction writers, in short stories such as Manik Bandyopadhyay's 'Aaj Kal Parshur Galpa' and, most famously, in the fiction of Indo-Anglian writer, Bhabani Bhattacharya, whose novel *So Many Hungers!* remains one of the best-known Indian famine narratives.

The particular historical context of the Bengal famine determined the nature of its literary representations in interesting ways. Originating, at least in part, in war measures and aggravated by government inefficiency and indifference, the famine was quickly to become, in Amartya Sen's words, 'a focal point of nationalist criticism of British imperial policy in India'.[54] From this perspective, famine constituted the climax of British rule – or misrule – in India; in Nehru's words, the final tragic act in Britain's long history of 'indifference, incompetence, and complacency', and hence a decisive argument for self-government.[55] Many of the famine authors whose work forms the subject of this chapter shared this viewpoint; in their writings, famine is part of a much longer story which extends back to the outbreak of war in 1939 and whose origins lie in the imperialist rule of India. As image of the consequences of imperial rule, famine also serves as inspiration and justification for the independence movement. Hunger and suffering become, most obviously in Bhabani Bhattacharya's work, metaphors, not only for political oppression and unjust deprivation, but also for a transcendent resistance. One of the most interesting features of such representations is the emergence of the hunger-strike as famine's obverse; the physical experience of hunger is now chosen as a mark of protest and spiritual resistance. Yet, as will be more fully explored in the next section, the strategies made available to men and women in famine texts are very distinct, with the issue of resistance displaying the most marked gender division.

Ann Dātā (I cannot die), by the Urdu writer Krishan Chandar, is one of the most powerful literary treatments of the Bengal famine. Published immediately after the famine, the narrative was translated into English by Kwaja Ahmad Abbas.[56] By the mid-1940s, Chandar was already a well-established literary figure, author of six collections of short stories and one of the most famous members of the Progressive Writers' Association, sharing the group's belief in a 'literature of purpose'.[57] According to his translator, *Ann Dātā* was quickly recognized as a 'land-mark' among stories of the Bengal famine in any Indian language, as well as 'recording the highest achievement in the realm of Urdu short story'. Abbas rightly emphasizes Chandar's power to render the catastrophe vivid and real, 'depicting a vast and horrible social phenomenon – the destitution of a whole people – in terms of individual human experience'; his success, reminiscent of O'Flaherty, a contemporary social realist, lies in 'personalizing the misery of the mass' without 'reducing the frightful proportions of the tragedy'.[58]

Chandar's text consists of three short stories, told from different points of view yet subtly linked. The first story, 'The Man with a Thorn in His Conscience', is told through a series of letters written by a foreign consul, stationed in Calcutta, to the head of his country's government. Ulluson, consul for the 'Republic of Silorica', describes events in Bengal from August to November 1943; through this device Chandar delivers a biting satire on official discourses regarding famine and destitution. As late as November, the Bengal government refuses to provide official confirmation that famine exists despite the presence of more and more corpses in the Calcutta streets. Although Ulluson himself witnesses dead bodies on the steps of the consulate, including a child 'trying to suckle the dried-up breast of his dead mother', and is haunted by the 'dead, stony, unmoving, unseeing eyes' of a musician's corpse, he enthusiastically employs the prevalent euphemism that the dying people are suffering from 'a strange and terrible disease'.[59] News on 25 August 1943 that the Bengal Assembly 'has decided that neither Calcutta nor the other districts of Bengal can be declared "famine areas"' is received 'with great satisfaction' by Ulluson and the other consuls; as he explains, 'if Bengal had been declared a "famine area" rationing would have had to be enforced and even we would have been affected'.[60] Proposals made to the consul that his government should provide famine relief are countered by the familiar argument against 'interference' in another country's affairs. The stereotype, frequent in famine representations, that the hungry are guilty of gluttony also appears; thus Ulluson concludes that 'the food shortage has been caused by the Indians' habit of over-eating'.[61] In November 1943, as starvation deaths have reached their peak and epidemics continue to spread, he leaves Calcutta, 'unable to answer' whether or not there is famine in Bengal.

The second and third stories tell of 'The Man Who Is Dead!' and 'The Man Who Is Alive'. The 'dead' man belongs to the upper classes of Bengal and briefly flirts with the notion of sacrificing his life to the service of his 'starving, ill-clad, dying fellow-countrymen'.[62] His plans quickly evaporate when faced with the reality of destitution, and the hollowness of his dedication is revealed. Chandar thus carefully locates responsibility for famine in two spheres: the international community which fails to intervene and the injustices and exploitation within Bengali society. His third story then moves to the perspective of a famine victim, a dead man who compels the attention of his listeners:

> Do not turn away from me with aversion and disgust. I am also a human being like you – a creature of blood and flesh and bones. It is true that now there are more bones than flesh in my body, that my tissues have begun to rot and an unhealthy odour rises from them. But this is after all the simple chemical process of decomposition. The only difference between your body and mine is that my heart action has stopped, my brain has refused to function and my stomach has caved in because of many days of starvation.[63]

In one of the most detailed portrayals of a famine victim, Chandar's story recounts the man's history as teacher of music to the daughter of a zamindar or landlord in a Bengali village, his marriage and the birth of his child. In 1943, rice soars in price and then vanishes; in the musician's words:

> the truth is what intervenes between growing and eating is by itself the whole history of man's evolution, the correct interpretation of his culture, his civilization, religion, philosophy and literature. Growing and Eating. Two simple words. But think of the deep gulf that separates them.[64]

The family, in desperation, join the 'army of ants' moving towards Calcutta. On this 'caravan of death', the narrator encounters husbands selling wives, mothers selling their daughters, brothers selling their sisters. His own wife dies before reaching the city: 'I did not bury her. I did not cremate her. I just left her by the road-side and, holding my child in my arms, marched on.' Soon after, his daughter dies, 'thirsting for a drop of milk'.[65] As the story nears the end, the musician starves on the steps of Ulluson's consulate.

In the final paragraphs, the fate of this one individual is juxtaposed with events on the world stage. Immediately after the musician has died, news vendors declare that 'The Big Three Meet in Tehran . . . A New World is Born!' The dead man's response is to question, 'Will the millions of us, the poor and the starving and the oppressed of the earth, also have a hand in the building of this

New World?'⁶⁶ On such an occasion, Chandar's style veers into melodrama and the understated tone of much of the story gives way to direct political rhetoric: 'So long as a single man goes without food, the whole world will starve; so long as there is a single man who is poor, all will remain poor; so long as there is a single man who is a slave every man in the world will remain in bondage.'⁶⁷ Yet, the story is ultimately quite successful in its individuation of famine, figuring what was to emerge as the death of millions through one 'single man' and tracing, with great precision, the operation of others' denial and evasion. In the context of its detailed depiction of a male victim, an infrequent focus in famine literature, it is striking that Chandar's portrayal includes a forceful political perspective; even in death, the man continues to voice a political analysis, so often denied to female figures.

The earliest novelistic depiction of the 1940s famine may be found in Tarasankar Bandyopadhyay's *Manwantar*, written in Bengali and first published in January 1944.⁶⁸ *Manwantar* (Epoch's end), is significantly less concerned with the individual experience; instead, its interest lies in the more impersonal forces which produce famine. Set in Calcutta, the first of Tarasankar's novels to have an urban location, it spans the period of December 1942 to March 1943, famine's prelude. The consequences of war are apparent: prices soar and 'gambling galore' develops in the markets, the urban poor are displaced by military camps, and Japanese air attacks on the city cause death and widespread damage. Panic-stricken city-dwellers, leaving Calcutta, meet an influx of destitutes entering the city, refugees from the cyclone in Midnapore and other migrants:

Calcutta's pavements offered a strange spectacle. Destitutes, with nowhere to lay their heads, sat there or spread themselves out in various postures of listless repose. Their clothes were tattered and hardly covered a woman's shame. The skeleton of a mother could often be seen, sitting with a vacant look in her eyes, with an infant crying at intervals and vainly trying to suck at her shrivelled breasts. Little nude children would stare at the city's strange sights, their natural curiosity and playfulness numbed by hunger and awe. Rows of men and women slept on the pavements, with no covering on their bodies and no roof to their heads, even when it was cold. They had organized a kind of life of their own, quarrelling, gossiping, begging, love-making with furtive desperation. Death on the streets had begun to happen.[69]

As hungry people pour into the city, 'war was being followed, inevitably, by famine'; a newspaper, marking the New Year of 1943, carries the following cartoon:

The ghoul of war was shown in a whirl – '39, '40, '41, '42, '43. And it snapped its fingers and from out of the earth was emerging a hideous skeleton, the figure of a female, wrathful, famishing and nearly nude, – it was famine. And just behind her peeped another spectre, the skin torn out of its face – it was pestilence. Up on the sky flew hordes of carrion-crows and vultures, shells burst, planes roared, the sun was hidden behind a sinister mist. The caption to the cartoon was – 'New Year, 1943'.[70]

In this sketch, famine itself is visualized as female: 'wrathful, famishing and nearly nude', with a focus on her angry force rather than pathetic consequence; as such, she embodies the 'wrath of Kali', a feature of Bengali representations to be explored in more detail later.

Tarasankar's vision, as this extract illustrates, is essentially apocalyptic, with war, famine and pestilence marking the 'epoch's end'. With the exception of the description of the city destitutes quoted above, the novel provides little characterization of famine's effects; instead famine exists as a symptom of a deeper crisis and prelude to an ultimate rebirth. Generational conflict unfolds between parents and children: Kanai, the novel's hero, frees himself from his once-rich, now decaying family; Geeta, whose family live in a bustee or mud-hut, is sold into prostitution by her father; the Communist reformers, Neela and Nepi, also become alienated from their families. These tensions are examples of a widespread breakdown, 'a mighty cataclysm', but one which heralds, for Tarasankar, another 'epoch', bringing 'freedom from injustice and oppression and exploitation'.[71] Writing in late 1943, with deaths from disease at their peak, Tarasankar looks beyond the immediate scene, presenting famine as a symptom of a deeper collapse and ultimate renewal. As the novel closes, the theme of famine gives way to hunger as a symbol of protest and liberation, embodied by Gandhi's fast in February 1943, and culminating in a final prophecy of independence: 'the great day when after the sacrificial rites the nectar of freedom will be churned by the people and a brave new world will ensue'.[72]

In stark contrast to *Manwantar*, the immediate and continuing impact of the famine and the urgency for rehabilitation are the central subjects of Ela Sen's *Darkening Days*, a collection of short stories written in English and first published in 1944.[73] Writing from Calcutta, in April 1944, Sen argues vehemently, in the foreword to her stories, against prevalent arguments that the famine is now over:

> The famine is not over. A cry has gone up that it is, and philan-thropists have begun to curtail their philanthropy. The sufferings of our people have been deposited beyond our vision to give credence that all is well once more. But the aftermath is upon us, the havoc created by famine has to be faced if the people of this province are ever again to live fully.[74]

The purpose of her narrative, therefore, is 'to show the urgency of our needs and on how large a scale relief is necessary if ever Bengal is to be reincarnated'. A detailed preface expands on the problems facing Bengal in the aftermath of famine: crops mortgaged to landlords, the 'spectral population' weakened and demoralized, the absence of 'concrete and strong' leaders:

> Leaderless and lost, all thoughts of nation or country drowned in the vital, gnawing, primeval pains of hunger, the population floundered on in a spirit of reckless bitterness. Many and sundry tried to minis-ter to their bodies, but nobody thought of the shrivelling up soul.[75]

Sen's stories reinforce this vision of a 'floundering', 'spectral population' through a focus on individuals' experience of famine, the survival strategies adopted by the poor and their ill-fated consequences. On occasion, they offer insight into the wider economic and political context but always from the perspective of an individual. Thus, in 'She Was Not Alone', Gouri realizes that the rich man who 'keeps' her has made his fortune through speculating in rice; she and many others are 'pawns' in his game of buying and selling.[76] In 'Two Sisters', Amina's resorting to prostitution is made possible by the nearby presence of an army base, while the general devastation experienced by her village also results from war measures – 'this strange thing, this war' which 'had leaped upon them as from behind an ambush'.[77] The suffering experienced by destitute women living on Calcutta's streets is portrayed by 'The Queue': one woman sells her body in a vain effort to save her child, another woman gives birth on the pavement, alone and unaided. Much of the strength of Sen's stories lies in their personal quality, detailing the desperate measures employed by villagers and city destitutes. Fishing folk sell their boats and nets, weavers sell their looms, women turn to prostitution, the conventions of caste and class are broken. Throughout, Sen focuses on the particular victimization of women, explaining and defending this emphasis in her foreword: 'This book is admittedly written from a woman's point of view, if on this account over-emphasis is laid on the vicissitudes of women during the dreadful days of last year it is not for want of appreciation of the sufferings of men.'[78] The plight of women, and specifically the consequences of widespread prostitution, emerges from *Darkening Days* as the most urgent problem facing Bengali society since, in Sen's words, 'Upon woman depends greatly the balance and morale of a nation, and therefore the seriousness of the calamity is of extraordinary significance.'[79]

Similarly, 'Aaj Kal Parshur Galpa', or 'A Tale of These Days', a short story by the Bengali writer Manik Bandyopadhyay, concerns the problems of return experienced by women who have worked as prostitutes during the time of famine.[80] Manik was, by the 1940s, a very established novelist, author of *The Boatman of the Padma* and *The Puppet's Tale*. In this story, set in the aftermath of the famine, he explores the demoralization and indifference of those who have survived: 'Almost all the common people were wounded, harassed, feeling socially discarded themselves; their spirits were broken along with their bodies.'[81] Few families are left intact, with many dead from starvation and disease; others 'lost track of – hardly two of a ten-member family tottering back home from their separate journeys for food'; and many young wives and girls 'picked up by procurers and traffickers'.[82] Manik's story evokes, with special power, the psychological condition of those who have survived: 'Not everybody who survived physically managed to survive mentally, to pick up the pieces of their cruelly broken lives. Very few were in a fit condition either to be brought back or to be brought back to.'[83]

On the one hand, stories such as those by Chandar, Ela Sen and Manik dramatize individuals' hunger and starvation and suggest that the dilemmas faced by famine victims continue long after the immediate crisis is over. Other narratives, such as Tarasankar's novel, explore the processes underlying the event of famine and offer some vision of transcendence. Clearly, in the year after the famine, differing interpretations of famine's origin and significance had already developed. In the preface and afterword to her stories, Sen engages with some prevalent views of famine's causation. Unambiguously, she locates the source of famine within the wider political structure, 'not "an act of God" but a political failure'.[84] Responsibility for this 'political failure' is shared among the provincial government, the central government, the Viceroy and the Secretary of State for India. In addition, those guilty of hoarding and profiteering are castigated: from the 'big trader' who sent 'millions of rupees worth of rice underground for the black market', the 'agricultural landlord' who held back rice from normal trade, to the 'upper class householders', people 'in our midst, among our relatives, our aunts and uncles' who panicked and 'kept large stocks in reserve for their consumption'.[85] Yet, underlying all of these factors, for Sen, is the view that 'it was the core that was rotten and therefore the flesh had grown poisonous'; in other words, 'as long as Whitehall rules over India, it is upon Britain that the final blame must rest'.[86] Once again, the depiction of famine leads to the conclusion that 'the entire edifice of imperialism' be destroyed and a 'truly national' government established.[87]

Some three years after the Bengal famine had ended, its most famous literary representation appeared. *So Many Hungers!*, written in English, was first published in 1947; its author, Bhabani

Bhattacharya, was later to become one of the best-known Indo-Anglian novelists.[88] Bhattacharya had previously and unsuccessfully attempted novel-writing; then, in his words, 'the great famine swept down upon Bengal. The emotional stirrings I felt (more than two million men, women and children died of slow starvation and a man-made scarcity) were a sheer compulsion to creativity. The result was the novel *So Many Hungers!*'[89] Elsewhere, the author recounts a more complex genesis for his novel, in which the inspiration for writing and the fortunes of the finished manuscript are critically influenced by contemporary political developments. Having written some chapters relating to the famine, he put the novel aside:

> Time passed. A year and more . . . Meanwhile, on the Indian political scene, history had been rapidly in the making. The fight with British imperialism was moving to its climax. How come that no creative writer was telling the great story? . . . The two stories of the time – the hungers and the Quit India movement – were intrinsically one. So I recovered the manuscript and went ahead . . . There it was. Done! But no Indian publisher could possibly accept it because of the risk involved. Publication abroad, if possible? There was the censorship on mail! At that point history came to my help. The British rulers quit.[90]

As the title indicates, Bhattacharya's narrative identifies the years of 1942 to 1943 as a time of 'many hungers': not alone for food but also revealing what the novelist has called 'the money hunger, the sex hunger' and, above all, 'the hunger to achieve India's political freedom'.[91] The story of famine is thus entwined with that of independence throughout the novel, unlike Sen's narrative in which discourse and story remain separate, or in Tarasankar's novel in which the political vision displaces the famine scene. The twinned stories of hunger and the movement for independence are characterized through two families, one urban and one rural. Rahoul, the wealthy son of a Calcutta speculator, is increasingly drawn to the nationalist sentiments of his grandfather; meanwhile, his grandfather has also become father-figure or 'Dadu' to the people of Baruni, a small Bengal coastal village. The novel traces in detail the coming of famine to Baruni, caused primarily by the government's 'scorched-earth policy' which ordains that the locals' boats be destroyed. In the words of one fisherman,

> Boats are the limbs of us folk. They are our legs, for without them we are lamed, we cannot move over the river highways from village to village or from islet to islet. They are our arms, for with them we reap the land, and some fish we eat and some we give for rice and salt and things on offer at the market-place. Boats are more than limbs for us folk: they are our blood and bone and heart and soul and all.[92]

The forced sale of food, together with the dispossession of people caused by the building of military camps, delivers a fatal blow to the village economy:

> It was man-made scarcity, for the harvest had been fair, and even if the Army bought up big stocks, with rationing at the right level there could be food for all. But there was no rationing. Forty thousand country boats wantonly destroyed. Many villages evacuated. The uprooted people pauperized. Inflated currency added the finishing touch.[93]

Anticipating the analysis of economists such as Amartya Sen, Bhattacharya argues that the collapse of traditional systems of production and distribution lies at the heart of famine, caused by the single-minded 'war effort' and exploited by private speculators. The belief by uneducated peasants that they were still ruled by the East India Company is shown to have a certain ironic validity; in 1943 a new 'Kompanee' is established to secure and hoard food, and its agents quickly spread all over the region – 'There had been nothing like this in Bengal – ever.'[94]

From an initial fatalism, Bhattacharya's rural characters develop a range of strategies to survive, searching for edible roots, selling their possessions, even their cattle. Traditional relationships come under threat: the small boy, Onu, and his friends 'are torn wide apart by their need for survival';[95] women sleep naked in order to protect their clothes from wear; women sell their daughters into sexual slavery. Focusing on the fate of Onu, Kajoli, his sister, and their mother, Bhattacharya presents a series of episodes which mark the growing desperation of the family. The 'mother' gives their cow to another mother who has contemplated killing her starving child; immediately afterwards she encounters another mother who has sold her daughter. Hoping to find Kajoli's husband who has left for the city, the family join the procession of hunger-marchers; on the way to Calcutta, Kajoli is raped. Over and over again in the narrative, the sexual debasement and exploitation of women is used to depict the ugliness and injustices of famine. Meanwhile, on the political scene, the 'Quit India' movement gathers force. The narrative's conclusion aims to keep these two stories entwined; thus Kajoli, who is about to support her family through prostitution, is 'redeemed' through hearing of the hunger-strike of the grandfather and other political prisoners. The hunger of starvation yields to hunger as a tool of political protest; from the famine scene comes a vision of the new epoch, 'the freedom to be free':

> This famine, this brutal doom, was the fulfilment of alien rule. The final commentary. Imagine two million Englishmen dying of hunger that was preventable, and the Government unaffected, uncensored, unrepentant, smug as ever! 'Quit India!' cried the two million dead of Bengal.[96]

The growing significance of resistance and its domination of the story of famine are most apparent in Bhattacharya's second famine novel, *He Who Rides a Tiger*.[97] The early part of the narrative recounts the story of a blacksmith, Kalo, who leaves his famine-stricken village to find work in Calcutta. The only employment available to him is as a 'harlot-house agent'; one evening, he discovers his daughter in the brothel, led there by his employers' deception. Resolved on 'hitting back', Kalo masquerades as a holy man, hoping to damn the souls of those who believe in him; likewise Lekha, his daughter, the girl who 'had almost fallen', is deified as the 'Mother of Sevenfold Bliss'.[98] The famine experience is quickly dispatched and serves more as prelude to the narrative's chief concern, one man's vengeance against those responsible for the exploitation of his daughter. When Kalo ultimately reveals the truth, the story of his act of deception becomes a 'legend of freedom' for the poor, along with the hunger-strikes and hunger-marches of the time.⁹⁹ Thus, the potential tension between famine, as story of victimization, and the story of national liberation is once again resolved, with hunger made the sign of resistance and rebellion.

SHAKTI, SATI, SAVITRI: THE FATE OF FEMALE FIGURES

In Hindu mythology, *shakti* means 'divine power or energy', personified as female.¹⁰⁰ Thus, the term is applied to the wife of a god, specifically the god Shiva, signifying the power and special efficacy of the deity manifested in and through his consort Shakti.¹⁰¹ The goddess Shakti is worshipped in a variety of forms: as Mother Goddess, as tender and devoted wife, or figure of terror. Her numerous incarnations as Shiva's wife include Parvati, goddess of beauty, and Sati, meaning 'true', the 'good wife' who, embodying devotion and piety, threw herself into a sacrificial fire and was consumed.¹⁰² Similar figures of fidelity are Savitri, a heroine of the *Mahabharata*, Sita, wife of Rama, and her incarnation, Lakshmi, spouse of Vishnu and goddess of good fortune and prosperity. Shakti's 'terror' aspects, as deity of destruction rather than devotion or prosperity, are personified by Durga, 'the invincible', later symbol of Bengal nationalism, and the related figure of Kali, 'the black', ugly and bloodthirsty goddess of death.

Although mythical figures such as Sati or Savitri are of ancient origin, their literary prominence as icons of the nation is much more recent. The emergence of this 'construct' and its role in nationalist ideology is the subject of a provocative essay by Partha Chatterjee, focusing on nationalist treatment of 'the women's question' in nineteenth-century Bengal:

> Whatever be its sources in the classical religions of India or in medieval religious practices, it is undeniable that the specific ideological form in which we now know the Sati–Savitri–Sita construct in the modern literature and arts of India today is wholly a product of the development of a dominant middle class culture coeval with the era of nationalism. It served to emphasize with all the force of

mythological inspiration what had in any case become a dominant characteristic of femininity in the new woman, viz. the 'spiritual' qualities of self-sacrifice, benevolence, devotion, religiosity, etc.[103]

Chatterjee demonstrates that the traditional dichotomies of home and the world, of inner and outer life, gained a special significance in nationalist thought. The world, as 'material sphere' and male domain, was where the claims of western civilization were most powerful, its superior technologies to be imitated by the East. The home, on the other hand, was where the 'spiritual essence of the national culture' – distinctive and superior – was located; as the 'true self' of the nation, this female domain must remain unchanged: 'No encroachments by the colonizer must be allowed in that inner sanctum. In the world, imitation of and adaptation to western norms was a necessity; at home, they were tantamount to annihilation of one's very identity.' Since the home served as the central expression of the nation's spiritual life and distinctive nature, women were given 'the main responsibility of protecting and nurturing this quality'. Hence nationalist writings celebrated women's 'godlike' qualities of self-sacrifice and spiritual purity, in contrast to the degenerate westernized woman or the common, promiscuous, lower-class woman. As Chatterjee summarizes:

> The new patriarchy advocated by nationalism conferred upon women the honour of a new social responsibility, and by associating the task of 'female emancipation' with the historical goal of sovereign nationhood, bound them to a new, and yet entirely legitimate, subordination.[104]

On women thus fell 'the burden of saving the nation', of preserving its distinctive character, through their self-sacrifice, purity and passivity.[105]

A related aspect of nationalist ideology is its emphasis on the maternal; in the words of Subhas Bose, 'The spiritual quest of Bengal has always been voiced through the cult of the Mother.'[106] Early nationalist poems and songs such as Bankimchandra Chatterjee's 'Bande Mātaram' (Hail to the Mother)[107] and, two generations later, Tagore's 'Āmār Sōnār Bānglā' (My Golden

Bengal)[108] characterized Bengal as motherland or 'Mother Bengal', a loving mother who provides her children with abundance. Later generations reinforced the religious character of the mother-figure; 'the Motherland' becomes 'the Mother Goddess, dominating the world of Gods and demanding the highest sacrifice from all'.[109]

The gendering of political identity as a strategy of oppression and resistance, what Ashis Nandy calls the 'homology of sexual and political dominance', forms a central theme in *The Intimate Enemy*, his study of the psychology of colonialism in India.[110] Nandy shows how the 'hypermasculinity' of colonialism was responded to, at first, by a similar emphasis on the part of the colonized subject. The significance of Gandhian ideology, he argues, lay in its reordering of femininity as superior to masculinity in power and activism, through the doctrines of *ahimsa* or non-violence; femininity, previously attributed to the colonized nation as a derogatory sign, was embraced and redefined; the 'sacrificial complex' became a vital strategy of resistance and ultimate liberation.[111] Yet as the work of Tanika Sarkar and others has shown, the extent of liberation offered to women by this celebration of the feminine principle was significantly limited.[112] Since patriotic struggle was characterized and internalized as a religious duty, any potential challenge to traditional gender roles arising from women's involvement in Indian political life could be restrained by an emphasis on nationalism's 'gentle, patient, long-suffering, sacrificial ambience' – 'particularly appropriate for the woman'.[113] A striking example is that of female members of the terrorist movement in Bengal who sought to locate their action within traditional models, primarily that of the sacrificing Sati figure; 'the woman terrorist in Bengal', Sarkar writes, 'seemed to claim equality in an act of sacrifice at an extraordinary crisis point, but did not extend this to a claim for equality in political choice and action'.[114]

With regard to literary representations of women, the familiar contradiction between mythical, idealized models of woman and women's inferior position in social and economic life is the subject of commentaries by a number of Indian literary critics. Critics such as Meena Shirwadkar and Shantha Krishnaswamy point to the disparity in Indian fiction between woman 'deified as the centre of culture' and women 'imprisoned in the walls of the family and shackled by tradition'.[115] Ujjal Dutta's discussion of 'Woman in Bengali fiction' explores how this disparity has evolved, arguing that 'the issue of woman's economic and social inferiority and her simultaneous elevation in the form of mother or *Grihalakshmi* or *Sakti* is basically one of imaginary mystification, that is, masking the reality with imaginary relation'; woman is thus compensated 'on the ideological plane for what she lost in actuality'.[116] Dutta's analysis includes a useful summary of the recurring female figures in Bengali narratives, characterizations which originate in, and sustain, mythical types:

> The woman is mother, taking care of her children, patient, self-sacrificing, abundant in her gifts like the mother earth: the woman is *Grihalakshmi*, symbolizing the prosperity of home: she is *Sahadharmini*, identifying herself with the dharma of her husband, her master: she is *Sati*, her life begins and ends with her husband's: she is *Kshetra*, an open field for her master's use: she is *Sakti*, the primal source of energy. The moment the woman is seen to lead her own life, to act in conformity with her own nature and not according to the specifications of the role assigned to her she loses favour with us, she is damned.[117]

Striking parallels exist between Dutta's work and recent critiques of 'woman as nation' in Irish literature, specifically Eavan Boland's highlighting of the objectification and idealization of women throughout Irish poetic representations.[118]

Drawing from these studies of female representations and their role in nationalist ideology, I wish to explore, in this section, what happens to images of women in the specific context of famine literature. Given the extremity of the subject, the difficulties of representation and the scale of suffering involved, what is the fate of the idealized female figure – whether Shakti, primal source of energy, or Lakshmi, goddess of abundance?

Literary representations of the Bengal famine demonstrate, once again, the primacy of maternity, with many depictions of acts of maternal self-sacrifice and self-denial. This idealization is most clearly evident in Bhabani Bhattacharya's portrayal, in *So Many*

Hungers!, of the mother of Kajoli and Onu. The mother functions both as an individual character and as symbol, 'mother to all', personifying to other characters the spirit of 'Mother Bengal'. Her child, Kajoli, is similarly 'daughter of earth'.[119] Famine's presence is signalled by the mother's inability to feed her family and by the conflict she experiences when she witnesses others' needs. Encountering a woman about to bury her child alive because she has no food to give it, 'the mother' gives to the younger woman the cow which is her family's last means of sustenance.[120] At the end of the narrative, she plans to commit suicide in order to improve her son's and daughter's chances of survival; 'It was hard enough to feed oneself; what misery to have to provide for a decrepit mother who ailed without cease and could not walk down to the free kitchen . . . Mother Ganges hailed her.' 'Hauling' herself up to the rail of the river-bridge, she remains suspended there – as individual character and as icon.[121] Shakti's traditional role of giver and protector of life, ensuring the continuity and vitality of her race, is thus tragically inverted; in one of the most recognizable images of crisis, the mother can secure her children's futures and, by extension, that of the patrilineage, only through yielding her own.

The emotional investment in the maternal ideal displayed by many writers appears with special vividness in Ela Sen's work. In her preface, Sen comments at length on the spectacle of 'mother-hood' during famine:

> Out of this ghastly panorama there emerged one beauty – mother-hood. Emaciated, broken in body, with a baby in her arms and three others, clustering round her ragged remnant of a *sari*, she trudged miles every day looking for food for the hungry little mouths . . . Through all the abnormality of her life the woman never forgot or grudged her motherhood. Wherever she went she kept her brood close at her heels; whatever she found was first for them though often she looked on with wolfish hunger in her eyes. In the midst of this primeval cry for food the gaunt and spectral mother with her brood of skeleton children epitomised the spirit of Bengal's women – undaunted and alive in the midst of death, pure as a flame amongst garbage. Was it a newer edition of Niobe

that greeted one? Or could it have been yet another version of the Madonna?[122]

Within Sen's apostrophe to the beauty of motherhood, physical details of women's suffering and emaciation are gradually displaced by an emphasis on their heroic spirit, 'undaunted and alive'. Analogies between this 'gaunt and spectral mother', epitome of 'Bengal's women', and Niobe or Madonna, other suffering mother-figures, complete the move into the symbolic sphere.[123]

The limitations of this maternal figure of famine, however, become immediately apparent; as the author continues, 'One question rises naturally from this – how then did they sell their children?'[124] Ela Sen's response is concise: the sale of children was only 'an extreme measure', employed by women 'when they felt that no longer could they do anything for them and that it was better they should get a proper life with somebody who could'.[125] The disturbing reality that parents sold, even killed, their children may thus be explained as actions which, however terrible, were well-intentioned:

> They passionately wanted their young to live, and for this they sold or 'deserted' their children in such convenient places where they felt they would be taken care of . . . A large number of women became bereft of their senses through privation and want, and rather than watch their children die slowly and in pain, they would put them out of their misery – in the same way as an animal will not allow a decrepit offspring to live.[126]

The terms used by Sen to describe the mothers' actions betray an uncertainty and vacillation common to treatments of this troubling and complex topic. The mothers are shown both as 'bereft of their senses' and as people who act with a rational motivation; the final analogy resolves this ambiguity by removing their actions from the human realm. A similar ambivalence continues in Sen's stories: on the one hand, they present a joyful reunion between a mother and child and a mother's determination to sacrifice all for her child; others tell of separation and abandonment. In one story, 'She Was Not Alone', the mother, Gouri, is described as taken over by 'some

ogre', 'bereft of all sense except the sting of hunger'.[127] She sets
down her child in order to fight for food; when she returns, the
child has been mauled by a pariah dog; and, although Gouri falls
'snarling' upon the animal, she is too late to save her child. Sen
terms the mother's actions in seeking food both 'mechanical' and
evidence of 'the desire to live', equivocating as to whether or not
they be deemed reprehensible, even comprehensible.[128]

The desperate actions and adaptive strategies which inevitably
form part of the story of famine thus severely test the idealizing
impulse to which writers like Bhattacharya and Sen are drawn. As
mentioned earlier, an event depicted again and again in Bengali
famine literature, in one of the most harrowing and challenging
visions of the destruction wrought in family relationships, is that of
parents selling their children in exchange for money and food.
References to the sale of young girls into prostitution by their
parents, most frequently by their mothers, occur in Tarasankar's
Manwantar, in Krishan Chandar's *Ann Dātā* and Bhattacharya's *So
Many Hungers!* In the latter novel, 'the mother' encounters a
woman who has sold her daughter into prostitution. A similar
offer is made to the mother for her daughter Kajoli; although she
determinedly refuses, the taunt delivered by the other woman is a
haunting one: 'You, too, will eat one day, for you have a daughter.'[129] Ulluson, the foreign consul who, in Chandar's opening
story, refuses to confirm famine's existence, encounters a woman
who seeks to sell her daughter for 'a rupee and a half' which, as the
narrator points out, is less than the price of 'a China doll'.[130] The
letter to his employer, in which Ulluson describes this prevalent
practice, includes a detailed calculation of the price and contemporary exchange-value of young girls:

> My chauffeur tells me that Sonagachi (where all the brothels are
> situated) is a regular slave-market. Hundreds of girls are being
> bought and sold every day. Parents sell them, and prostitutes buy
> them. The usual price is a rupee and a quarter. But if the girl is
> good-looking she might fetch four or five or even ten rupees. Rice
> costs about a rupee a pound. So if a family can sell two of its girls, it
> has enough rice for a week or two. And the average Bengali family
> has more than two girls.[131]

In Chandar's third story, the selling of children is made even more immediate. The narrator, rural peasant and unemployed musician, recounts how all around him families were selling their women-members – wives, sisters and daughters: 'Religion, morality, spiritualism, motherhood – all the strongest ideals and emotions of humanity had been stripped off.'[132] Finally, his own wife proposes the sale of their daughter. Deeply shocked by this suggestion, the narrator, soon himself to become one of famine's fatalities, ponders on the fate of 'motherhood':

> What horrible power had killed her motherhood, crushed her soul? . . . Her wild hair was matted with dust, her sari was in tatters, the sore in her right foot was bleeding . . . That incomparable beauty in which was summed up all the majesty of the Taj, the fascination of Ellora, the immortality of Asoka's edicts! Where was it today? Why was this beauty, this soul, this majesty of motherhood lying today in the dust like a trampled, disfigured corpse? . . . If it is true that Woman is a miracle, a faith, that she is the essence and the truth of life, then I say that this faith, this truth, this miracle is born of a grain of rice and without that it dies![133]

Chandar's story vividly demonstrates, on one hand, the fatal challenge delivered by famine to the 'majesty of motherhood'. Yet the language through which this breakdown is conveyed also betrays a tendency, shared by many famine authors, to replace the lost maternal ideal with equally stereotypical characterizations. The narrator's wife, no longer of 'incomparable beauty' and fallen from the pantheon of goddesses, changes from 'sea-nymph' to 'witch'.[134] Sen's stories demonstrate a similar descent: women who depart from the 'beauty' of motherhood are presented in animalistic terms; no longer Niobe or Madonna, they become less rather than super-human. Throughout famine narratives, both Irish and Bengali, the inability of the maternal ideal to accommodate the 'fearful realities' of the time, when such a failure is acknowledged, can be spoken only in the most generalized of terms; rarely does the challenge thus posed to representations result in a characterization of subtlety and complexity.

On some occasions, the collapse of the ideal produces the heroic mother's 'monstrous' opposite. A striking example of this process occurs towards the end of Bhattacharya's *So Many Hungers!* in which the picture of a mother and child comes to epitomize the social consequences of famine. Rahoul, while flipping the pages of a newspaper, lingers at one particular illustration:

> A woman sat on the pavement eating from a bowl while her famished child sat by and gazed. The camera had done its work well. The child, a skeleton with unwinking eyes, perhaps too feeble to cry, gazed on while the hunger-mad mother ate with ravenous gulps.[135]

This 'cruel picture' reminds him of a story in the papers: 'A starving mother with a child at her breast was given food at a kitchen. While she ate, the child died in her lap. But the mother ate on. She finished her meal, and then left with her dead child.' The 'story' referred to by Bhattacharya would appear to be that published in the *Hindusthan Standard*, on 11 October 1943. Writing from Chandpur region, the correspondent relates that:

> A report has reached here from the cooked food distribution center at Asta-Mahamaya, within P. S. Faridgunj, opened by the Bengal Relief Committee there, that a starving mother with a child in her lap, was taking food distributed at the center. In the meantime the child died in her lap. The mother did not stop to take her food and after finishing her meal she left with the dead child.[136]

In Bhattacharya's narrative, these 'grim pictures' have a wider implication, making manifest an 'inner degradation' and 'emotional hardening' among the people of Bengal which will render famine's legacies long and painful. Thus Rahoul, musing on the picture of the 'hunger-mad' mother and her child, imagines a scene, one year ahead, when this mother has returned to her village home and, one day, discovers the newspaper picture:

> She has recognized her dead child – for the image of him ever fills her eyes – and though she cannot see herself in the evil shape in

the picture, she knows it is none other. There she is, a mother filling her hunger-swollen belly while her skeleton child looks on beggingly. He died. Maybe those mouthfuls would have saved him. A monster, not a mother. A monster that ate its child . . . she sits with the picture in her lap, crazy with her shame and her anguish.[137]

The mother's identification of the 'evil shape' as her own self serves not to explain her actions but only to intensify the condemnation: 'A monster, not a mother. A monster that ate its child.' Far from the pole of 'Good Mother', source of nurture and protection, the famine woman becomes 'Terrible Mother', guilty not only of rejection and deprivation but of devouring, Kali-like, her own child.

The crisis of famine, when figured in maternal terms, marks the collapse of Lakshmi, goddess of prosperity and abundance: the mother/land unable to sustain her children, the mother unable to feed her child. In the mythology of Bengal, as Paul Greenough explains, 'Lakshmi is typically portrayed as a compassionate mother who takes pity upon poor and suffering persons', her principal roles being 'remover of sorrows and destined provider of subsistence'.[138] Her presence, and also the fatal challenges posed to her role, are movingly suggested in an episode in Bhattacharya's *So Many Hungers!* in which the mother encounters another, younger mother about to bury her child alive:

> The woman turned aside and picked up the bare-limbed baby boy, rocking him in her arms as he whimpered faintly, and coaxing, warm and tender: 'No more hurt in the belly, my sweet one, my godling. You will sleep.' And she laid the child in the trench, folded his reedlike arms over the bony chest and pushed the eyelids down as though to put the child to sleep, and then with hurried hands she began to pile the earth back into the grave.[139]

The author's simplicity of language and quietness of tone have a special power, though the difficulties involved in narrating the act of infanticide are also evident. The woman's actions must, once again, be termed less than rational; she is described as under 'a veil of stupor', her eyes 'dull' and 'sunken', until the rescue of the child marks the restoration of her humanity: 'The veil of stupor had lifted from her feelings. She was living again. And how she needed the little one, her child, her godling!'

Mother and child are saved by the other mother who gives Mangala, her cow, as sustenance for the child. Lakshmi succeeds in relieving sorrow and providing succour, yet, in this famine narrative, only through sacrificing the food needed both by herself and by her own children. The mother's identity is thus a complex one – giver of aid but also herself in need, taking from her own children what is given to others. Acts of generosity and of nurture, traditional in times of abundance or even sufficiency, collapse in famine times: children are sold and abandoned, even killed by their parents. Fearful exchanges evolve, in which the survival of one or some is directly at the expense of another, in which Lakshmi's act of giving is simultaneously one of deprivation.

Read in these terms, Bhattacharya's pairing of the famine mothers, one who attempts to sacrifice her child in order to save it from suffering, the other who sacrifices herself and her family for another mother and child, is richly suggestive of the dilemmas experienced by famine's victims. Yet the structure of the episode may have another effect. To some extent, famine emerges as an enclosed event between female victims, an exchange of victimization isolated from the wider sphere.[140] Such scenes remain difficult to evaluate: is this type of episode to be read, and welcomed, as an image of the social crisis caused by famine, reflecting the appalling choices necessary for survival? Or does it produce an individuation of famine's effects which, at best, obscures and, at worst, undermines a broader analysis of why famine has occurred?

A further example of the challenges posed by famine to the female ideal is evident in the treatment of prostitution by famine authors. Earlier in nationalist ideology, the figure of the prostitute or lower-class woman had served to emphasize the purity of her higher-class sister, the 'new' woman through whose spiritual purity was reflected the spirit of the nation.[141] In famine literature, however, women's sale of their bodies in the desperation of hunger and as a strategy of survival is a feature of the contemporary crisis impossible to avoid. Over and over again, journalists and other commentators comment on the scale of the problem and the great difficulties faced in rehabilitating its victims. As early as August 1943, the *Statesman* noted:

> There is a further great evil, about which men have spoken cautiously in public. Many young people, homeless and friendless, have disappeared, probably sucked or dragged into the vice of a large city. How in their misery can they resist those who would profit by them? What refuge and resource have they? Numbers of them will never see their village again, and those who do will probably not be useful and welcome members of it; misery and the town will have robbed even the best of them of their village ways and made them aliens and outcasts.[142]

A meeting of Calcutta women, in January 1944, reiterated the existence of 'mass prostitution among village women, who on occasions formed as much as half of the total population, who have been left destitute as a result of famine'.[143] T. C. Das, professor of anthropology in Calcutta and director of the survey of Calcutta destitutes conducted in 1943, noting the small number of girls, as against boys, in the age group of ten to fifteen years, concluded that this situation mainly resulted from the absorption of girls into city brothels.[144] By early 1944, the Government of Bengal itself expressed 'grave concern at reports received from various sources that young destitute women were being collected by certain persons in various parts of the province with facile promises and were then being sent to different places for the purposes of prostitution'.[145]

Similarly, Ela Sen, in the preface to *Darkening Days*, written in early 1944, argues that prostitution and the resulting disintegration of family life have 'assumed such alarming proportions that Bengal's entire womanhood stands menanced'.[146] The narrative's concluding 'facts and figures' include an estimate that 'about 30,000 from Calcutta's 125,000 destitutes alone have gone into brothels, 1 in 4 of them being young girls'.[147] The consequence, in Sen's view, since 'upon woman depends greatly the balance and morale of a nation', is that post-famine Bengal is threatened with 'social disintegration'.[148]

Echoing other observers, Sen initially deems such young girls and women to be the victims of trickery and deception:

It is true also that the ranks of prostitution swelled and this was due to two reasons – mainly because young and middle-aged women were won by the chicanery of procurers who lured them with smooth promises of food and shelter, which to the destitute meant heaven itself; and because women unwittingly sold their young daughters to the agents of brothels promising to look after them in a good home.[149]

Later in the narrative, however, prostitution emerges more as a survival strategy, chosen as a last resort, but proof of women's greater determination to resist demoralization and despair:

> for somehow in spite of the odds against them they clung tenaciously to life and were not willing victims of demoralization. The men suffered a queer psychological reverse on their reduction to beggary, and their mortification and humiliation was so great at having to revert from honest toil to begging that they rather welcomed death than continue the struggle for existence. Women fought against this apathy and instead of allowing the whirlpool to drag them down, they struggled to get out of it. It left them worn, battered and bruised, mere wraiths of their former selves, but they lived.[150]

This characterization of women's resistance to demoralization and apathy, in spite of odds stacked against them, echoes observations made in relation to the Irish 1840s famine in interesting ways. Women are those on whom famine's repercussions fall most severely, as Sen's preface outlined, yet also the most visible famine survivors; tenacious fighters though especially vulnerable. This combination of determination and fragility is embodied in Sen's story, 'Two Sisters', through the character of Amina: 'her youth demanded that she live and pointed the only way'. Amina's explanation is clear: 'I want to live, and I have nothing to sell but my youth and my body.' The tragic consequence of her efforts 'to live' through prostitution is made painfully clear: the 'laughing gentle-eyed sister' becomes 'an old, old woman with wrinkles under her eyes, hollowed cheeks and matted hair'.[151]

To describe Amina's actions as 'a choice' seems hardly apt; in Sen's words, 'prostitution or death became the twin possibilities for these women'.[152] In her story, 'The Queue', a woman resorts to prostitution only to save her child; when this attempt fails, she is left 'empty', her body compared to 'a husk out of which the best had been squeezed out'.[153] Part of the achievement of Sen's stories, as has been discussed, is their interweaving of individual actions with the wider economic and political context, identifying the power politics which underlie and determine these women's fates. 'She Was Not Alone' thus tells of a woman, Gouri, 'kept' by a man who has made his fortune from hoarding rice. As the story comes to an end, Gouri comes to recognize how her situation relates to the wider exploitation of the famine poor: '"All these people like us have been made pawns in your game of buying and selling. People like you, who have no cares but to make money and hoard it, have bartered away the food from the mouths of our children."'[154] In 'Two Sisters', the presence of a military camp near the coastal village offers 'ugly possibilities' to local women.[155] An ironic dichotomy develops between women's intention and their fate; as Sen declares, women 'wanted to live, to labour and to perform their share of national life, and they were condemned to the penal servitude of brothels'.[156] A further irony is apparent when one recalls the claims made by nationalism to reform and redeem 'the degenerate condition of women'.[157]

The most successful individuation of the problem of prostitution and its aftermath is provided by Manik Bandyopadhyay's powerful and moving story, set immediately after the Bengal famine. 'A Tale of These Days' intimates the extent of the social crisis facing the region through the story of one couple, Rampada and Mukta. At the beginning of the story, Mukta returns to the village, having been 'rescued' by the 'city ladies and gentlemen' who were now 'bringing her back home'. Husband and wife were separated first by Rampada's departure to find food and, later, by Mukta's departure for the city, following the death from hunger of their child: 'By the time she left, Mukta had looked like a skeleton draped in dirty rags'; 'there was now flesh between her skin and her bones'. Manik, gently and with great economy, narrates the strain of their re-encounter:

After eleven months of separation and terrible happenings, the biggest barrier was not knowing what to say to each other, being so much alone with the burden of one's thoughts. Hesitating about saying anything was only natural, but not saying anything was now painful. The thoughts and the terrible memories stirred in Mukta's mind. Her baby boy was seven months old when Rampada went away. What happened to the baby after he left was something that she could tell him and lighten her mind a little. Haltingly, she started. 'The baby died after eating food that a baby should not have. After my milk dried up, I fed him gruel of ground rice for some time. Then the rice was finished. I had nothing to give him except the wild greens that I boiled for myself. That's what killed him! What could I do?'. . .

'Nobody in the village tried to help you?' he now asked her.

'Das-babu offered to give milk for the baby, food and clothing for me if I obliged him. How would I know then that this was going to happen to me? If I had known, I would have taken his offer. At least the baby would have lived. I was ruined anyway and I lost the baby.'

She wiped her eyes and tried to calm herself. She now had to explain her actions to him without tears. She had decided not to plead for his pity with tearful accounts of what drove her out. She was not looking for justice either. She wanted Rampada to decide on his own, to do as he thought right. Calmly she started the account of what happened.

'The baby was dead, and you still were not back. Das-babu was sending Nedi's mother to me every day to find out if I would give in. I didn't have anything to eat for days. Then one night two men came for me. I bit their hands and ran away. I hid in the forest for a few days. Then I was at the end of my wits and went to the town.'[158]

Following Mukta's return, and her acceptance by Rampada, Ghanashyam, grain merchant and 'social pillar of the area's poor community', attempts to generate moral outrage among the other villagers and summons Mukta to a public trial. His plans fail, owing to the general listlessness and apathy of the village's inhabitants. The pervasiveness of experiences such as Mukta's further hinders any potential protest.

> With the terrible things that had happened all around, with so many
> dead of starvation and sickness, so many families splintered and
> members lost track of – hardly two of a ten-member family
> tottering back home from their separate journeys for food – with so
> many young wives and girls picked up by procurers and traffickers,
> who would bother? Who would have fussed, in the midst of all this,
> about whose wife came back home after surviving for a few months
> by immoral means. It would be like bothering about who was
> dirtying whose tank at a time after a catastrophic flood.[159]

Ghanashyam's hypocrisy is ultimately exposed by his mistress, Giri,
whose own mother has 'gone out of her mind' with grief. 'A Tale
of These Days' subtly conveys the changes wrought by famine, not
only in the family relationships of husband and wife but also in
traditional structures of power. Yet, while the blow delivered to
Ghanashyam's status in the community appears a positive change,
as does the undermining of traditional methods of judgement, the
overall story does not support an optimistic conclusion. Instead
what lingers from Manik's tale is the sense of lives which have
been 'cruelly broken', both physically and emotionally; in the
closing lines, Giri's mother fails even to recognize her daughter.

The crisis posed by famine to personal and family values is a
central feature of Bhabani Bhattacharya's famine novels. In response
to a critic's observation that 'the importance of women', both 'as
individuals and symbols', was a striking aspect of his fiction, the
novelist himself has contended: 'I think the women of India have
more depth, more richness than the men. The transition from the
old to the new, the crisis of value adaptation, strikes deeper into
the lives of our women than our menfolk.'[160] This 'crisis of value
adaptation', experienced by women, takes a variety of forms in *So
Many Hungers!* Mothers are driven to sell or abandon their
children; traditional notions of maternity and nurture come into
crisis. As the novel develops, the sexual exploitation of women and
young girls becomes a dominant theme, sign of the various
'hungers' with which the novel is concerned. Sir Abalabandhu, the
'moving spirit' behind 'Cheap Rice, Ltd' and specialist in hoarding
rice, is also the novel's most depraved character. His 'pleasures'
include relating to his colleagues tales of his 'sex adventures' which

are thinly disguised as those of a 'friend' – stories of 'frank, smooth brutality' towards destitute girls which sicken his fellow specu-lators.[161] On the streets of Calcutta, 'alien soldiers' may purchase photographs taken with Indian girls, as 'mementos' of India: 'Every photo showed a group of two – grinning alien soldier with a grey-faced wench on his knees . . . They earned two rupees a day, just for sitting gaily on the knees of an alien in khaki uniform for the brief pose.'[162] The terrible conjunction of need and exploita-tion is succinctly summarized in a passage from *He Who Rides a Tiger*, Bhattacharya's later novel:

> Two great hungers had struck the land of Bengal in the wake of war: the hunger of the masses of people uprooted from their old earth and turned into beggars, and the hunger of the all-owning few for pleasure and more pleasure, a raging fever of the times. Uprooted women with their own kind of hunger had to soothe the other hunger, had to cool the raging pleasure-fever with their bodies.[163]

The depiction of these 'two great hungers' serves in turn to sharpen and support a third, arguably for Bhattacharya, the most significant: the hunger for freedom.

This conjunction appears most graphically in *So Many Hungers!* in the scene of Kajoli's rape. The rapist is a soldier, a Punjabi sepoy who had joined the army to save his family from want. From his perspective, 'The war was good, this mobilization. In peace-time he never had enough to eat – with the landlord and the moneylender sated, little was left to him of his harvest. But now he had bread in abundance.'[164] That this man, who 'had known hunger in his body', should exploit another's hunger and rape a starving, pregnant woman forms one of the most disturbing episodes in the novel. Because of the rape, Kajoli miscarries, and a jackal crouches over her 'prostrate body' until driven away by her young brother. Immediately after, the soldier is stricken with remorse; through his perspective, a forceful complaint is delivered against the political structures which have given him food and hence power:

> Why were these innocent people doomed to hunger and death
> while the Army had food and rice to squander? Who but the
> peasants had created the foodgrains − . . . When you came to
> think of it, the peasants were as much in the war as the makers of
> shots and shells and those firing the missiles − who could fight with
> no food in the stomach? And he, himself a peasant, had made use
> of the undeserved bread he possessed to do wrong to a famished
> peasant girl, pregnant.[165]

Bhattacharya's intention is clearly to bring to the foreground the
political processes which have turned the fellow-peasant into a
rapist; his action serves as symptom of the wider injustices of
imperialism. Yet this involves a troubling appropriation of the
individual's experience and its sacrifice to political metaphor.

Later in the narrative, in an episode intended as a counterpoint
to Rahoul's meditation on the deadening of maternal instinct and,
by extension, of Bengal's 'innate humanity', another figure of
imperial exploitation is constructed. Walking through the streets of
Calcutta, Rahoul encounters a group of white soldiers purchasing
views of the naked body of a young destitute girl. One by one, the
soldiers drop a rupee into the woman's begging-bowl:

> She said no word, rose to her feet, languid, slender of limb, no
> taller than Kajoli. Arms folded upon her bosom, she stood erect
> and lifted her face starward, the moulding of her neck revealed . . .
> Then the arms unfolded, stripping the garment from her breast. So
> she stood bare, the hooded street light full upon her, a bronze
> image with eyes reaching starward . . . The crowd gaped, but no
> word was spoken, no titters came. Moments went by, and the girl
> dropped her face and drew the sari back to her bosom and sank on
> her knees. She hung her head. She looked shamed.
>   Another rupee clinked into the bowl. The girl stared at it for a
> long moment, then rose once more and bared herself to the
> flooding light, arms up-flung, bronze, again, a different mould.
> And the ravages of hunger showed on her flesh . . .
>   The cruel clink in the bowl once more.[166]

The narration of this episode itself constructs a spectacle of the
woman, disturbingly close to what Laura Mulvey has called a

moment of 'erotic contemplation'.[167] The full significance of the scene is revealed when Rahoul follows the young woman and discovers that the coins which she has received are used by her to feed other destitutes. The woman thus becomes symbol of self-sacrifice, devoted to her people; with obvious similarities to Yeats's Countess Cathleen, she sacrifices her honour to feed others. As figure of the spirit of Bengal, she embodies the experience of exploitation but also of resistance, having risen 'to a tremendous crisis' through an inner resilience of spirit. Deemed by 'the convention-bound moron' to have 'abased the body's sanctity', to Rahoul she is proof of 'the sanctity of the human spirit'.[168] Through her figure, the suffering and self-sacrificing Sati of tradition gains a new, contemporary form.

These episodes from Bhattacharya's novel suggest that mythical and idealized figures such as Shakti and Lakshmi, while severely challenged by the crisis of famine, may also encompass it, through adapting to its circumstances. Throughout famine literature, the self-sacrificing character of women remains crucial in conveying a sense of the enduring resilience of Bengal. Yet, as *So Many Hungers!* also demonstrates, the limits to adaptation are clear when the narrative moves to the theme of physical resistance, culmination of the hunger for freedom. In the closing chapter, Kajoli has just accepted the offer of a life of prostitution in Calcutta when she hears the news that her grandfather and other political prisoners have begun a hunger-strike. This news causes her to be overwhelmed by shame:

> She saw him in jail-house in the garb of a convict, wielding his body's hunger like a sword, strong as ever, and true and deathless.
> And she, dadu's grand-daughter. Hunger-trapped, she had sold herself.
> What if dadu knew one day? This, the final gesture of her life, would hurt him more than all the oppression he suffered in jail-house and all the pangs of his hunger-battle – [169]

The hungers experienced by male prisoner and female destitute are explicitly linked but their use of that weapon is markedly different. Kajoli's only 'power' is to add to her grandfather's suffering through knowledge of her shame. That her actions also constitute a form of active resistance and, in Ela Sen's words, her 'share of national life',[170] is not considered; instead she is described as being in a 'stupor' from which the others' actions have awakened her. To further emphasize the point, Kajoli's future is assured by becoming vendor of newspapers, selling others' news. The hunger experienced by men thus carries a very different meaning from that of women: men's fasting from food is a weapon of change and liberation; women remain tied to their bodies, receiving only the option of prostitution and its mark of shame. The only transcendence usually allowed to famine women is an access to spiritual 'sanctity' through acts of sacrifice; political resistance and heroism remain men's preserve.[171]

FAMINE AS FEMALE: THE FATE OF KALI

While Sati, and the related figures of Savitri and Lakshmi, represents the positive face of Shakti, her power also takes a darker form, that of Kali, the black goddess, who 'brings in her train bloodshed, pestilence, terror and death' and whose relevance to famine is acutely clear.[172] Armed with her weapons of destruction, Kali threatens to devour all beings; as symbol of eternal life, she is both the giver and destroyer of life. Thus, she represents 'in its most grandiose form' what Erich Neumann calls 'the experience of the Terrible Mother': 'dark, all-devouring time, the bone-wreathed Lady of the place of skulls'.[173] The figure of Kali shadows two Indian short stories, published many years after the events of the 1940s, but whose representations of famine provide a suggestive postscript to this chapter. The first, entitled 'The Leader', a short story written by the Bangladeshi journalist and author Abu Jafar Shamsuddin and published in 1967,[174] is set during the Bengal famine, while Mahasweta Devi's 'Daini', or 'The Witch-Hunt', published twelve years later, is set in south-eastern Bihar in the mid-1970s.[175]

In 'The Leader', the hypocrisy and shallowness of political figures is the subject of a biting satire. The male narrator, a member of a left-wing political party, has become 'a sort of minor leader' due to his oratorical abilities.[176] His skills are quickly marshalled by his 'comrades' and, with the additional enticement of Tara, sister of one of his colleagues, he is brought to speak about 'the food problem', at a distant village. Having begun to 'pontificate' on 'national and international issues', his speech is interrupted by 'a strange sight'. 'A host of people', gradually revealed to be women, come to seek food. The sight of these 'living skeletons', like 'sub-terranean legendary monsters', terrifies the narrator and he flees: 'How to save my own skin was my sole preoccupation as I fled . . . These living skeletons, possessed by the devil, would be on earth for only a little while and then vanish but I would once again be in the midst of good times and plenty.'[177] Shamsuddin's story is clearly designed to expose the hollowness and self-serving motivation behind contemporary political rhetoric, through the perspective, not, as in Chandar's story, of a foreign official but of a Bengal activist. As his translator and editor, Ranjana Ash, notes, 'the bland irony' through which 'the political posturing of the radicals' is conveyed, contrasts sharply with the 'elaborate imagery' used to describe famine victims.[178] Yet the precise language used by Shamsuddin deserves closer attention; as one of the most detailed examples of a feminization of famine, it throws light on its literary predecessors in very interesting ways.

The narrator's description of the famine 'host' begins, as follows:

As they came closer their forms became clearer. They were women. In tattered clothes covered with dust, they leaned forward as they walked. The wind blew against them and as they could not stand up to the force of the wind, they leaned forward like hunchbacks. Some seemed to have their heads touching the ground in front of them. Their hair, long deprived of oil, was dust-covered and matted. As no sari covered their heads, their hair was blowing about wildly like falling leaves. Their ragged clothes were flying around. The outline of their ribs stood out from their dark, copper-coloured bodies. Their stomachs seemed to have merged with their backs. Women's breasts – cups that contain nectar – were shrivelled and hanging like bats or like the torn pockets of a shirt. Some of the women had children in their arms or on their backs.[179]

The collapse of traditional conventions of dress and decorum is painfully apparent from this passage. The women's hair, uncovered, is deprived of oil and blows like 'falling leaves'; their 'ragged clothes' fail to shield their emaciated bodies. A further breakdown is thus laid bare, the women's breasts now shrivelled and empty. Shamsuddin's description suggests another famine figure with 'matted locks' and skeletal appearance – the classical Famine of whom Ovid wrote : 'her skinny hip-bones bulged out beneath her hollow loins, and her belly was but a belly's place; her breast seemed to be hanging free and just to be held by the framework of the spine'.[180]

The gradual advancement of the 'host' towards the petrified spectator is marked by an explosion of simile and metaphor as the narrator struggles to capture in words the overwhelming spectacle. Animal imagery predominates: their movement is like that of a 'nest of snakes', their eyes those of a 'reptile', their teeth 'like the serried teeth of a crocodile'. Threatening to 'devour' all before them, they are 'ominous black banks of clouds ranged in columns in the sky', 'surging to devour the entire human race to satisfy their perennial hunger'.[181] The scene becomes almost apocalyptic, the women like 'some subterranean legendary monsters', an engulf-ing 'deluge':

> Dancing a dance of destruction, like Shiva's tandav, they would consume the entire world with the supreme indifference of cold-blooded creatures. Like the lizard on the wall that swallows flies and gnats with a flick of its tongue, their voracious hunger would spare neither you, me nor anyone else.[182]

The narrator is, at first, immobilized by fear of this 'voracious hunger' – their 'tentacles, ready to coil round their prey and imprison it in their powerful net; giant crabs opening their long pincers to snare their food'.[183] The moving figures seem 'living skeletons', come from 'the nether world to consume human civilization'. Their sudden screams, calling for food, break the spell and he 'escapes', determined to save himself; though 'running away then or since will never erase the horrific memory'.[184]

Shamsuddin's narrative documents the fear which the spectacle of famine may inspire, not just in one character-spectator but, more fundamentally, in all viewers. The language chosen by his narrator is especially revealing. At first, as in so many famine texts, animal images are employed to keep the famine victims at bay; in this narrative, analogies with snakes and reptiles locate the victims of hunger in a primordial and subhuman world. But these 'monsters' continue to move forward, spreading their tentacles, ready to 'ensnare'.[185] The threatening power which the host of women possesses, to ensnare through their tentacles and then 'devour', thus exemplifies the dark and deadly functions of Kali as 'Terrible Mother': 'her devouring-ensnaring function, in which she draws the life of the individual back into herself'.[186] In Shamsuddin's narrative, fear of the female is also the fear of hunger. Hunger is 'voracious' and 'perennial'; its insatiable nature threatens to consume the entire world and, more specifically, the viewer. If, as Maud Ellmann has argued, the spectacle of hunger 'deranges the distinction between self and other', this occurs, as this story vividly demonstrates, less through 'an appeal to our forgotten past' and much more from the terror of being ensnared by, and made part of, what is seen.[187] In order to withstand such a danger, the spectator must marshal familiar self-justifications, the most blatant and fundamental example, as Shamsuddin's narrative shows, being the belief in one's superior right to survive.

In Shamsuddin's narrative, through the representation of the starving poor in female form, archetypes of hunger are revealed and fears as to the spectator's relationship with what is seen are laid bare. Mahasweta Devi's story, 'The Witch-Hunt', provides a suggestive counterpoint; the narrative begins with a study of the fears and superstition generated by hunger and deprivation and proceeds to expose the power-structures operating within but also disguised by these beliefs. Devi's work is set in south-eastern Bihar in the mid-1970s, and thus is removed from the famine which has provided the subject of this chapter.[188] Yet her stories, in particular 'The Witch-Hunt', are not only vivid and detailed portrayals of the continuing hunger in post-independence India but crucial investigations of the ways in which famine is represented and understood.

'The Witch-Hunt' is set during a period of acute drought, in a region of Bihar populated by tribes such as the Oraon and Munda and members of the untouchable castes.[189] As the story begins, popular belief that the drought has been caused by the presence of a witch is fuelled by a vision experienced by Hanuman Misra, Brahmin priest and one of the area's most powerful men, in economic and political terms.

> When he emerged from the meditation, he told them that the deity had granted him a vision in the form of a terrible figure. It was the figure of a dreadful female, dark and completely naked, flying atop a blood-red cloud and saying 'I'm the famine.' From the almanac he had figured out that she was indeed the witch. They would have to find her and drive her away. If she were hit and bled, or if she were burned, then even more terrible things might happen.[190]

Misra's vision spreads great fear among the villages; husbands, fathers, brothers and sons are asked to keep constant watch over the women in their families. One old woman is driven away from her begging-station and dies; another old woman is left broken-hearted having being suspected and reported by her son. In Devi's words, 'Human nerves are not made to tolerate the constant pressure of unknown, unspecific terror. If to the unknown terror of the witch is added the known terror of an approaching famine, the stress is too much to bear.'[191] Pregnant and menstruating women are the subject of particular suspicion; some women come to suspect themselves. Finally, 'the witch' is seen: 'an ugly dark young woman, naked', eating the raw meat off a bird; her 'ferocious howls' resemble the 'bellowing of a buffalo'.[192] Others encounter her with 'face smeared with blood', and hear a 'strange laugh' followed by an 'inhuman scream'.[193]

The news of the witch-hunt generates much interest from outside the area. Devi's treatment of the falsification involved in media representations, how the story of the witch is exploited for external consumption, is particularly adept: in one magazine story, a black-painted Western woman and 'ashram devotee' named Eileen Bharati is photographed as the witch; though 'eating a fried chicken leg', she is captioned as 'the witch eating a bird raw'.[194] A movie-version is planned, to be shot in the 'similar landscape' of Arizona, with whites playing Indian characters and Indians playing white characters. Devi also constructs the complex character of

Mathur, a local Brahmin schoolteacher who is drawn to the villagers, accompanying them on a witch-hunt and himself glimpsing 'a dark naked young woman, her belly horribly swollen'. It is Mathur who recognizes the reality of the people's emotional reactions – their fear and the resulting 'vengeful anger' – regardless of the witch's 'real' existence.[195] Yet he also remains separate from the action, like a 'spectator, watching an exotic drama being played out': 'He was in the battle, and yet he was not. He was also observing himself, an academic who even in the midst of a battle could instinctively stand apart and judge it, analyze it for his own purpose of obtaining a Ph.D.'[196]

The conclusion of Devi's story brings a double revelation. The 'witch' proves to be the deaf and dumb daughter of a local villager, made pregnant by a son of Hanuman Misra and abandoned by him. Somri's scream in childbirth, followed by 'an incredible sound, the pure and helpless cry of the newborn', are the means through which her human identity is finally restored.[197] Misra's 'vision' is thus exposed as a deliberate lie, intended to disguise his son's abuse of the young woman. Even before this revelation occurs, Mathur comes to a special understanding:

> Listening to them Mathur suddenly understands a crucial and terrible truth about their life. He sees that these people have no place at all in the economic world. They are left out of all the economic progress surrounding them – the steel industry and the coal mines, the lumber business, the railways, the grain-laden irrigated lands. They are totally excluded from the man-made bounty and control of technology and abandoned to nature at its most fickle. Unwanted by the rest of the country, they would be wiped out if nature turns against them. So when nature's breasts turn dry, they blame it on the witch because they don't understand their man-made deprivation.[198]

Abandoned to nature, the villagers are totally dependent on its vicissitudes; yet behind this, and disguised by it, lies the reality of 'their man-made deprivation'.

Hunger continues in the present, 'post-independence' society; thus one character reminds another, 'You always cried "I'm still hungry." The same words always. Our children said it; our grand-children will say it.'[199] At the end of the story, however, the beginnings of resistance may be glimpsed, as the villagers pledge to oppose Hanuman Misra's power, refusing to work for him and preventing others from doing so.

What Devi's story highlights is of central significance to this study. An emphasis on famine's 'natural' character may cover over its deeper political nature, its 'man-made' economic structures obscured by manipulable beliefs and stock female figures. Both 'Mother Nature' and her witch-opposite emerge as restrictive, though potent, types. While mythical figures reappear in Devi's narrative – the 'wrathful' Kali, Ovid's bellied female – the 'femi-nization of famine' ultimately proves to have a very particular, human truth. This recovery of the individual female experience, within myth and superstition, is also, crucially, the means through which famine's political character is restored.

NOTES AND REFERENCES

1. Wallace Ruddell Aykroyd, *The Conquest of Famine* (London, 1974), p. 75.

2. See Paul Greenough, *Prosperity and Misery in Modern Bengal* (Oxford and New York, 1982), appendix A; a significant exception is the 1770 famine which decimated Bengal and Bihar and is estimated to have caused some ten million deaths.

3. Quoted in Aykroyd, *The Conquest of Famine*, p. 72; as Aykroyd observes, these districts were among the hardest hit in 1943–44.

4. Amartya Sen, *Poverty and Famines: An Essay on Entitlement and Deprivation* ([1981]; Oxford, 1982), p. 79. Significant studies of the Bengal famine include Paul Greenough's *Prosperity and Misery*, Sen's *Poverty and Famines* (chapter 6), and Aykroyd's discussion in *The Conquest of Famine* (chapter 7). An early study, written almost contemporaneously with the famine, is Kali Charan Ghosh's *Famines in Bengal: 1770–1943* (Calcutta, 1944; reprinted, with a foreword by Amartya Sen, in 1987).

5. Sen, *Poverty and Famines*, p. 79.

6. Ibid., p. 55.

7. *The Statesman*, a British-owned paper, was published both in New Delhi and Calcutta, and thus possessed a significant influence over both the provincial and central governments. On 22 August, the paper published a page of photographs of famine destitutes; similar photographs were published on 29

August, accompanied by one of its many forceful editorials, entitled 'An All-India Disgrace'. *Monsoon Morning*, the autobiography of its editor, Ian Stephens (London, 1966), contains an interesting discussion of the newspaper's reporting of the famine (chapters 13 and 14).

8. Aykroyd, *Conquest of Famine*, pp. 70, 78; the obvious parallel with Ireland is also recognized by Aykroyd: 'In the Irish famine, one hundred years earlier, the word "famine" was not used in official correspondence from Whitehall, "distress" being preferred' (p. 70).

9. Sen, *Poverty and Famines*, pp. 195–202.

10. Ibid., pp. 53, 57.

11. Ibid., p. 58; the winter (*aman*) crop, harvested in December 1942, was less than normal owing to a number of factors including the destruction caused by an October cyclone and torrential rain in some parts of Bengal. Yet, reinforcing Sen's argument, Aykroyd, in his 1974 study, recalls the view of the commission that the 1943 supply was 'probably sufficient for about forty-nine weeks, which meant an absolute deficiency of about three weeks requirements' and observes that this suggests that 'sheer lack of rice was a less important cause of starvation and death than its enormous price' (p. 74).

12. Sen, *Poverty and Famines*, p. 76.

13. David Arnold, *Famine: Social Crisis and Historical Change* (Oxford and New York, 1988), pp. 44–45.

14. Ibid., p. 46.

15. B. M. Bhatia, *Famines in India: 1860–1965* (2nd [1963]; Bombay, 1967), p. 318.

16. Quoted in ibid., p. 315.

17. By orders issued in May, boats capable of carrying ten or more passengers were removed, in order to 'deny' them to the Japanese; see Greenough, *Prosperity and Misery*, p. 89, and Sen, *Poverty and Famines*, p. 67.

18. Greenough, *Prosperity and Misery*, pp. 90–94.

19. Bhatia, *Famines in India*, p. 324.

20. Sen, *Poverty and Famines*, pp. 54–55, and Sugata Bose, *Agrarian Bengal: Economy, Social Structure, and Politics, 1919–1947* (Cambridge, 1986), p. 89.

21. Aykroyd, *Conquest of Famine*, p. 79.

22. Greenough, *Prosperity and Misery*, p. 125.

23. See Cormac Ó Gráda, *Ireland Before and After the Famine: Explorations in Economic History, 1800–1925* (Manchester, 1988; revised edition, 1993), chapter 3.

24. Aykroyd, *Conquest of Famine*, p. 78.

25. Sen, *Poverty and Famines*, pp. 76–77, and Bhatia, *Famines in India*, pp. 333–39.

26. Bhatia, *Famines in India*, pp. 337–39.

27. Sen, *Poverty and Famines*, p. 79.

28. See J. S. Bright, *Before and After Independence* (New Delhi, 1950), pp. 351–52.

29. Jawaharal Nehru, *The Discovery of India* (1946), pp. 4–6, quoted in Dorothy Norman (ed.), *Nehru: The First Sixty Years; Passages from Nehru's Writings* (London, 1965), ii, p. 140. An interesting link between Ireland and India,

with regard to the issue of famine relief, is worth noting here: in April 1846, one of the first sums subscribed for Irish relief, some £14,000, had come from Calcutta; see Cecil Woodham-Smith, *The Great Hunger: Ireland 1845–1849* ([1962]; London, 1987), p. 156. Christine Kinealy notes that, in 1847, further sums of £2,500 and £3,000 came, via the Society of Friends, from Calcutta and Bombay; see *This Great Calamity: The Irish Famine, 1845–1852* (Dublin, 1994), p. 163.

30. Aykroyd, *Conquest of Famine*, p. 77.

31. The anthropology department of Calcutta university, as early as February 1944, suggested that famine-related mortality would reach over three and a half millions; this figure was later adjusted by Chattopadhyaya, leader of the group, to an estimate of 2.7 million; see Sen, appendix D, 'Famine Mortality: A Case Study', in *Poverty and Famines*, pp. 195–216, and Greenough, *Prosperity and Misery,* pp. 237–60, 299–315.

32. Paul Greenough's suggested figure is of 3.5 to 3.8 million between 1943 and 1946: 'at least one million of these deaths occurred in the last half of 1943, which means that for six months more than 5,400 victims died daily', *Prosperity and Misery*, p. 237.

33. Sen, *Poverty and Famines*, p. 215 [author's emphases].

34. Ibid., pp. 70–75, 209–10. However, as Sugata Bose emphasizes, a significant decline in entitlements also occurred among small-holding peasantry, many of whom became landless during the famine period (*Agrarian Bengal*, p. 94).

35. T. Das, *The Bengal Famine of 1943, as Revealed in a Survey of the Destitutes in Calcutta* (Calcutta, 1949), quoted by Sen, *Poverty and Famines*, p. 211.

36. The anthropology department's report, published in February 1944, claimed that, even in less affected areas, 'nearly twice as many adult men have died as adult women' and 'in the more affected areas, the proportion of men has been even higher'. The consequences of this, as identified by the report, included the loss of wage-earners for families, the resulting vulnerability of women and children, and an increase in prostitution. See Ghosh, appendix G, *Famines in Bengal*, pp. 183–85, and Sen, *Poverty and Famines*, p. 211, n. 29.

37. Greenough suggests an average mortality rate for males of 4.18 per cent, as compared with a female rate of 3.21 per cent; see *Prosperity and Misery*, pp. 309–15.

38. Ibid., p. 239.

39. Sen, *Poverty and Famines*, p. 211. Sen's findings pose a significant challenge to the general supposition that Indian famines have a lower impact on women, a typical example being the view recorded by one nineteenth-century official that 'all the authorities seem agreed that women succumb to famine less easily than men' (quoted by Sen, pp. 210–11).

40. Ibid., p. 211, n. 30.

41. Examples of such 'contrived explanations', drawn by Sen from comments in the 1911 *Census of India*, include women's employment as maid-servants, their

possession of ornaments which may be sold and their access to household stores, with 'no scruple' in availing themselves of this 'advantage' (See *Poverty and Famines*, pp. 211–12, n. 32.) Others, offered by J. N. Uppal in his *Bengal Famine of 1943: A Man-Made Tragedy* (Delhi and Lucknow, 1984), are that men's work ate into their physical reserves more quickly, that men suffered from greater internal resistance to availing of the relief measures and that young females had a better chance of survival through 'immoral traffic' (p. 225).

42. The role of gender in determining entitlements to food has been analyzed by Jean Drèze and Amartya Sen in *Hunger and Public Action* (Oxford, 1989), pp. 48–50.

43. Greenough, *Poverty and Famines*, p. 138.

44. Ibid., pp. 11, 215–17.

45. Ibid., p. 275. Similarly, the department of anthropology's report on deaths due to famine in 1943 emphasized the widespread collapse of family structures: 'Husbands have driven away wives and wives have deserted ailing husbands; children have foresaken aged and disabled parents and parents have also left home in despair; brothers have turned deaf ears to the entreaties of hungry sisters and widowed sisters, maintained for years together by their brothers, have departed at the time of direct need', quoted in Ghosh, *Famines in Bengal*, p. 81.

46. Ela Sen, *Darkening Days: Being a Narrative of Famine-Stricken Bengal* (Calcutta, 1944), pp. 26–28.

47. Sir John Shore (1770), quoted in Ghosh, *Famines in Bengal*, p. 92.

48. Ghosh, *Famines in Bengal*, pp. 83–92.

49. Contemporary accounts and photographs, from newspapers such as the *Hindusthan Standard* and the *Amrita Bazar Patrika*, are reproduced in Uppal, *Bengal Famine*, and in Ghosh, *Famines in Bengal*. Extracts from contemporary observers together with numerous photographs and contemporary cartoons, up to December 1943, are collected by Kasturiranga Santhanam in *Cry of Distress: a first-hand description and objective study of the Indian famine of 1943* (New Delhi, 1943). The majority of photographs are of city destitutes, with graphic images of starving children and of despairing women holding their dying infants; the caption from one image of a mother and child, published in the *Hindusthan Standard* (1943) and reproduced by Ghosh and Santhanam, reads 'Rank despair on face and a dead child on lap she waits for what she does not know'.

50. Sen, *Poverty and Famines*, p. 63.

51. Ibid. pp. 208–09; however, as Sen notes, in the later epidemic-phase of famine, Calcutta had 'its own share of casualties', continuing when rural famine destitutes had left or been repatriated.

52. By October, 'the number of starving and sick destitutes in Calcutta was estimated to be "at least 100,000"' (Sen, p. 57). Later that month, the controversial Bengal Destitute Persons (Repatriation and Relief) Ordinance was passed, ordering the removal of destitutes from the city.

53. Other literary treatments of the Bengal famine include a famine play, *Nabanna* (The festival of the harvest) by Bijon Bhattacharya, first staged by the Indian People's Theatrical Association in 1944, and a number of films, including Satyajit Ray's *Asani Sanket* (Distant thunder), produced in 1973, and Mrinal Sen's *Ākāler Sandhāney* (In search of famine), first screened in 1982. The script of Sen's film was reconstructed and translated by Samik Bandyopadhyay, and published in Calcutta in 1983. Other stories, discussed later in the chapter, are Abu Jafar Shamsuddin's Bengali short story, 'The Leader' (1967), and Mahasweta Devi's story of drought and famine in south-eastern Bihar, 'The Witch-Hunt' (1979). More generally, twentieth-century Indian 'novels of hunger' include Mulk Raj Anand's *Coolie* (London, 1936) and Kamala Markandaya's powerful story, *Nectar in a Sieve* (Bombay, 1955). See Ramesh K. Srivastava, 'The Theme of Hunger in Bhattacharya and Markandaya', in R. K. Dhawan (ed.), *Explorations in Modern Indo-English Fiction* (New Delhi, 1982), pp. 172–83.

54. Sen, *Poverty and Famines*, p. 78.

55. Jawaharlal Nehru, quoted by Arnold, *Famine*, p. 117. See also Nehru, *The Discovery of India* (Calcutta, 1946; abridged edition, Delhi and Oxford, 1989): 'The tragedy of Bengal and the famines of Orissa, Malabar, and other places, are the final judgement on British rule in India' (p. 264). In contrast, the famine was argued by opponents to independence as demonstrating, through the failures of the provincial government, Indian inability for self-rule.

56. Krishan Chandar, *I Cannot Die: A Story of Bengal* (*Ann Dātā*), (Poona, 1944/5), translated from Urdu by Kwaja Ahmad Abbas, with cover design and illustrations by Rathin Motra. *Ann Dātā* and its English translation were published between 1944 and 1945.

57. Chandar (variant spelling, 'Chander') was born in Lahore in 1914 and became a leading Urdu short-story writer and novelist (d. 1977). His literary output includes many novels and film scripts, and a body of short stories whose number is estimated to lie between three and five hundred. His work has been translated into many languages including English, German, Russian, Chinese, Japanese, Arabic and Czech. See Kedar Nath Sud, 'Urdu fiction and Krishan Chandar', in *Indian Literature*, 20, 4 (1977), pp. 122–27, and Muhammed Sadiq, *Twentieth-Century Urdu Literature* (Karachi, 1983).

58. Kwaja Ahmad Abbas, preface to *I Cannot Die*, pp. 4–5.

59. Chandar, *I Cannot Die*, p. 11.

60. Ibid., p. 14.

61. Ibid., p. 19.

62. Ibid., p. 27.

63. Ibid., p. 36.

64. Ibid., p. 41.

65. Ibid., pp. 47–49.

66. Ibid., p. 51. The reference is to the meeting of Roosevelt, Churchill and Stalin in Tehran on 4 December 1943.

67. Ibid., p. 52.
68. *Manwantar (Epoch's End)* was first published in Calcutta in January 1944. The popularity of the novel is evident in the release of a third reprint by June 1945; the novel was translated into English by Hirendranath Mookherjee in 1950. Tarasankar Bandyopadhyay (alternate spellings include Tarashankar and Banerjee or Banerji) was born in West Bengal in 1898 and as a youth was jailed for political activities. Moving to Calcutta in 1933, his literary career began; he later became president of the anti-fascist writers' and artists' movement, known as the Progressive Writers' Association from its foundation in 1936, and, after 1942, as the A.F.W.A.A. Before his death in 1971, he had produced over fifty novels and numerous short stories. See Mahasweta Devi, *Tarasankar Bandyopadhyay* (New Delhi, 1975), and Kalpana Bardhan (ed.), *Of Women, Outcastes, Peasants and Rebels: A Selection of Bengali Short Stories* (California, 1990), pp. 22–24.
69. Tarasankar Bandyopadhyay, *Epoch's End*, pp. 293–94.
70. Ibid., p. 271.
71. Ibid., p. 312.
72. Ibid.
73. Ela Sen, *Darkening Days: Being a Narrative of Famine-Stricken Bengal* (Calcutta, 1944), with illustrations by Zainul Abedin. Ela Sen (1899–?) was also a well-known translator and biographer. Her works include *Testament of India* (London, 1939), a biography of *Gandhi* (Calcutta, 1945) and of *Indira Gandhi* (London and Bombay, 1973). Her *Wives of Famous Men* (Bombay, 1942) includes profiles of Kamal Nehru, Kasturbai Gandhi, Eleanor Roosevelt, Mrs Churchill, Madame Stalin, Mrs Bernard Shaw and Mrs de Valera. After 1947, Sen lived in England.
74. Sen, *Darkening Days*, foreword, p. 7.
75. Ibid., p. 12.
76. Ibid., pp. 76–85.
77. Ibid., p. 105.
78. Ibid., foreword, p. 7.
79. Ibid., p. 169.
80. Manik Bandyopadhyay (1908–1956) is described by Kalpana Bardhan as an 'unsparing reporter of the lower depths – the disintegrating petty bourgeoisie and the proletariat-in-formation'. Made famous in his twenties by *The Boatman of the Padma* (1936) and *The Puppet's Tale* (1936), he produced over fifty novels and collections of short stories before his early demise. His story 'A Tale of These Days' was published in 1963, seven years after the author's death; it was translated and published by Kalpana Bardhan in *Of Women, Outcastes, Peasants and Rebels*, pp. 135–47. See also Bardhan's introduction, pp. 18–22, and Buddhadeva Bose, *An Acre of Green Grass: A Review of Modern Bengali Literature* (Calcutta, 1948), pp. 85–87. A recent collection of Manik's stories, selected and introduced by Bardhan, is *Wives and Others* (New Delhi, 1979).
81. Ibid., p. 141.

82. Ibid., p. 138.
83. Ibid., p. 146.
84. Sen, *Darkening Days*, p. 31.
85. Ibid., pp. 24–26, 31.
86. Ibid., pp. 31, 175–77.
87. Ibid., pp. 31, 177.
88. Bhabani Bhattacharya (1906–1988) was the author of six novels and a number of short stories, and a well-known essayist. With Kamala Markandaya and R. K. Narayan, he ranks as one of the best-known Indo-Anglian novelists. The many critical studies of Bhattacharya's work include K. R. Chandrasekharan, *Bhabani Bhattacharya* (New Delhi, 1974); Dorothy Shimer, *Bhabani Bhatta-charya* (Boston, 1974); K. K. Sharma, *Bhabani Bhattacharya: His Vision and Themes* (New Delhi, 1979) and Ramesh K. Srivastava (ed.), *Perspectives on Bhabani Bhattacharya* (New Delhi, 1984).
89. See Srivastava's interview with the author, 'Bhattacharya at Work', in Srivastava (ed.), *Perspectives on Bhabani Bhattacharya* , p. 229.
90. Quoted by S. C. Harrex, entry on 'Bhabani Bhattacharya' in James Vinson and D. L. Kirkpatrick (eds.), *Contemporary Novelists* (4th ed; London and New York, 1986), pp. 98–100.
91. Ibid., p. 79.
92. Bhattacharya, *So Many Hungers!* ([1947]; New Delhi, 1978), pp. 53–54.
93. Ibid., p. 105.
94. Ibid., p. 62.
95. Ibid., p. 115.
96. Ibid., p. 202.
97. *He Who Rides a Tiger* (New York, 1954) was Bhattacharya's third novel to be published, following *Music for Mohini* (New York, 1952). It was republished in 1988, and its many translations include Russian, Polish, Danish, French, German, Finnish, Chinese and Spanish versions.
98. Ibid., p. 220.
99. Ibid., p. 232.
100. As Benjamin Walker notes, 'Many Hindu cults of very ancient provenance, some incorporating features anterior even to the Aryan invasion of India have been devoted to the worship of Shakti', in *Hindu World: An Encyclopedic Survey of Hinduism* (London, 1968), ii, p. 336.
101. Ibid.
102. Hence *sati*, or Anglicized 'suttee', refers to widows or wives who immolated themselves. See Lata Mani, 'Contentious Traditions: The Debate on *Sati* in Colonial India', in Kumkum Sangari and Sudesh Vaid (eds.), *Recasting Women: Essays in Colonial History* (New Delhi, 1989), pp. 88–126.
103. Partha Chatterjee, 'The Nationalist Resolution of the Women's Question', in Sangari and Vaid (eds.), *Recasting Women*, pp. 248–49.
104. Ibid., p. 248.

105. Susie Tharu, 'Tracing Savitri's Pedigree: Racism and the Image of Woman in Indo-Anglian Literature', in Sangari and Vaid (eds.), *Recasting Women*, p. 263. Tharu shows how the figure of Savitri was used by writers in late nineteenth and early twentieth-century India to combat negative images projected by the British and to support, through the doctrine of self-sacrifice, an emerging nationalism.

106. Quoted by Tanika Sarkar, 'Politics and Women in Bengal: The Conditions and Meaning of Participation', in J. Krishnamurty, *Women in Colonial India: Essays on Survival, Work and the State* (Delhi, 1989), p. 239.

107. According to Ashis Nandy, Bankimchandra was the first 'to introduce the theme of the great mother into Indian nationalism' ; see Nandy, *The Intimate Enemy: Loss and Recovery of Self under Colonialism* (Delhi, 1983), p. 92. See also Tanika Sarkar, 'Nationalist Iconography: Image of Women in Nineteenth-Century Bengali Literature', in *Economic and Political Weekly*, 21 November 1987, pp. 2011–15.

108. Tagore's 'My Golden Bengal' was later to become the national anthem of Bangladesh.

109. Sarkar, 'Politics and Women', p. 238.

110. Nandy, *The Intimate Enemy*, p. 4.

111. Nandy also demonstrates how Gandhian concepts of womanhood continued the traditional Indian belief in 'the primacy of maternity over conjugality in feminine identity' (*The Intimate Enemy*, p. 54).

112. See Sarkar, 'Politics and Women', pp. 238–39, and Joanna Liddle and Rama Joshi, *Daughters of Independence: Gender, Caste and Class in India* (London and New Delhi, 1986), p. 200.

113. Sarkar, 'Politics and Women', p. 239.

114. Ibid., p.240.

115. See Meena Shirwadkar, *Image of Woman in the Anglo-Indian Novel* (New Delhi, 1979), and Shantha Krishnaswamy, *The Woman in Indian Fiction in English, 1950–1980* (New Delhi, 1986); the quoted phrases are from Shirwadkar's preface.

116. Ujjal Dutta, 'Woman in Bengali Fiction: An Inquiry', in C. D. Narasimhaiah and C. N. Srinatu (eds.), *Women in Fiction and Fiction by Women* (Mysore, 1986), pp. 23–24.

117. Ibid., p. 20.

118. See Eavan Boland, *Object Lessons: The Life of the Woman and the Poet in Our Time* (Manchester, 1995) and 'A Kind of Scar: The Woman Poet in a National Tradition', LIP pamphlet (Dublin, 1989).

119. Bhattacharya, *So Many Hungers!*, p. 90.

120. Ibid., pp. 117–24.

121. Ibid., pp. 192–94. In the last moments of the novel, Rahoul observes, from the police-wagon in which he is journeying to prison, a woman 'pause, flop to her feet. He saw her face turn about on the stem of her neck as though seekingly. Pulled from her frenzied desperation? Saved?' (p. 204).

122. Sen, *Darkening Days*, pp. 17–18.

123. The allusion to Niobe refers to the killing of eleven of her children by Apollo and Artemis; in sorrow, Niobe turned to marble. A number of the characters in Sen's stories are named after Hindu goddesses; thus Durga is the middle-class woman who sacrifices her respectability in order to save her children in 'Impulse', while Lakshmi is the barren woman who becomes foster-mother to her husband's child in 'The Co-wife'.

124. Sen, *Darkening Days*, p. 18. According to Ghosh, 'In August reports of sale of children in the famine and flood-stricken areas of Burdwan and Nadia became known to the public. At Khulna, a woman sold her daughter for Rs. 15 only on October 20, 1943. The father of the girl had left the family in quest of food and never returned. A girl of only three months was offered for sale for Rs. 5 at Burdwan at the end of October, but was prevented from being sold by local people. On November 15, 1943, reports of destitute mothers selling their children or abandoning them on the road-side, husbands deserting their ailing wives were received from Dacca' (*Famines in Bengal*, p. 77). Contemporary accounts of the sale and abuse of children are also included in Greenough, *Prosperity and Misery*, pp. 221–23.

125. Sen, *Darkening Days*, p. 18. Similarly, Ghosh writes: 'Outwardly, the motherly instinct disclosed in its ugliness where the primordial necessity made it appear in its most hideous form. But the real mother never failed her. If she had sold her child, it was more for the welfare of the latter than for the advantages of a few coins to herself . . . If she had thrown her child before the running train or into the well, if was primarily for the consoling thought that the act will shorten its sufferings' (*Famines in Bengal*, pp. 72–73).

126. Sen, *Darkening Days*, pp. 18–19.

127. Ibid., p. 78.

128. Ibid.

129. Bhattacharya, *So Many Hungers!*, p. 125.

130. Chandar, *I Cannot Die*, p. 16.

131. Ibid., pp. 16–17.

132. Ibid., p. 45.

133. Ibid., p. 46.

134. Ibid., p. 47.

135. Bhattacharya, *So Many Hungers!*, p. 181.

136. Reproduced in Ghosh, *Famines in Bengal*, p. 72.

137. Bhattacharya, *So Many Hungers!*, p. 182.

138. Greenough, *Prosperity and Misery*, pp. 23–25.

139. Bhattacharya, *So Many Hungers!*, p. 121.

140. As chapter three has shown, this type of structure also appears in Irish famine narratives and the difficulty of evaluation is similar.

141. See Chatterjee, 'Nationalist Resolution', p. 245.

142. *Statesman*, 13 August 1943; quoted by Ghosh, *Famines in Bengal*, pp. 75–76.

143. Quoted by Ghosh, *Famines in Bengal*, p. 81.

144. Das, *Bengal Famine*, p. 44; see also Uppal, *Bengal Famine of 1943*, p. 229.

145. Cited by Ghosh, p. 81; see also Greenough, *Prosperity and Misery*, pp. 155–57 and 177–78 for contemporary reports and first-person accounts of prostitution.

146. Sen, *Darkening Days*, p. 29.

147. Ibid., p. 169.

148. Ibid.

149. Ibid., p. 19.

150. Ibid., p. 28.

151. Ibid., pp. 103–19.

152. Ibid., p. 29.

153. Ibid., p. 71.

154. Ibid., p. 83.

155. Ibid., p. 107.

156. Ibid., p. 30.

157. See Chatterjee, 'Nationalist Resolution', p. 245.

158. Bandyopadhyay, 'A Tale of These Days', pp. 139–40.

159. Ibid., p. 138.

160. See Marlene Fisher, 'The Women in Bhattacharya's Novels', in *World Literature Written in English*, 11, 1 (1972), p. 95; also quoted by Shirwadkar, *Image of Woman*, p. 33.

161. Bhattacharya, *So Many Hungers!*, pp. 173–76.

162. Ibid., p. 179.

163. Bhattacharya, *He Who Rides a Tiger*, p. 53.

164. Bhattacharya, *So Many Hungers!*, p. 143.

165. Ibid., p. 149.

166. Ibid., p. 184.

167. Laura Mulvey, 'Visual Pleasure and Narrative Cinema', in *Screen* 16, 3 (1975), pp. 6–18.

168. Bhattacharya, *So Many Hungers!*, p. 186.

169. Ibid., p. 195.

170. Sen, *Darkening Days*, p. 30.

171. The parallels between Bhattacharya's text and Gerard Healy's *The Black Stranger* (1945) are particularly striking. In Bhattacharya's later novel, *He Who Rides a Tiger*, which is only partially a famine story, some interesting progressions are apparent in his treatment of female figures. The idealization of Lekha as 'Mother of Sevenfold Bliss' is exposed as a fiction, constructed by her father in order to obtain vengeance. Yet, although the novel demonstrates, through the character of Lekha, how human qualities are suppressed by the divine ideal, her experience, as 'legend of freedom', ultimately serves, as in Healy's play, as a spur for others' resistance.

172. See Walker, *Hindu World*, p. 509: 'She is black of visage, and is frequently represented wearing a necklace of human skulls; in two of her hands she holds a sword and a dagger, and in the other two are severed heads dripping with blood. Her long tongue hangs out of her mouth and blood trickles

down her chin and neck as she gorges herself at her cannibal feasts . . . Her worship is particularly widespread in Bengal where the great temple of Kalighata marks the centre of an ancient Kali cult.'

173. Erich Neumann, *The Great Mother: An Analysis of the Archetype* (trans., London 1955), pp. 148–53. As previously mentioned, an early manifestation of Kali in Bengali famine literature is Tarasankar Bandyopadhyay's 'cartoon' of famine in *Epoch's End*: 'a hideous skeleton, the figure of a female, wrathful, famishing and nearly nude' (p. 271).

174. Abu Jafar Shamsuddin (1911–) is a well-known Bangladeshi writer who began his career as a journalist in 1930s Bengal. His story, 'The Leader', was first published in his collection *Shreshta Galpa* (Dacca, 1967); it was translated from Bengali by Ranjana Ash and published in *Short Stories from India, Pakistan and Bengal*, edited by Ranjana Ash (London, 1980), pp. 59–64 (the original Bengali title of 'The Leader' is not available).

175. Mahasweta Devi, 'The Witch-Hunt (1979), translated and published by Kalpana Bardhan in *Of Women, Outcastes, Peasants and Rebels*, pp. 242–71.

176. Shamsuddin, 'The Leader', p.59.

177. Ibid., p. 63.

178. Ranjana Ash, editor's note, *Short Stories from India*, p. 59.

179. Shamsuddin, 'The Leader', pp. 61–62.

180. Ovid's *Metamorphoses*, translated by Frank Justus Miller, Loeb Classical Library (London, 1916), pp. 460–63; see introduction, pp. 1–2.

181. Shamsuddin, 'The Leader', p. 62.

182. Ibid., pp. 62–63.

183. Ibid., p. 63.

184. Ibid.

185. Neumann interprets both the crab and the octopus as symbols of the Great Mother's devouring and ensnaring power; see *The Great Mother*, pp. 177–81.

186. Ibid., pp. 71–72.

187. Maud Ellmann, *The Hunger-Artists: Starving, Writing and Imprisonment* (London, 1993), p. 54.

188. Devi (b. 1926) is the author of numerous novels, short stories and plays, many of which are based on her work with tribal peoples and the 'untouchable' caste. She is also a well-known journalist and activist, connected, as Susie Tharu and K. Lalita note, with 'several tribal and Harijan grassroot-level organisations'. See Tharu and Lalita, *Women Writing in India*, *vol.* II (London and Delhi, 1993), pp. 234–36, and Kalpana Bardhan, introduction to *Of Women, Outcastes, Peasants and Rebels*, pp. 24–28. Three stories by Devi are published in *Imaginary Maps*, translated by Gayatri Chakravorty Spivak (New York and London, 1995), together with Spivak's interview with Devi.

189. As Kalpana Bardhan, translator of 'The Witch-Hunt', notes in her introduction to *Of Women, Outcastes, Peasants, and Rebels*, these 'semilandless tribals and untouchables' are 'effectively denied the rights guaranteed by the

Constitution, even a legal minimum wage, and marginalized by the process of economic development' (p. 25).

190. Devi, 'The Witch-Hunt', p. 243.
191. Ibid., p. 245.
192. Ibid., pp. 252–53.
193. Ibid., p. 261.
194. Ibid., p. 257.
195. Ibid., p. 263.
196. Ibid., p. 262.
197. Ibid., p. 269.
198. Ibid., p. 268.
199. Ibid., p. 258.

Postscript:
Contemporary Images of Famine and Disaster

In our use of the female as sign, in text and in image, we need to generate a philosophy of possibilities, not reaction . . . That broadening can come only through the creative energy of imaginative empathy, to draw us into the subject of a figure, make us feel inside the body on whose exterior we have until now scribbled the meanings we wanted.

Marina Warner[1]

In October 1992, Ireland's President, Mary Robinson, paid a three-day visit to famine-stricken Somalia. Her visit to Baidoa, Mogadishu and Mandera received extensive coverage from the Irish media, and later that year President Robinson's diary of her visit was published under the title *A Voice for Somalia*.[2] In light of the famine representations examined in this study, the president's narrative is especially interesting. It begins with the admission that her text is inevitably 'a flawed and incomplete account' by one not among 'the participants in the horror', but one of the 'visitors to it'.[3] The issue of language's adequacy in depicting famine, so frequently a prefacing disclaimer to famine depictions, is directly confronted:

> However much I felt the grief of what was happening, however stricken to wordlessness I felt at certain times – and I candidly describe my reactions here – I am as sure now as I was then that grief and silence are luxuries which we in the West cannot indulge if men and women and children are to survive. They need our action, not our tears; our practical, downright, problem-solving help, and not our wordless horror.[4]

The warning delivered by Primo Levi, as to the 'dangerous vicious circle' encouraged by theories of 'incommunicability', finds a significant echo here.[5]

The diary proceeds to describe many of the famine victims seen: children 'dying at the very feeding stations that were trying to give them supplementary feeding', mothers whose 'milk had dried up', 'beside children who were covered in sores with no oil to put on their children', a 'skeletal father' trying to feed 'an emaciated boy who was too ill or too listless to respond'.[6] It emphasizes, with deliberate detail, the presence of Somali aid workers and their 'central role in feeding, medical services and the operation of the centres . . . doctors, nurses, teachers, civil servants, part of a decimated middle class, now working voluntarily on behalf of their people' and recounts meetings with representatives of local women's organizations, women who 'wanted to play a role in the reconstruction of their society'.[7]

Both Mary Robinson's visit and her later narrative demonstrate a successful negotiation of forces often separated, sometimes opposed, in the famine literature studied in this volume. In speeches at the time and later, Robinson combined vivid and disturbing descriptions of people's suffering with strong, hard-hitting political analysis of the causes of their hunger. Her Nairobi press conference, made memorable to its spectators by the speaker's visible emotion, ended with a call for 'new strategies, new lateral thinking about our relationship with the continent of Africa';[8] similarly *A Voice for Somalia* moves from graphic images of hunger to a series of challenges delivered to the United Nations, to other organizations, and to each observer. Her narrative's combination of affective power and political analysis makes it one of the few texts to approach Paul Ricoeur's definition of the role to be played by 'literature of horror' through a combination of 'individuation' and 'historical explanation': so that those struck by the 'horror' of events will seek to understand them.[9]

Robinson's 'act of witness', carefully and successfully negotiated, demonstrates the great symbolic potential of her role, though also its limitations. Her visit was the first by a European head of state, but a head of state without any decision-making or policy-shaping function. A certain *déjà-vu* surrounds the location of women's power primarily in the symbolic sphere, separated from the political sphere. Yet in her visit to Somalia, Robinson exploited the full potential of her symbolic presence, specifically her identity as woman and mother. With some echoes of the rhetoric employed by another famous woman, depicting the famine-stricken districts of Mayo less than one hundred years before, the president spoke of her outrage as a woman and, especially, as a mother: 'Now I found that as a mother it was totally unacceptable talking to a mother beside her dying children and she herself looking too under-nour-ished and frail and very desolate and often without energy because that diminishes our human sense, and we share this world.'[10] These features were also seized upon by media commentators at the time. Over and over again, articles praise Robinson's 'heart-felt' speech, the 'tears of a mother', her struggle to 'contain her emotion' and her 'touching maternal instinct' – phrases, by now, extremely familiar to readers of famine narratives. In particular, the headlines employed by Irish newspapers make striking reading: 'President's cry from the heart' (*Sunday Press*), 'Two visions of Irish woman-hood' (*Irish Independent*), 'They have given us back our humanity' (*The Star*) and 'A return to old decency' (*Irish Independent*).[11]

These headlines, especially when read at some distance, have troubling, and occasionally farcical qualities. The *Star*'s article, 'They have given us back our humanity', concluded that though Somali people 'were thanking us for the little we did' we 'should be thanking THEM, all the starving of Somalia, for what they have done for US'. The self-reflexive nature of such newspaper cover-age, saying, in many ways, more about 'us' than 'them', highlights the ways in which Robinson's visit also became the occasion for a type of self-congratulation and complacency about Ireland's role, the importance of Irish aid workers, the generosity of Irish chari-table donations, etc.[12] Through the figure of Mary Robinson, the 'ministering angel' or 'angel of mercy', one of the oldest characters in famine literature, gained a new life. Yet the difficulties raised by this character and by philanthropy in general, questions discussed in this volume in the context of Trollope's *Castle Richmond* (chapter one), women's famine philanthropy (chapter two) and 'Big House' literature (chapter three), remain. The ministering angel clearly stands for her class or nation, representing their benevolence and their partaking in the suffering of famine; she also serves to cover over more troubling questions of power and responsibility. In this context, Mary Robinson is such an ambivalent figure, not because of who she is, but because of who she represents: a western country whose role on the world stage is now that of donor and not, despite issues of folk-memory, potential victim – possessing the power to intervene or to look away. With the widespread media preference for showing Irish 'angels of mercy' in coverage of international famine and disaster, thus mediating images of starving or suffering people through the 'human interest' angle of a single, white figure, questions continue as to what exactly this 'ministering angel' represents.

Media commentators today share many of the difficulties which characterized writers' attempts to treat the subject of Irish and Bengal famines. The sense of a crisis in representation pervades journalists' writings, a crisis not lessened by the predominance of visual media and the ease of transmitting such images. How to individuate a large-scale and overwhelming event, to render the individual experience while retaining a focus on its collective nature, to avoid exploitation and stereotype, are still central dilemmas. A disaster affecting a million people, the orchestrated murder of up to one million men, women and children, consists of the experience of one million 'ones': can this ever be conveyed, given what Primo Levi has called 'our providentially myopic senses'?[13] Related obstacles concern the difficulty of securing and retaining a spectator's interest. Writing of his work in 1940s Bengal, Ian Stephens, editor of the *Statesman*, a newspaper with a key role in 'announcing' famine, dryly observed:

> Death by famine lacks drama. Bloody death, the deaths of many by slaughter as in riots or bombings is in itself blood-bestirring; it excites you, prints indelible images on the mind. But death by famine, a vast slow dispirited noiseless apathy offers none of that. Horrid though it may be to say, multitudinous death from this cause looked at merely optically, regarded without emotion as a spectacle, is until the crows get at it, the rats and kites and dogs and vultures very dull.[14]

Meantime, the media's role in highlighting famine and disaster is often quite selectively applied: in late 1984, while drought in Brazil remained virtually unreported, Ethiopian famine dominated the news, a prominence aided by rivalry between television channels, newspaper battles, and media-driven charity appeals.[15]

Present-day reporting of African politics is summarized succinctly by Fergal Keane in *Season of Blood*, a narrative of his experiences as a journalist in Rwanda:

> Where television is concerned, African news is generally only big news when it involves lots of dead bodies. The higher the mound, the greater the possibility that the world will, however briefly, send its camera teams and correspondents. Once the story has gone 'stale', i.e. there are no new bodies and the refugees are down to a trickle, the circus moves on. The powerful images leave us momentarily horrified but largely ignorant, what somebody memorably described as 'compassion without understanding'.[16]

In Mrinal Sen's film, *In Search of Famine*, one devastating scene shows the film-crew, temporarily unable to proceed with their film of the 1943–44 Bengal famine because of heavy rains, occupying themselves by guessing from which famine various photos of emaciated figures have come: 1943, 1959, or 1971 – 'Bangladesh. Do you remember?'[17]

The current methods for depicting famine and disaster once again involve the construction of spectacle, frequently with a focus on the female victim. An extract from Keane's book provides one memorable example:

> Begin with the river. From where I stand near the bridge it looks like a great soup. It is brown with upland silt and thick with elephant grass. It has come swirling down from the far reaches of the land and is fat with rain. I am arguing with Frank . . . The talk goes on like this for several more minutes. It is pleasantly distracting. So much so that at first I do not notice them. And then I turn around and for the first time I see two bodies bobbing along. Then three more. They nudge in and out of the grass and the leaves and are carried towards the falls. One swirls in towards the bank and I notice that it is a woman who has been chopped and hacked. But it is not the gash in her head, the gouges in her back and arms, that frighten and offend. Rather, I am shocked by her nakedness. Like the others she is

bloated and her bare body turns and drops and turns and drops in the current. Near the bridge the current picks up and I watch her tumble down into the white water, disappearing fast. She comes up again, head first, and is bounced against the rocks.

'Don't worry man. Don't be surprised,' says Frank. 'They've been coming through in their hundreds.' I look down directly on to the falls and see that there are two bodies wedged tight into the rocks. One is that of a man wearing a pair of shorts. He appears to be white, but this is because the days in the water have changed his colour. Near by there is a baby, but I can only make out the head and an arm. The infant is tossed around by the falling water but is tangled in the weeds that cover the lower part of the rocks. The force of the water is unable to dislodge the baby and so it bounces up and down in the foam. At this I turn and walk away from the bridge and quietly take my place in the back of the car.[18]

Keane's account is profoundly shocking and disturbing; as observer and narrator, he directly acknowledges the aspects of the scene to which his gaze is drawn: the woman's 'nakedness', the man's strange colour, the awful movement of the baby. More simplistically, though predictably, this is the extract chosen for the book's dust-cover; the second paragraph is deleted, with the exception of Frank's comment and the closing line, the result being that, in presenting the book for the scrutiny of prospective readers, even greater focus is placed on the woman's naked body.

The visual images of catastrophe, reproduced in newspapers and shown on television screens, demonstrate some of the most troubling features of contemporary media. Prevalent are images of emaciation and of suffering, of helplessness and hopelessness, suggesting the victims' powerlessness and inability to help themselves. The demeaning nature of these images also reinforces a division between spectator and scene, with significant consequences. As David Arnold writes, 'Famine grants one the honoured role of benefactor and donor while conferring upon the other the permanent and demeaning status of the begging-bowl.'[19] Rarely are the strategies employed by people in order to withstand famine given attention; like many of the images of the 1840s famine made available at the time, the famine victim is on the point of death, or has just died, never receives a voice and usually remains unnamed. In contrast, some of the more successful twentieth-century literary texts, both of the Irish and Bengal famine, explore what people may have done to survive, with moving and memorable consequences.

Simplistic and shocking images are sometimes defended because of their claimed affective power, their ability to 'move' the spectator, and, more specifically, to generate financial donations. Their role is thus, as one commentator has sardonically observed, to 'nourish western appetites for charity'.[20] Similarly, Fintan O'Toole notes, in the context of a discussion of Tom Murphy's play, that 'all our images of starvation, even the most compassionate journalistic representations, are images of the suffering to be consumed by the relatively comfortable'.[21] To what extent shocking and intrusive images are justified by their income-generating role remains fiercely disputed.[22] Certainly some of the images employed for fund-raising today equal the most voyeuristic and intrusive famine spectacles highlighted by this study. The nakedness of women is a frequent and particularly troubling feature; the dangerous configuration of issues of sexuality and charity, highlighted in the reading of *Castle Richmond*, returns to mind here. Other common objects of scrutiny are the exposed bodies of the dead. Given that some of the most moving of the famine texts explored in previous chapters concern the efforts of people, themselves starving or diseased, to bury or, at least, cover their dead, the absence of sensitivity to this need, among present-day commentators and journalists, is made even more striking.

The political consequences of these images should not be underestimated. As other commentators have highlighted, they present apathy as the primary characteristic of those who are starving; by extension, Africa appears as a continent waiting to be fed. On the part of the spectator, they promote a fatalism regarding what is seen: people's hunger emerges as somehow inevitable. The function which may be played by female images is particularly significant in this regard. Scenes of women unable to feed their children, of a child suckling at the dry breast of its mother or a despairing mother holding her dead child, are chosen to convey the breakdown in a primary or 'natural' order; in the words from Tom Murphy's *Famine*, 'where is a woman with childre when nature lets her down'. A disjunction results, similar to that highlighted in Murphy's play and present as early as Carleton's *The Black Prophet*, whereby the individuation of famine's effects, however moving or affective, may work against an understanding of why this has occurred. The resulting implication, that famine is a natural rather than a political or economic event, is itself a political message, regrettable but also convenient.

Deep ambivalences exist within the female figure; this double-ness can be glimpsed in many famine texts and is acknowledged by some of the more reflective writers. The mother gives life but also death; she may heroically seek to safeguard her child's life or endanger it; she is fatally passive and furiously active; her actions, in turn, have a double form: heroic sacrifices made by Shakti, the good mother, or the threatening and dangerous force of Kali, her 'terrible' other. The various anxieties which thus underlie the famine image and threaten the spectator's own well-being can be comforted and contained by the spectator's assumption of the philanthropic role, by 'compassion' and 'charity'.

The representations examined in this study, especially those of a maternal figure, have an obvious affective dimension, part of their 'appeal' being their evocation of primary, psychological needs, shared by the observer and the figure seen. Yet another, perhaps dominant, function, far from undoing the separation between spectator and scene, seeks its reinforcement. For all their graphic and shocking qualities, many aspects of famine images serve to remove rather than establish immediacy. The victim's plight is located within the realm of 'nature', with occasional subhuman or superhuman features, safely removed from the 'human' and poli-tical spheres.

A final issue is the spectator's potential 'fatigue' and inurement to any image, however graphic. What commentators today call 'famine fatigue' is not a recently-discovered syndrome. On 2 May 1846, an editorial from the *Illustrated London News*, speaking on behalf of the 'British Empire', reads as follows:

> We are stopped on the road to commercial prosperity by the gaunt and fever-stricken figure of our sister country, like a fat and wealthy citizen arrested, on his way to 'Change' by an importunate mendicant, all rags and hunger; and the man of wealth cannot help feeling his own prosperity as a

sort of reproach, in the presence of such an embodiment of misery; a twinge of conscience crosses him – a doubt, whether his wretched fellow-subject can have had fair play; so he grasps a handful of silver, bids the poor object take it, and buy bread, and goes his way to his merchandise. But, in the course of time, the same figure crosses his path, bearing about it additions and variety of wretchedness, and the same process of relief is repeated, causing dissatisfaction on one side, and humiliation on the other, till both are weary of it, and begin to ask whether more and better cannot be done? It is this question which is now being asked in a thousand forms. It seems long and tedious; but there is a long arrear of neglect and error to be made up; it is not one session, or many sessions, or even generations of those who make sessions and Parliaments that can remedy evils which have been the growth of centuries. Time is the last thing we should grudge in the process.[23]

Generations later, 'whether more and better cannot be done' has a poignant ring: the 'fat and wealthy citizen' and 'wretched', 'importunate mendicant' taking new yet analogous forms.

Returning briefly to the issue of aesthetics with which I began, the 'feminization of famine' emerges as a key strategy employed by writers to counter the feared impossibility of representation, with various consequences. In the late 1990s, the commemoration of the hundred and fiftieth anniversary of the Great Irish Famine yields interesting new depictions, in many different genres. A focus on performing or staging famine, as an event to be not only retold but seen, unites a number of different art forms: theatre, multi-media, and the big screen.[24] With screen adaptations of famine stories completed and promised, the vexed questions of the unspeakable and the unspoken gain a new urgency, encompassing what can and what should be seen. The images offered to us today, whether of present-day disaster or restagings of the past, are the most recent in a long tradition of famine portrayals. Other parts of that history, and specifically the role of female signs, have been examined in these chapters. The female figure has been made, in the course of famine representations to bear various meanings and to disguise others; embodying death and survival, horror and heroism, her form is an important reminder that the most 'moving' of images may fail to move understanding. The politics of famine may be covered over, or exposed, by the image chosen. My hope is that this study will contribute to an ongoing critique of how famine is depicted, sharpening our gaze as spectators, both of the past and of the present.

NOTES AND REFERENCES

1. Marina Warner, *Monuments and Maidens: The Allegory of the Female Form* ([1985]; London, 1987), p. 332.
2. Mary Robinson, President of Ireland, *A Voice for Somalia* (Dublin, 1992).
3. Ibid., preface.
4. Ibid.
5. Primo Levi, *The Drowned and the Saved* (1986), trans. Raymond Rosenthal (London, 1989), pp. 68–69.
6. Robinson, *A Voice for Somalia*, pp. 38, 65.
7. Ibid., pp. 19, 45–46.
8. The text of this address in the Nairobi Press Conference, 5 October, is reproduced in *A Voice for Somalia*, pp. 64–69. Interestingly, the diary also recounts her initial fear that this 'wall of emotion' had worked against her aims: 'In the event, because I was hit by a wall of emotion, of frustration and anger as I tried to convey what I had seen, I thought I had blown the opportunity . . . However, I wasn't just a barrister pleading a case. I was the President of Ireland giving a personal witness and responding to the people of Somalia. Above all, I was a human being devastated by what I had seen. In that context it was impossible not to show emotion.' (p. 64)
9. Paul Ricoeur writes: 'The more we explain in historical terms, the more indignant we become; the more we are struck by the horror of events, the more we seek to understand them', in *Time and Narrative* ([1985]; Chicago, 1988), iii, p. 188.
10. Robinson, *A Voice for Somalia*, pp. 65–66.
11. In 'Two visions of Irish womanhood' (*Irish Independent*, 10 October 1992), the columnist compared Mary Robinson with another Irishwoman 'in the headlines': Sinéad O'Connor, who, that week, had 'torn up a picture of the Pope on American television'. The headline, 'A return to old decency', accompanied an article on Robinson's visit written by Conor Cruise O'Brien (*Irish Independent*, 3 October 1992). A controversial, dissenting voice was that of Eamon Dunphy; in his article 'Misguided mission of mercy' (*Sunday Independent*, 11 October), he castigated the making of Somalia into a type of 'Caring Olympics'.
12. Among some media commentators, this complacency involved careless and inaccurate comment; one example is the description of the visit as the first by a 'head of state', rather than 'western head', ignoring the visit by President

Musseveni of Uganda some time before. Rarely did newspaper articles consider the more complex relationship between Africa and the west, evidenced, for example, by the structure of debt repayments, whereby significantly more money flows to the 'developed world' from the 'developing world', than vice versa. See Andy Storey, 'Comments on "Controversies over Conditionality" by Georg Sorensen' in *Irish Studies in International Affairs*, 5 (1994), pp. 49–52: 'Developing countries transfer $150 billion per annum in debt repayments to the developed world, three times the level of aid from rich to poor.'

13. Levi, *The Drowned and the Saved*, p. 40.

14. Ian Stephens, *Monsoon Morning* (London, 1966), p. 184.

15. See William Boot, 'Ethiopia: feasting on famine', in *Columbia Journalism Review*, 23 (1985), pp. 47–48.

16. Fergal Keane, *Season of Blood: A Rwandan Journey* (London, 1995), p. 7.

17. Mrinal Sen, *In Search of Famine* (1982); script reconstructed and translated by Samik Bandyopadhyay (Calcutta, 1983), p. 35. The presence of the film crew in the village causes huge increases in the price of food and shortages of many items; as one old man remarks, 'They came to take pictures of a famine and sparked off another famine' (p. 47). In addition, the recruiting of a local girl to play the part of a woman who turned to prostitution during the 1940s famine causes outrage among the villagers.

18. Keane, *Season of Blood*, pp. 73–74.

19. David Arnold, *Famine: Social Crisis and Historical Change* (New York and Oxford, 1988), p. 73. See also Sandra Burman's 'Innocents Abroad: Western Fantasies of Childhood and the Iconography of Emergencies', in *Disasters*, 18, 3 (1994), pp. 238–53, and John Sorenson, *Imagining Ethiopia* (New Jersey, 1993).

20. Adrian Hart, 'Images of the Third World', in Michelle Reeve and Jenny Hammond, *Looking Beyond the Frame*, Links series, 34 (Oxford, 1989), p. 16.

21. Fintan O'Toole, 'Some Food for Thought', *Irish Times*, theatre guide, 1 October 1993, p. 4.

22. See, for example, the campaign for less stereotyped media coverage of the 'Third World' launched by Comhlámh, a voluntary association of returned development workers (Eilish Dillon, *Irish Times*, 18 December 1995) and the Complete Picture Campaign's *Guidelines for Good Practice in Charity Advertising in Ireland* (Dublin, 1995).

23. *Illustrated London News*, 2 May 1846.

24. These include the video installations of Alanna O'Kelly; Radio Telefís Éireann's adaptation (1996) of Michael Harding's story 'The Poorhouse', first published in 1986; the screening by the British Broadcasting Corporation, in conjunction with RTÉ, of a four-part television drama, *The Hanging Gale* (1995); and a planned screen adaptation of Liam O'Flaherty's novel, *Famine*.

Bibliography

Abel, Elizabeth (ed.), *Writing and Sexual Difference* (Brighton, 1982).

Achebe, Chinua, *Arrow of God* (London, 1964).

Adorno, Theodor, *Prisms* (1955), trans. Samuel and Shierry Weber (Cambridge, Mass., 1981).

Alloula, Malek, *The Colonial Harem: Images of Subconscious Eroticism* (1981); trans. Myrna Godzich and Wlad Godzich (Manchester, 1987).

Arnold, David, *Famine: Social Crisis and Historical Change* (Oxford and New York, 1988).

Aykroyd, Wallace Ruddell, *The Conquest of Famine* (London, 1974).

Ash, Ranjana (ed.), *Short Stories from India, Pakistan and Bengal* (London, 1980).

Bandyopadhyay, Manik, 'Aaj Kal Parshur Galpa' (A Tale of These Days), (1963); translated and published by Kalpana Bardhan in *Of Women, Outcastes, Peasants and Rebels: A Selection of Bengali Short Stories* (California, 1990), pp. 135–51.

——, *Wives and Others*, selected and translated by Kalpana Bardhan (New Delhi, 1979).

Bandyopadhyay, Tarasankar, *Manwantar* (*Epoch's End*) (Calcutta, 1944); trans. Hirendranath Mookherjee (Calcutta, 1950).

Banville, John, *Birchwood* ([1973]; London, 1987).

Bardhan, Kalpana (ed.), *Of Women, Outcastes, Peasants and Rebels: A Selection of Bengali Short Stories* (California, 1990).

Bennett, William, *Narrative of a recent journey of six weeks in Ireland in connexion with the subject of supplying small seed to some of the remoter districts . . .* (London and Dublin, 1847).

Berens, Louise, *Steadfast unto Death: A Tale of the Irish Famine of Today* (London, 1880).

Bhabha, Homi, 'The Other Question . . . Homi Bhabha Reconsiders the Stereotype and Colonial Discourse', *Screen*, 24, 6 (1983), pp. 18–36.

——, 'Of Mimicry and Men: The Ambivalence of Colonial Discourse', *October*, 28 (1984), pp. 125–33.

Bhatia, B. M., *Famines in India: 1860–1965* (2nd [1963]; Bombay, 1967).

Bhattacharya, Bhabani, *So Many Hungers!* ([1947]; New Delhi, 1978).

——, *He Who Rides a Tiger* (New York, 1954).

Boland, Eavan, *A Kind of Scar: The Woman Poet in a National Tradition*, LIP pamphlet (Dublin, 1989).

——, *Selected Poems* (Manchester, 1989).

——, *Outside History* (Manchester, 1990).

——, *In a Time of Violence* (Manchester, 1994).

——, *Object Lessons: The Life of the Woman and the Poet in Our Time* (Manchester, 1995).

Boot, William, 'Ethiopia: feasting on famine', *Columbia Journalism Review*, 23 (1985), pp. 47–48.

Bose, Buddhadeva, *An Acre of Green Grass: A Review of Modern Bengali Literature* (Calcutta, 1948).

Bose, Sugata, *Agrarian Bengal: Economy, Social Structure, and Politics, 1919–1947* (Cambridge, 1986).

Boyle, Phelim P. and Cormac Ó Gráda, 'Fertility Trends, Excess Mortality, and the Great Irish Famine', *Demography*, 23, 4, (1986), pp. 543–559.

Brew, Margaret (M. W.), *The Burtons of Dunroe* (3 vols; [1880]; reprinted, with an introduction by Robert Lee Wolff, New York and London, 1979).

——, *The Chronicles of Castle Cloyne; or, Pictures of the Munster People* (3 vols; [1884]; 1885 edition reprinted, with an introduction by Robert Lee Wolff, New York and London, 1979).

Bright, J. S., *Before and After Independence* (New Delhi, 1950).

Brown, Malcolm, *The Politics of Irish Literature* (London, 1972).

Brown, Stephen J., *Ireland in Fiction, Volume I* ([1915]; second edition 1919, reprinted Shannon, 1968).

Burman, Sandra (ed.), *Fit Work for Women* (London, 1979).

——, 'Innocents Abroad: Western Fantasies of Childhood and the Iconography of Emergencies', *Disasters*, 18, 3 (1994), pp. 238–53.

Burritt, Elihu, *A Visit of Three Days to Skibbereen and Its Neighbourhood* (London, 1847).

——, *Elihu Burritt: a memorial volume containing a sketch of his life and labors . . .*, (ed.) Charles Northend (New York, 1879).

Buttimer, Neil, 'A Stone on the Cairn: The Great Famine in Later Gaelic Manuscripts', in Christopher Morash and Richard Hayes (eds.), *'Fearful Realities': New Perspectives on the Famine* (Dublin, 1996), pp. 93–109.

Byrd, Elizabeth, *The Famished Land* (London, 1972).

Cardozo, Nancy, *Maud Gonne: Lucky Eyes and a High Heart* (London, 1978).

Carleton, William, *The Black Prophet: A Tale of Irish Famine* ([1847]; Shannon, 1972, facsimile of 1899 edition).

——, *The Squanders of Castle Squander* (2 vols; London, 1852).

——, 'Fair Gurtha; or, The Hungry Grass: A Legend of the Dumb Hill', *Dublin University Magazine*, XLVII (1856), pp. 414–35.

Carty, James, *A Class-book of Irish History* (Dublin, 1929).

Central Relief Committee, *Transactions of the Central Relief Committee of the Society of Friends during the Famine in Ireland, in 1846 and 1847* (Dublin, 1852).

——, *Distress in Ireland: Address of the Committee to the Members of the Society of Friends in Ireland, 13 November 1846.*

Census of Ireland for the Year 1851, V, part 1, H. C. 1856, [2087–I], xxix.

Chandar, Krishan, *Ann Dātā (I Cannot Die: A Story of Bengal)* (Poona, 1944/5), translated from Urdu by Kwaja Ahmad Abbas, with cover design and illustrations by Rathin Motra.

Chandrasekharan, K. R., *Bhabani Bhattacharya* (New Delhi, 1974).

Chatterjee, Partha, 'The Nationalist Resolution of the Women's Question', in Kumkum Sangari and Sudesh Vaid (eds.),

Recasting Women: Essays in Colonial History (New Delhi, 1989), pp. 23–54.

Cobbe, Frances Power, *Life of Frances Power Cobbe By Herself* (2 vols; London, 1894).

Connolly, James and Maud Gonne, *The Right to Life and the Rights of Property* (Dublin, 1898).

Connolly, James, *Labour in Irish History* (Dublin, 1910).

Conyngham, David Power, *Frank O'Donnell: A Tale of Irish Life* (Dublin, 1861), reprinted in America as *The O'Donnells of Glen Cottage* (New York, 1874).

Cooper, George, 'The Irish Mother's Lament over Her Child', *Howitt's Journal*, 23 October 1847.

Coxhead, Elizabeth, *Daughters of Erin* (London, 1965).

Correspondence from July 1846 to January 1847, relative to the Measures adopted for the Relief of Distress in Ireland (Board of Works series), First Part (London, 1847), reprinted in Irish University Press, *Famine* Series, VI (Shannon, 1970).

Crawford, E. Margaret (ed.), *Famine: The Irish Experience, 900–1900* (Edinburgh, 1989).

Crosfield, Joseph, *Distress in Ireland: Letter from Joseph Crosfield, containing a Narrative of the first week of William Forster's Visit to some of the Distressed Districts in Ireland* (London, 1846).

Crosthwaite, C. H., *Thakur Pertab Singh and Other Tales* (Edinburgh, 1913).

Cullingford, Elizabeth Butler, *Gender and History in Yeats's Love Poetry* (Cambridge, 1993).

Cummins, Nicholas, letter to *The Times*, 24 December 1846, p. 6.

Cusack, Mary Frances, *Tim O'Halloran's Choice; or, from Killarney to New York* (London, 1877).

——, *The Case of Ireland stated: a plea for my people and my race* (Dublin, 1881).

——, *The Nun of Kenmare: An Autobiography* (London, 1889).

Daly, Mary, *The Great Famine in Ireland* (Dublin, 1986).

Darby, Mildred (pseud. Andrew Merry), *The Hunger* (London, 1910).

Das, T., *The Bengal Famine of 1943, as Revealed in a Survey of the Destitutes in Calcutta* (Calcutta, 1949).

Deane, Seamus (ed.), *The Field Day Anthology of Irish Writing* (3 vols; Derry, 1991).

Denvir, Gearóid, *Cadhan Aonair* (Dublin, 1987).

Devi, Mahasweta, *Tarasankar Bandyopadhyay* (New Delhi, 1975).

——, 'The Witch-Hunt', trans. from Bengali by Kalpana Bardhan in *Of Women, Outcastes, Peasants and Rebels: A Selection of Bengali Short Stories* (California, 1990), pp. 242–71.

——, *Imaginary Maps*, trans. by Gayatri Chakravorty Spivak (New York and London, 1995).

Dhawan, R. K. (ed.), *Explorations in Modern Indo-English Fiction* (New Delhi, 1982).

Dinneen, Patrick, *Creideamh agus Gorta: traghidheacht bhaineas le haimsir an drochshaoghail* (Faith and Famine: a tragic drama relating to the famine) (Dublin, 1901).

——, *Teachtaire Ó Dhia* (A Messenger from God) (Dublin, n. d.).

Doane, Mary Ann, Patricia Mellencamp and Linda Williams (eds.), *Re-Vision: Essays in Feminist Film Criticism* (Maryland and Los Angeles, 1984).

Donnelly, James S., 'The Administration of Relief, 1846–7', and 'The Administration of Relief, 1847–51', in W. E. Vaughan (ed.), *A New History of Ireland: Volume 5: Ireland under the Union, I, 1801–1870* (Oxford, 1989), pp. 294–331.

Donovan, D., 'Observations on the peculiar diseases to which the famine of the last year gave origin . . .', *Dublin Medical Press*, XIX (1848), p. 67.

Drèze, Jean and Amartya Sen, *Hunger and Public Action*, WIDER studies in development economics (Oxford, 1989).

Dufferin, Lord and Hon. G. F. Boyle, *Narrative of a Journey from Oxford to Skibbereen during the Year of the Irish Famine* (Oxford, 1847).

Dutta, Ujjal, 'Woman in Bengali Fiction: An Inquiry', in C. D. Narasimhaiah and C. N. Srinatu (eds.), *Women in Fiction and Fiction by Women* (Mysore, 1986), pp. 20–30.

Eagleton, Terry, *Heathcliff and the Great Hunger: Studies in Irish Culture* (London, 1995).

Edgeworth, Frances, *A Memoir of Maria Edgeworth with a Selection from Her Letters* (3 vols; London, 1867).

Edgeworth, Maria, correspondence with the Central Relief Committee in Dublin relating to distress in the Edgeworthstown area, 1847–8, in Edgeworth Papers (National Library, Dublin), Ms. 989.

——, letters to Joseph Harvey and others on the Benevolence of the Society of Friends (January and February 1847), in Ballitore Papers (National Library, Dublin).

——, letters to Rev. Richard Jones, 1833–49, in Edgeworth Papers (National Library, Dublin).

Edwards, R. D. and T. D. Williams (eds.), *The Great Famine: Studies in Irish History, 1845–1852* (Dublin, 1956).

Ellmann, Maud, *The Hunger-Artists: Starving, Writing and Imprisonment* (London, 1993).

Field, Louise (E. M.), *Denis: A Study in Black and White* (London, 1896).

Fisher, Marlene, 'The Women in Bhattacharya's Novels', *World Literature Written in English*, 11, 1 (1972), pp. 95–108.

Fitzpatrick, David, 'Women and the Great Famine', in Margaret Kelleher and James H. Murphy (eds.), *Separate Spheres?: Gender and Nineteenth-Century Ireland* (Dublin, forthcoming 1997).

Forster, William Edward, *Distress in Ireland: Narrative of William Edward Forster's Visit to Ireland* (London, 1847).

Foucault, Michel, *The History of Sexuality: An Introduction* (1976), trans. Robert Hurley (London, 1979).

Fox, Emily (pseud. Toler King), *Rose O'Connor* (Chicago, 1880).

Fox, R. Barclay, *Distress in Ireland: Narrative of R. Barclay Fox's Visit to some parts of the West of Ireland* (London, 1847).

Frayne, John (ed.), *The Uncollected Prose of W. B. Yeats* (2 vols; London, 1970).

Freiligrath, Ferdinand, 'Ireland' (trans. Mary Howitt), *Howitt's Journal*, 3 April 1847.

Gallop, Jane, *Thinking Through the Body* (New York, 1988).

Gamman, Lorraine and Margaret Marshment (eds.), *The Female Gaze* (London, 1988).

Gerard, Jessica, 'Lady Bountiful: Women of the Landed Classes and Rural Philanthropy', *Victorian Studies*, 30 (1987), pp. 183–210.

Ghosh, Kali Charan, *Famines in Bengal: 1770–1943* (Calcutta, 1944; second edition, 1987, with a foreword by Amartya Sen).

Ginzberg, Lori D., *Women and the Work of Benevolence: Morality, Politics, and Class in the Nineteenth-Century United States* (New Haven and London, 1990).

Gledhill, Christine, 'Pleasurable Negotiations', in E. Deidre Pribram (ed.), *Female Spectators: Looking at Film and Television* (London and New York, 1988), pp. 64–89.

——, 'Recent Developments in French Film Criticism', *Quarterly Review of Film Studies*, 3, 4 (1978), reproduced in Doane et al., *Re-Vision*, pp. 18–48.

Gonne, Maud (Maud Gonne MacBride), 'Relief Work in Erris', *Freeman's Journal*, 9 March 1898, and 'The Distress in the West', *Freeman's Journal*, 30 March 1898.

——, 'Reine de la Disette', republished as 'The Famine Queen' in *United Irishman*, 7 April 1900.

——, *Dawn*, first published in *United Irishman*, 29 October 1904, republished in Hogan, Robert (ed.), *Lost Plays of the Irish Renaissance* (Dixon, Calif., 1970).

——, *A Servant of the Queen: Reminiscences* (London, 1938).

Gonne, Maud and James Connolly, *The Right to Life and the Rights of Property* (Dublin, 1898).

Goodbody, Roy, *A Suitable Channel: Quaker Relief in the Great Famine* (Bray, 1995).

Greaves, C. Desmond, *The Life and Times of James Connolly* (London, 1961).

Greenough, Paul, *Prosperity and Misery in Modern Bengal* (New York and Oxford, 1982).

Gregory, Lady Augusta, 'An Explanation', *Arrow*, 1 June 1907.

Harding, Michael P., 'The Poorhouse', in *Priest: A Fiction* (Belfast, 1986).

Hare, Augustus J. C., *The Life and Letters of Maria Edgeworth* (2 vols; London, 1894).

Hart, Adrian, 'Images of the Third World', in Michelle Reeve and Jenny Hammond (eds.), *Looking Beyond the Frame*, Links series, 34 (Oxford, 1989), pp. 12–18.

Hatton, Helen, *The Largest Amount of Good: Quaker Relief in Ireland, 1654–1921* (Kingston and Montreal, 1993).

Hayden, Mary, *A Short History of the Irish People from the Earliest Times to 1920* (Dublin, 1921).

Healy, Gerard, *The Black Stranger* (Dublin, 1950).

Heaney, Seamus, *Death of a Naturalist* (London, 1966).

Hennedy, Hugh, 'Love and Famine, Family and Country in Trollope's *Castle Richmond*', *Éire-Ireland*, 7, 4 (1972), pp. 48–66.

Hewitt, John, *Out of My Time: Poems 1967–1974* (Belfast, 1974).

Hewitt, Nancy A., 'Beyond the Search for Sisterhood: American Women's History in the 1980s', *Social History*, 10, 3 (1985), pp. 299–319.

Hildebidle, John, *Five Irish Writers: The Errand of Keeping Alive* (Cambridge, Mass., 1989).

Hoare, Edward, *Some account of the early history and genealogy with pedigrees from 1330, unbroken to the present time, of the families of Hore and Hoare, with all their branches* (London, 1883).

Hoare, Mary Anne, *Shamrock Leaves; or, Tales and Sketches of Ireland* (Dublin and London, 1851).

——, 'The Mysterious Sketch', *Temple Bar*, 34 (1872), pp. 212–24.

Hogan, Robert, *After the Irish Renaissance: A Critical History of the Irish Drama since* The Plough and the Stars (London and Melbourne, 1968).

——, (ed.), *Lost Plays of the Irish Renaissance* (Dixon, Calif., 1970).

Hogan, Robert and James Kilroy, *The Abbey Theatre: The Years of Synge, 1905–1909* (Dublin, 1978).

Homans, Margaret, *'Bearing the Word': Language and Female Experience in Nineteenth-Century Women's Writing* (Chicago and London, 1986).

Hone, Joseph, *W. B. Yeats, 1865–1939* (London, 1942).

Hurst, Michael, *Maria Edgeworth and the Public Scene: Intellect, Fine Feeling and Landlordism in the Age of Reform* (London, 1969).

Innes, C. L., *Woman and Nation in Irish Literature and Society: 1880–1935* (London, 1993).

Ireland in Prose and Poetry, Junior and Senior Books (Dublin, 1930).

Irish University Press, 'Famine Series' (8 vols; Shannon, 1968–70).

Jardine, Alice, *Gynesis: Configurations of Woman and Modernity* (Ithaca and London, 1985).

Jeffares, A. N., *W. B. Yeats: A New Biography* (London, 1988).

Jeffares, A. N. and A. S. Knowland, *A Commentary on the Collected Plays of W. B. Yeats* (London, 1975).

J. L., introduction to Asenath Nicholson, *Annals of the Famine in Ireland, in 1847, 1848, and 1849* (New York, 1851).

Kaplan, E. Ann, *Women and Film: Both Sides of the Camera* (London, 1983).

Kavanagh, Patrick, *The Great Hunger* (Dublin, 1942).

——, *Lough Derg* (Curragh, 1978).

Keane, Fergal, *Season of Blood: A Rwandan Journey* (London, 1995).

Keary, Annie, *Castle Daly: The Story of an Irish Home Thirty Years Ago* (3 vols; London, 1875); first published in *Macmillan's Magazine*, XXIX–XXXII (1874–75); reprinted, with an introduction by Robert Lee Wolff (New York and London, 1979).

Keary, Eliza, *Memoir of Annie Keary by her Sister* (London, 1882).

Kelleher, Margaret and James H. Murphy (eds.), *Separate Spheres?: Gender and Nineteenth-Century Ireland* (Dublin, forthcoming 1997).

Kelleher, Margaret, 'Anthony Trollope's *Castle Richmond*: A "Horrid Novel"?', *Irish University Review*, 25, 2 (1995), pp. 242–62.

——, 'The Female Gaze: Asenath Nicholson's Famine Narrative', in Christopher Morash and Richard Hayes (eds.), *'Fearful Realities': New Perspectives on the Famine* (Dublin, 1996), pp. 119–30.

——, 'Irish Famine in Literature' in Cathal Póirtéir (ed.), *The Great Irish Famine* (Cork and Dublin, 1995), pp. 232–47.

Kerben, Linda K., 'Separate Spheres, Female Worlds, Women's Place: The Rhetoric of Women's History,' in *Journal of American History*, LXXV, I (1988), pp. 9–39.

Killen, John, *The Famine Decade: Contemporary Accounts, 1841–1851* (Belfast, 1995).

Kinealy, Christine, *This Great Calamity: The Irish Famine, 1845–52* (Dublin, 1994).

Kipling, Rudyard, 'William the Conqueror' in *The Day's Work* ([1898]; London, 1988).

Kissane, Noel, *The Irish Famine: A Documentary History* (Dublin, 1995).

Knelman, Judith, 'Anthony Trollope: English Journalist and Novelist, Writing about the Famine in Ireland', *Éire-Ireland*, 23, 3 (1988), pp. 57–67.

Krishnamurty, J. (ed.), *Women in Colonial India: Essays on Survival, Work and the State* (Bombay, 1989).

Krishnaswamy, Shantha, *The Woman in Indian Fiction in English, 1950–1980* (New Delhi, 1984).

Kristeva, Julia, 'Stabat Mater' (1977), reprinted and translated in Toril Moi (ed.), *The Julia Kristeva Reader* (Oxford, 1986).

——, *Powers of Horror: An Essay on Abjection* (1980), trans. L. S. Roudiez (New York, 1982).

Lane-Poole, Stanley, 'Annie Keary', *Macmillan's Magazine*, 42 (1880), pp. 259–67.

Langer, Lawrence L., *The Holocaust and the Literary Imagination* (New Haven and London, 1975).

Lawless, Emily, *Ireland* ([1887]; London, 1912).

——, *With Essex in Ireland* ([1890]; New York and London, 1979).

——, *Traits and Confidences* ([1897]; New York and London, 1979).

Leventhal, A. J., review of *The Black Stranger*, *Dublin Magazine*, XX (1945), p. 44.

Levi, Primo, *The Drowned and the Saved* (1986), trans. Raymond Rosenthal (London, 1989).

Liddle, Joanna and Rama Joshi, *Daughters of Independence: Gender, Caste and Class in India* (2nd, London and New Delhi, 1986).

Lowe-Evans, Mary, *Crimes Against Fecundity: Joyce and Population Control* (New York, 1989).

Luddy, Maria, 'Prostitution and Rescue Work in the Nineteenth Century', in Luddy and Murphy (eds.), *Women Surviving*, pp. 51–84.

——, *Women and Philanthropy in Nineteenth-Century Ireland* (Cambridge, 1995).

——, *Women in Ireland, 1800–1918: A Documentary History* (Cork, 1995).

Luddy, Maria and Clíona Murphy (eds.), *Women Surviving: Studies in Irish Women's History in the Nineteenth and Twentieth Centuries* (Dublin, 1989).

M. L., review of *Famine*, *Irish Book Lover*, XXV (1937), pp. 22–23.

MacBride, Maud Gonne, see under Gonne, Maud.

MacBride White, Anna and A. Norman Jeffares, *The Gonne–Yeats Letters, 1893–1938: 'Always your Friend'* (London, 1992).

MacGrianna, Seosamh, *An Grá agus An Ghruaim* (Dublin, 1929).

McHugh, Roger, 'The Famine in Irish Oral Tradition', in R. D. Edwards and T. D. Williams (eds.), *The Great Famine: Studies in Irish History* (Dublin, 1956), pp. 391–436.

Mac Lochlainn, Antain, 'The Famine in Gaelic Tradition', *Irish Review*, 17/18 (1995), pp. 90–108.

McLoughlin, Dympna, 'Workhouses and Irish Female Paupers, 1840–70', in Maria Luddy and Clíona Murphy (eds.), *Women Surviving* (Dublin, 1989), p. 117–47.

Macken, Walter, *The Silent People* (London, 1962).

Mahony, James, engravings in *Illustrated London News*, 13 and 20 February 1847.

Mani, Lati, 'Contentious Traditions: The Debate on Sati in Colonial India', in Kumkum Sangari and Sudesh Vaid (eds.), *Recasting Women: Essays in Colonial History* (New Delhi, 1989), pp. 88–126.

Marcus, Steven, *Representations: Essays on Literature and Society* ([1975]; New York, 1990).

Markandaya, Kamala, *Nectar in a Sieve* (Delhi, 1955).

——, *A Handful of Rice* (London, 1966).

Mayne, Judith, 'The Woman at the Keyhole: Women's Cinema and Feminist Criticism', *New German Critique*, 23 (1981), pp. 27–43, republished in Doane et al., *Re-Vision*, pp. 49–66.

Meredith, Susanna, *The Lacemakers: Sketches of Irish Character with Some Account of the Effort to Establish Lace-Making in Ireland* (London, 1865).

Michie, Helena, *The Flesh Made Word: Female Figures and Women's Bodies* (New York and Oxford, 1987).

Moi, Toril (ed.), *The Julia Kristeva Reader* (Oxford, 1986).

Morash, Christopher (ed.), *The Hungry Voice: The Poetry of the Irish Famine* (Dublin, 1989).

——, *Writing the Irish Famine* (Oxford, 1995).

Morash, Christopher and Richard Hayes (eds.), *'Fearful Realities': New Perspectives on the Famine* (Dublin, 1996).

Morrison, Toni, *Beloved* (New York, 1987).

——, 'Site of Memory', in William Zinsser (ed.), *Inventing the Truth: The Art and Craft of Memoir* (Boston, 1987).

——, *Playing in the Dark: Whiteness and the Literary Imagination* ([1992]; London, 1993).

Mulholland, Rosa (Lady Gilbert), *The Haunted Organist of Hurly Burly and Other Stories* (London, 1891).

——, 'The Hungry Death' in W. B. Yeats (ed.), *Representative Irish Tales* (2 vols; New York and London, 1891), ii, pp. 285–327.

Mullen, Michael, *The Hungry Land* (New York and London, 1986).

Mulvey, Laura, 'Visual Pleasure and Narrative Cinema', *Screen*, 16, 3 (1975), pp. 6–18.

Murphy, Tom, *Famine* (Dublin, 1977).

——, *Plays: One* (London, 1992).

Nandy, Ashis, *The Intimate Enemy: Loss and Recovery of Self under Colonialism* (Delhi, 1983).

Nangle, Edward, article on Asenath Nicholson, *Achill Missionary Herald and Western Witness*, 25 June 1845, p. 65.

Narasimhaiah, C. D. and C. N. Srinatu (eds.), *Women in Fiction and Fiction by Women* (Mysore, 1986).

Nehru, Jawaharal, *The Discovery of India* (Calcutta, 1946; abridged edition, Delhi and Oxford, 1989).

Neumann, Erich, *The Great Mother: An Analysis of the Archetype*, trans. Ralph Manheim (London, 1955).

Nic Eoin, Máirín, 'Ar an Trá Fholamh – an Gorta Mór in Litríocht Ghaeilge na hAoise seo' in Cathal Póirtéir (ed.), *Gnéithe den Ghorta* (Dublin, 1995), pp. 107–30.

Nicholson, Asenath, *Ireland's Welcome to the Stranger; or, Excursions through Ireland in 1844, and 1845, for the purpose of personally investigating the condition of the poor* (London, 1847).

——, *Lights and Shades of Ireland, in Three Parts* (London, 1850).

——, *Annals of the Famine in Ireland in 1847, 1848 and 1849* (reprint of part three of *Lights and Shades of Ireland*), with an introduction by 'J. L.' (New York, 1851).

——, *The Bible in Ireland* (abridged version of *Ireland's Welcome*), edited with an introduction by Alfred T. Sheppard (London, 1926).

Norman, Dorothy (ed.), *Nehru, The First Sixty Years: Passages from Nehru's Writings* (2 vols; London, 1965).

Ó Cadhain, Máirtín, *An tSraith ar Lár* (Dublin, 1967).

O'Connell, Catherine M., *Excursions in Ireland during 1844 and 1850* (London, 1852).

O'Connor, Frank, *A Short History of Irish Literature: A Backward Look* (New York, 1967).

O'Faolain, Sean, review of *Famine, Ireland Today*, II, 2 (1937), pp. 81–82.

O'Flaherty, Liam, *Famine* ([1937]; Dublin, 1979).

Ó Gráda, Cormac, *The Great Irish Famine* (London, 1989).

——, *Ireland Before and After the Famine: Explorations in Economic History, 1800–1930* ([1988]; Manchester, 1993).

——, *An Drochshaol: Béaloideas agus Amhráin* (Dublin, 1994).

——, '"Making History" in Ireland in the 1940s and 1950s: The Saga of *The Great Famine*', *Irish Review*, 12 (1992), pp. 87–107.

O'Grady, Hubert, *The Famine* (1886), republished in the *Journal of Irish Literature*, 19 (1985), pp. 14–49.

O'Leary, Philip, *The Prose Literature of the Gaelic Revival, 1881–1921: Ideology and Innovation* (Pennsylvania, 1994).

O'Neill, Kevin, *Family and Farm in pre-Famine Ireland: The Parish of Killashandra* (Madison, 1984).

O'Neill, Tim P., 'The Persistence of Famine in Ireland', in Cathal Póirtéir (ed.), *The Great Irish Famine* (Cork and Dublin, 1995), pp 204–19.

O'Rourke, Canon John, *The History of the Great Irish Famine of 1847, with notices of earlier Irish famines* (Dublin, 1875; reprinted Dublin, 1989).

Osborne, Sidney Godolphin, letters to *The Times*, 14 and 21 June, 5 and 9 July 1849.

——, *Gleanings in the West of Ireland* (London, 1850).

O'Toole, Fintan, *The Politics of Magic: The Work and Times of Tom Murphy* (Dublin, 1987).

——, 'Some Food for Thought', *Irish Times*, 1 October 1993, p. 4.

Ovid, *The Metamorphoses, Book VIII*, trans. by Frank Justus Miller (Loeb Classical Library [1916]; London, 1977).

Parnell, Anna, *Old Tales and New* (Dublin and London, 1905).

Pelly, Patricia and Andrew Tod (eds.), *The Highland Lady in Ireland, Journals 1840–1850: Elizabeth Grant of Rothiemurchus* (Edinburgh, 1991).

Póirtéir, Cathal, 'Folk Memory and the Famine', in *The Great Irish Famine* (Cork and Dublin, 1995), pp. 219–31.

——, *Famine Echoes* (Dublin, 1995).

—— (ed.), *The Great Irish Famine* (Cork and Dublin, 1995).

—— (ed.), *Gnéithe den Ghorta* (Dublin, 1995).

Poovey, Mary, *Uneven Developments: The Ideological Work of Gender in Mid-Victorian England* (Chicago, 1988).

Preston, Margaret H., 'Lay Women and Philanthropy in Dublin, 1860–1880', *Éire-Ireland*, 28, 4 (1993), pp. 74–85.

Pribram, E. Deidre (ed.), *Female Spectators: Looking at Film and Television* (London and New York, 1988).

Prochaska, F. K., *Women and Philanthropy in Nineteenth-Century England* (Oxford, 1980).

——, *The Voluntary Impulse: Philanthropy in Modern Britain* (London, 1988).

Read, Charles A. and T. P. O'Connor (eds.), *The Cabinet of Irish Literature: Selections from the Works of the Chief Poets, Orators, and Prose Writers of Ireland. With Biographical Sketches and Literary Notices* (4 vols; London, Glasgow, Edinburgh and Dublin, 1879–80); new ed. by Katherine Tynan Hinkson (London, 1902–3).

Rich, Adrienne, *Of Woman Born: Motherhood as Experience and Institution* ([1976]; London, 1992).

Ricoeur, Paul, 'Narrative Time', *Critical Inquiry*, 7, 1 (1980), pp. 169–90.

——, *Time and Narrative* (3 vols; 1983–5), trans. K. Blamey and D. Pellauer Chicago, 1984–8).

Ringelheim, Joan, 'The Holocaust: Taking Women into Account', *Jewish Quarterly*, 39, 3 (1992), pp. 19–24.

Rivers, J. P. W., 'The Nutritional Biology of Famine', in G. Harrison (ed.), *Famine* (Oxford, 1988).

Robinson, Mary, *A Voice for Somalia* (Dublin, 1992).

Rose, Jacqueline, *Sexuality and the Field of Vision* (London, 1986).

Ryder, Seán, 'Reading Lessons: Famine and the *Nation*, 1845–1849', in Chris Morash and Richard Hayes (eds.), *'Fearful Realities': New Perspectives on the Famine* (Dublin, 1996), pp. 151–63.

Sadiq, Muhammed, *Twentieth-Century Urdu Literature* (Karachi, 1983).

Sadlier, Mary Anne, *New Lights; or, Life in Galway* (New York, 1853).

Sangari, Kumkum and Sudesh Vaid (eds.), *Recasting Women: Essays in Colonial History* (New Delhi, 1989).

Santhanam, Kasturiranga (ed.), *Cry of Distress: a first-hand description and objective study of the Indian famine of 1943* (New Delhi, 1943).

Sarkar, Tanika, 'Politics and Women in Bengal: The Conditions and Meaning of Participation' in J. Krishnamurty (ed.), *Women in Colonial India: Essays on Survival, Work and the State* (Delhi, 1989), pp. 231–41.

——, 'Nationalist Iconography: Image of Women in Nineteenth-Century Bengali Literature', *Economic and Political Weekly*, 21 November 1987, pp. 2011–15.

Scally, Robert, *The End of Hidden Ireland* (New York and Oxford, 1995).

Scott, Joan W., 'Gender: A Useful Category of Historical Analysis', in *American Historical Review*, XCI (December 1986), pp. 1053–75.

Sen, Amartya, *Poverty and Famines: An Essay on Entitlement and Deprivation* ([1981]; Oxford, 1982).

Sen, Ela, *Darkening Days: Being a Narrative of Famine-Stricken Bengal* (Calcutta, 1944), with illustrations by Zainul Abedin.

——, *Wives of Famous Men* (Bombay, 1942).

Sen, Mrinal, *Ākāler Sandhāney* (*In Search of Famine*) (1982); script reconstructed and translated by Samik Bandyopadhyay (Calcutta, 1983).

Shamsuddin, Abu Jafar, 'The Leader' (1967), translated from Bengali by Ranjana Ash and published in Ash (ed.), *Short Stories from India, Pakistan and Bengal* (London, 1980), pp. 59–64.

Sharma, K. K., *Bhabani Bhattacharya: His Vision and Themes* (New Delhi, 1979).

Sharpe, Jenny, *Allegories of Empire: The Figure of Woman in the Colonial Text* (Minnesota, 1993).

Sheeran, Patrick, *The Novels of Liam O'Flaherty* (Dublin, 1976).

Shimer, Dorothy, *Bhabani Bhattacharya* (Boston, 1975).

Shirwadkar, Meena, *Image of Woman in the Indo-Anglian Novel* (New Delhi, 1979).

Showalter, Elaine, 'Feminist Criticism in the Wilderness', *Critical Inquiry*, 8, 1 (1981), pp. 179–205.

—— (ed.), *The New Feminist Criticism* (New York, 1985).

Sidnell, M. J., 'Yeats's First Work for the Stage: The Earliest Versions of the *Countess Kathleen*' in Desmond E. Maxwell and S. B. Bushrui (eds.), *W. B. Yeats, 1865–1935: Centenary Essays* (Ibadan, 1965).

Sims, William Dillwyn, *Distress in Ireland: Narrative of the Fifth and Sixth weeks of William Forster's journey to some of the Distressed Districts in Ireland* (London, 1847).

Smalley, Donald (ed.), *Trollope: The Critical Heritage* (London and New York, 1969).

Smith, Elizabeth (Grant), see Patricia Pelly and Andrew Tod (eds.), *The Highland Lady in Ireland*, and David Thomson and Moyra McGusty (eds.), *The Irish Journals of Elizabeth Smith*.

Somerville, Edith and Martin Ross, *Irish Memories* (London, 1917).

——, *The Big House of Inver* ([1925]; London, 1978).

Sorenson, John, *Imagining Ethiopia* (New Jersey, 1993).

Srivastava, Ramesh K., 'The Theme of Hunger in Bhattacharya and Markandaya', in R. K. Dhawan (ed.), *Explorations in Modern Indo-English Fiction* (New Delhi, 1982), pp. 172–83.

——, *Perspectives on Bhabani Bhattacharya* (New Delhi, 1984).

Steiner, George, *Language and Silence: Essays, 1958–1966* ([1967]; London, 1985).

Stephens, Ian, *Monsoon Morning* (London, 1966).

Storey, Andy, 'Comments on "Controversies over Conditionality" by Georg Sorensen', *Irish Studies in International Affairs*, 5 (1994), pp. 49–52.

——, 'Who tells us what about the "Third World"?', *Irish Times*, 14 February 1996, p. 21.

Sud, Kedar Nath, 'Urdu fiction and Krishan Chandar', *Indian Literature*, 20, 4 (1977), pp. 122–27.

Summers, Anne, 'A Home from Home – Women's Philanthropic Work in the Nineteenth Century', in Sandra Burman (ed.), *Fit Work for Women* (London, 1979), pp. 33–63.

TeBrake, Janet, 'Personal Narratives as Historical Sources: The Journal of Elizabeth Smith', *History Ireland*, 3, 1 (1995), pp. 51–56.

Thakurta, Tapati Guha, 'Women as "Calendar Art" Icons: The Emergence of Pictorial Stereotype in Colonial India', *Economic and Political Weekly*, 26 October 1981, pp. 91–99.

Tharu, Susie, 'Tracing Savitri's Pedigree: Racism and the Image of Woman in Indo-Anglian Literature', in Kumkum Sangari and Sudesh Vaid (eds.), *Recasting Women: Essays in Colonial History* (New Delhi, 1989), pp. 254–68.

Tharu, Susie and K. Lalita, *Women Writing in India: 600 B.C. to the present* (2 vols; London and New Delhi, 1991 and 1993).

Thomson, David and Moyra McGusty (eds.), *The Irish Journals of Elizabeth Smith: 1840–1850* (Oxford, 1980).

Tignay, Lance (ed.), *The Irish Famine: Six Letters to the Examiner, 1849–1850* (London, 1987).

Trench, W. Steuart, *Realities of Irish Life* (London and New York, 1868).

Trevor, William, *Fools of Fortune* (New York, 1983).

——, *The News from Ireland and Other Stories* (London, 1986).

——, *The Silence in the Garden* (London, 1988).

Trollope, Anthony, *The Macdermots of Ballycloran* (3 vols; London, 1847); reprinted in Garland series (New York and London, 1979).

——, *The Kellys and the O'Kellys* (3 vols; London, 1848); reprinted in Garland series (New York and London, 1979).

——, *Castle Richmond* (3 vols; London, 1860); reprinted in Garland series (New York and London, 1979), and as single-volume edition (Oxford, 1989).

——, *An Eye for An Eye* (2 vols; London, 1879); reprinted in Garland series (New York and London, 1979).

——, *The Landleaguers* (3 vols; London, 1883); reprinted in Garland series (New York and London, 1979).

——, *An Autobiography* (London, 1883).

——, *The Irish Famine: Six Letters to the Examiner, 1849–1850*, (ed.) Lance Tignay, (London, 1987).

Tuke, James Hack, *Distress in Ireland: Narrative of the Second, Third and Fourth Weeks of William Forster's visit to some of the Distressed Districts in Ireland* (London, 1847).

Ua Laoghaire, Peadar, *Mo Sgéal Féin (My Own Story),* (Dublin, 1915).

Uppal, J. N., *Bengal Famine of 1943: A Man-Made Tragedy* (Delhi and Lucknow, 1984).

Vaughan, Megan, *The Story of an African Famine: Gender and Famine in Twentieth-Century Malawi* (Cambridge, 1987).

Vinson, James and Kirkpatrick, D. L. (eds.), *Contemporary Novelists* (4th ed; London, 1986).

Walker, Benjamin, *Hindu World: An Encyclopedic Survey of Hinduism* (2 vols; London, 1968).

Walsh, Louis, *The Next Time: A Story of Forty-Eight* (Dublin, 1919).

Walshe, Elizabeth Hely, *Golden Hills: A Tale of the Irish Famine* (London, 1865).

——, *The Manuscript Man; or, The Bible in Ireland* (London, 1869).

Ward, Margaret, *Maud Gonne: Ireland's Joan of Arc* (London, 1990).

Warner, Marina, *Alone of All Her Sex: The Myth and Cult of the Virgin Mary* ([1976]; London, 1985).

——, *Monuments and Maidens: The Allegory of the Female Form* ([1985]; London, 1987).

Watt, Stephen and Julia Williams, 'Representing a "Great Distress": Melodrama, Gender and the Irish Famine', in Michael Hays and Anastasis Nikolopoulou (eds.), *Culture and Society in Twentieth-Century Melodrama* (New York, forthcoming 1996).

Williams, Linda, 'When the Woman Looks', in Mary Ann Doane, Patricia Mellencamp and Linda Williams (eds.), *Re-Vision: Essays in Feminist Film Criticism* (Maryland/Los Angeles, 1984), pp. 83–99.

Wittig, E. W., 'Trollope's Irish Fiction', *Éire-Ireland*, 9, 3 (1974), pp. 97–118.

Woodham-Smith, Cecil, *The Great Hunger: Ireland, 1845–1849* ([1962]; London, 1987).

Woods, Christopher, 'American Travellers in Ireland before and during the Great Famine: A Case of Culture-Shock', in H. Kosok (ed.) *Literary Interrelations: Ireland, England and the World* (Tübingen, 1987), iii, pp. 77–84.

Yeats, W. B. (ed.), *Representative Irish Tales* (2 vols; New York and London, 1891).

——, *Poems* ([1895]; London, 1927).

——, *Collected Plays* ([1952]; London, 1982).

——, *Letters to the New Island: Collected Works of W. B. Yeats*, vol. VII ([1934]; New York, 1989), eds. George Bornstein and Hugh Witemeyer.

——, *The Uncollected Prose of W. B. Yeats* (2 vols; London, 1970), ed. John Frayne.

Index